DAUGHTERS OF THE DREAM

EIGHT GIRLS FROM RICHMOND WHO GREW UP IN THE CIVIL RIGHTS ERA

TAMARA LUCAS COPELAND

INSPIRE

TITLES DISTRIBUTED IN
NORTH AMERICA
UNITED KINGDOM
WESTERN EUROPE
SOUTH AMERICA
AUSTRALIA
CHINA
INDIA

DAUGHTERS OF THE DREAM

EIGHT GIRLS FROM RICHMOND WHO GREW UP IN THE CIVIL RIGHTS ERA

TAMARA LUCAS COPELAND

DAUGHTERS OF THE DREAM

EIGHT GIRLS FROM RICHMOND WHO GREW UP IN THE CIVIL RIGHTS ERA

TAMARA LUCAS COPELAND

HARDCOVER ISBN: 9781937592813
PAPERBACK ISBN: 9781937592820

PUBLISHED BY INSPIRE

A NONFICTION IMPRINT FROM ADDUCENT

WWW.ADDUCENTINC.COM

AUTHOR'S NOTE: I am not a historian or academic, so what I share in this book is from my personal reading and study and how it fits within the story—mine and my friends—I wanted to share. Please forgive any errors or omissions as they are unintentional.

FRONT COVER (starting at 12 o'clock, licking her fingers) -- Jeannie Petties, Renee Mills, Deborah Smith, Tamara Copeland, Hope Herring, Debbie Riddick, Debby Smith and Gloria Reid

BACK COVER -- Standing L to R: Marsha Ware, Debby Smith, Madeline Swann, Debbie Riddick, Renee Mills, Veronica Abrams. --Seated L to R: Tamara Copeland, Jeannie Petties

TABLE OF CONTENTS

DEDICATION

Daughters of the Dream is dedicated to my mother, Edna Olivia Charity Lucas.

In the 1960s, my mom started work on a genealogical history of the Charity family. She didn't drive, so doing the research—pre-Internet—was a challenge. I can remember my dad taking her to the Virginia State Library or to talk with families in Charles City, Virginia, the ancestral home of her family. Her commitment to this project was unceasing, and in 1982 she published *Old Births and Old Residents of Charles City County (1671-1880)*. With so much information and desire to learn more about the genealogical roots of the family, she kept going. Eventually, she published *The Descendants of James and Keziah Charity of Charles City County, Virginia*, fondly referred to by the family as the 'green book' because of its bright green cover. I may not have consciously known it, but my mother's drive to understand her family's roots was a subliminal prod for me to write this book.

The real push, however, came from my forever friends, the Valianettes who ultimately became the Divas. Renée Fleming Mills planted the seed of a book about our friendship. Madeline Bruce Swann nurtured that desire and celebrated the book's name in many ways from notepads to needlepoint. Renée and Madeline along with Debby Anderson Smith, Marsha Ford Ware, Debbie Johnson Riddick, Veronica Dungee Abrams and Jean Johnson Petties are the stars of the story (together we form the Daughters of the Dream). So, I wrote a version of the manuscript several years ago and then got stuck. I took a writing class to move me along, then hired a grad student to fact check so I could say I was making progress. But I was still stuck. A big thank you to Dennis Lowery who with a critical eye affirmed that ours was a solid story and then guided me through revisions to get to where we are today.

And lastly, to my family, AJ Copeland, Nicki Lombardo, Tom Lombardo and the munchkins—Sam, Belle and Eli—and my family of dear friends, especially Janice Bowie and Isaiah Robertson, thank you for your unfailing support and caring. And, daddy, I feel your love every day. You were there, too. Every step of the way.

TAMARA LUCAS COPELAND
MAY 2018

ADVANCE COMMENTS

"Rarely does a personal account so intimately speak to the journey faced by many African-Americans in this country. *Daughters of the Dream* is one such story, to which even I recalled fond familial memories of our resilient heritage. In telling her own story, Ms. Copeland has captured the pure essence of a people and of a nation striving to achieve a more perfect union."

-LONNIE G. BUNCH III, FOUNDING DIRECTOR,
NATIONAL MUSEUM OF AFRICAN-AMERICAN HISTORY & CULTURE

"*Daughters of the Dream* chronicles the ordinary lives and friendship of eight African American girls from their school days after the Brown v. Board of Education decision to their maturation as women in the present. This book is real life storytelling at its very best, of eight women relentlessly moving together towards racial justice."

-DR. IBRAM X. KENDI, NATIONAL BOOK AWARD-WINNING AUTHOR OF
STAMPED FROM THE BEGINNING: THE DEFINITIVE HISTORY OF RACIST IDEAS IN AMERICA

"I read with pleasure Tamara Lucas Copeland's weaving of Richmond's racial history with her story of a decades-long friendship. When we share the rich stories of the African-American experience, we fill a void in our understanding of America. This is a must-read for many, but definitely for anyone with roots in Richmond."

-REV. DWIGHT C. JONES, FORMER MAYOR, RICHMOND, VIRGINIA

"*Daughters of the Dream* is a quiet book, no drama, no suspense, simply a straightforward story of the ongoing quest for racial justice. It resonates with me as a daughter of the South myself, someone who devoted the recent past in my professional life to the value of reading and as someone who fully understands the power of public policy. This is an important new lens on America's story."

-CAROL HAMPTON RASCO, CEO, READING IS FUNDAMENTAL (2001-2016)
DOMESTIC POLICY ADVISOR TO PRESIDENT WILLIAM JEFFERSON CLINTON (1993-1996)

FOREWORD

Each of us has a history that makes us who we are. It can be described as our own personal set of 'tapes' that play over and over in our minds as we go through life, experiencing even more that is added to our history. These tapes are really the life lessons learned that make us unique beings and are influenced—formed even—by our physical environment, our family, our friends and our experiences.

African-Americans raised in the mid-20th century were also impacted by the state-mandated laws of separate-but-equal of the South or the de facto segregation of the North. In some ways, in those times, there was comfort being surrounded by people who looked like you and whose experience was similar. Living in neighborhoods that included all manner of people from laborers to professionals. The knowing that Mr. Jones, the owner of the corner store was also your Uncle Jim when he came to visit your home. The adults of these communities were all your extended family and were treated with the same level of respect you gave your parents.

There was caring, safety and genuine love in those communities. There was both a desire and an expectation that the next generation would achieve even more for their race. That success was not individual but communal. The safety of the cocoon of those segregated communities nurtured the growth and development of relationships that endure the tests of time. Childhood friendships fostered in a time when the broader society said you could not, but your close circle told you, "the sky is the limit!" And ultimately, the quality of our lives is based on the quality of our relationships.

Parenting African-American children in that era meant you did your best to shield your children and your friends' children from the overt racism and bigotry of the time. It was a time when adults talked about adult things, while children played and were, well, children. But, exposure to the ignorance of people and the discriminatory laws of the time often had an impact not realized until years later. The question of 'why?' continues to linger and insidiously molds us over time. It is *our* American experience.

This book—the story you are about to read—speaks to this... it tells of this experience as it pertained to eight girls raised in a bastion—still so decades after the end of the Civil War—of Southern heritage.

After the Civil Rights era, we find ourselves longing for the safety of those communities as we now have the legal right to live, work and play where we like. But the institutional and structural racism ingrained in society remains an albatross—a burden—we must bear on a daily basis.

Each of us carries that weight and responds differently to the adversity and opportunities that life has dealt—deals—us. Our real challenge is to use the lessons learned in life, adversities included, to our advantage. To emerge as butterflies, spreading our wings to soar to new heights, just as the girls in *Daughters of the Dream*!

-TERRI LEE FREEMAN, PRESIDENT, THE NATIONAL CIVIL RIGHTS MUSEUM

PROLOGUE

Any journey begins with desire—a personal ambition—to move from one place to another. Sometimes that journey is geographic, moving from one place to another, but more often, that journey is intellectual, a learning journey if you will, a growth in understanding of something, how it came to be and the impact it is having on you, your family or your community.

Understanding race in America — its history of oppression, inequality, inequity, prejudice, and discrimination—has been a journey, even for me, a black person who has lived through it. So, much of the story I'm about to share with you is about my journey, my growing understanding of what I experienced, what my friends experienced, and how those events, not only shaped us as adults, but shaped, and continue to develop our country.

Given the title of this book, you may have a preconceived idea of what it's about. Since I grew up in the '50s and '60s in Richmond, Virginia, not just any southern city, but the capital of the Confederacy, a city still with significant vestiges of that heritage, you may expect stories of mistreatment based on race. But that is only the backdrop, not the core. At its heart, the book is about family and friends, cocoons of love and support. And rising above what was intended to hold us back.

Friends often ask me, "How could you have grown up in segregated Richmond, Virginia in the era of a stark *separate-but-equal* environment without witnessing overt signs of segregation?"

Their question stems from a truth I've shared with many: I have no memory of seeing whites-only and colored-only water fountains. No time when I was denied access to restaurants. No riding in the back of the bus. None of that. As a child, I did not understand that my world was defined by race. People don't believe me when I tell them this, but it's true.

Some suggest that my mind has blocked the negative images or memories. I don't believe that. I think there is a far more powerful explanation: Edna Charity Lucas and Howard Edward Lucas, my parents. In hindsight, I know they went to great lengths, as many black parents did, to ensure I never felt any level of second-class citizenship. Another thing: they did not talk about discrimination, at least not where I could hear. I think that was important in shaping my reality.

My mom would pack a delicious lunch for our trip to visit family in New York. Then halfway there, my dad would pull the car over to a roadside picnic area. No one commented that we were doing this because we couldn't eat in restaurants along the way. My parents pulled out our lunch, put a tablecloth on the wooden picnic table, and we played games, like looking for cars with license plates from different states and naming the capital city, as we ate and enjoyed what we now think of as quality family time. And when my dad stopped at the Esso, now Exxon, service station to buy gas, we would go to the bathroom. I thought nothing of it. But his lifelong loyalty to Exxon was born from that company being the first to let blacks use the restroom facilities in their service stations, a reality I learned from books, not from my dad telling me.

There was one childhood incident that probably was exposure to *separate-but-equal*, but I didn't know it at the time. My mom and I had entered the train station to travel to visit relatives. I remember skipping ahead toward a seat. Mom took my hand and gently directed me to another area. I now suspect that she was leading me to the 'colored' area. No conversation, just a subtle re-direction. I don't recall ever noticing it. The possibility/probability of this being a *separate-but-equal* memory only surfaced as an adult when friends questioned my experience of segregation as a child. Again, the important point was there was no preamble as I was being led away from where I was headed. At no time, did anyone tell me that there was something I couldn't do or someplace I couldn't go.

I lived in a segregated neighborhood and attended a segregated school, but I didn't know I was being denied anything. My community was lovely, and I never felt as supported in any educational environment as I did in that school. My point, simply, is that the harshness of segregation as a reality that makes someone superior to you never consciously entered my psyche. Was this level of insulation by my parents positive or did it cause me to have an unrealistic sense of the world? I'm not sure.

All I know is that when whites entered my world via integration, I didn't fear them, nor did I dislike them. I did not feel they were the persecutor and I was the victim. I think that is the most important point. Victims are powerless. Being a victim wears you down. You are continually looking for injustice, looking for where/how you have been wronged. It causes physical and mental stress. I am not saying that prejudice has not been a part of my life. It has, but that is not the frame I start out with every day. Whites had, and have, more power than I do, but I have always approached my interactions with them as equals, even as a teen when around white teenagers. Now, as an adult, injustice surrounds me in the governmental processes and structures that have, with intentionality, disadvantaged me and my community. It is in the media that often portray negative images of black people. It is in the rhetoric of the current president of the United States. It is truly in the air I breathe. But, I am still not a victim.

My parents wisely, and bravely, chose to deflect—but not deny—segregation's impact on me even as they raised me within its confines. They dealt with reality, all the while telling me I could do anything I wanted to do.

My understanding of how other people of color were affected by segregation came about in stages as I grew older. And with that came awareness of how much had been denied us.

It was in college we (my seven friends—that I tell you about in this story—and I) became black. Black in the sense of a heightened sense of racial identity, no longer a brown reflection of whites, but understanding what it meant to be black. It had started in high school, but these thoughts, these realizations, matured in college. We thought about our past. We had been immersed in the history and heritage of European whites: their innovations, their contributions to our nation, but knew very little of our own history, our contributions and nothing of African history. Some celebrated the natural kinkiness of our hair and to wear the afro hairstyles that were becoming popular across the country. And, like many others, we too joined the protests. We were no longer protesting for access to goods, services, and opportunities. Our issues had become more nuanced as some vocally and aggressively advocated for African studies programs or additional black faculty. Others protested the Vietnam War, wondering why blacks were fighting in a war that cost the United States funds needed for programs to help the poor. Or why black kids were fighting for rights for the Vietnamese that weren't enjoyed by blacks in the southern part of their own country. As college was meant to do, our minds were being expanded. Richmond, Virginia and our families were no longer at the center of our thinking. Our upbringing would forever be fundamental to who we were, but we were being exposed to the experiences and thoughts of others from all over the country and even from around the world. Their ideas and life's lessons were affecting our understanding of many issues and were shaping how we viewed the world and how we thought about the events of the day.

America's journey continues. There is much work to do to get to where we should be by this day in the 21st century United States. But, this story is not about growing up a black victim in the Jim Crow South. It's about how eight girls grew up in that era—understanding the context and importance of the times—and still created successful lives. It's about friends growing up believing in the dream and being strong enough to help make it a reality.

* * *

It was my friend Renée's idea to write a book about our friendship. In 2001, she'd been laid off. With time on her hands, she thought about capturing the experiences we had shared and the bond that had grown between us. But life got in the way. Renée hadn't had the time to write. As time passed, every now and then the idea of the book would re-surface whenever we got together. Tentatively, I decided to bring it up again in a conversation between the two of us. I didn't want to be perceived as trying to take over Renée's project. But, I thought it was a terrific idea and wanted to see it happen. "Hey, Renée, are you still thinking about writing our story?" I asked. She was but didn't know when she could get started. "Do you want a co-author?" She did, and a brief partnership was born. Renée's involvement with her church, her sorority, her family, and her new job filled every minute of the day, and this book became my project. I'm so glad it did. When the book evolved in my mind, I realized it wasn't only about our friendship. Our bond had emerged, strengthened and solidified within the dominant framework of the civil rights movement, the black power movement, and the more modern-day discussions of equity, inclusion, and diversity. And it was more than Renée and me. A group of us grew up together in that era, and our six other close friends were part of the story I wanted to tell. You'll get to know us as it unfolds, but since I'm your narrator, you first need to know who I am.

I am Tamara Lucas Copeland, the only child of Howard and Edna Charity Lucas.

HOWARD LUCAS

EDNA CHARITY LUCAS

I am the divorced mom of one son and stepmom to a daughter. I am also nana to three lovely munchkins. I have worked in children's public policy and association leadership throughout my career. I live in Washington, D.C. and think of myself as the quiet one. The group disagrees. They have labeled me the classy one. These are my dear friends, who form the core of this story.

THE VALIANETTES

INTRODUCTION

The story begins at Albert V. Norrell Elementary School in the Northside section of Richmond, Virginia. The year was 1956. A racially-charged bus boycott in Montgomery, Alabama was only a few months old. Those things were happening in the Deep South, hundreds of miles and cultural chasms away from our home. In Richmond, no one could have predicted the country was on the cusp of significant changes for African-Americans, changes that would transform our lives. And we didn't know we were beginning a friendship that would last and grow stronger for over 50 years.

Segregation, integration, and a powerful bond of friendship have combined to shape who we are. Living it, we didn't think our story was that unique. But every time we told someone about our friendship, they would remark on how unusual it was. And every time we talked about our experiences: the transition from attending an all-black school to being a significant minority in another; the effort to stop 'Dixie' from being our high school's fight song or how an ordinary day at a state park becomes extraordinary... there was always a thread of prejudice and of racial pride. From the Brown v. Board of Education decision right before we started elementary school to the election of the first African-American president right before our 60th birthdays, we have lived, and continue to live through, the emergence of rights and equity for African-Americans. The legal and societal changes were massive and transformational in our younger years, at a point in our lives when we didn't, and couldn't, understand the enormity of what was happening. Now, as adults, we reflect on and discuss what we perceive as the current lack of a powerful voice for African-Americans and the popular fallacy that we are living in a post-racial time because of the election of President Obama. We talk about the declining enrollment of black men in colleges at the same time their numbers grow in jails and prisons. When we gather and talk about the latest movie or a new ache as our bodies age, opportunity, and oppression also enter the conversation. Race will always be the defining element of our lives, and our friendship will forever bind us.

So, we think it is time to tell our story: how eight Negro girls negotiated the complexities of integration and the simplicity of everyday life to become eight strong, African-American women. Our maiden names were, Debbie Johnson, Debby Anderson, Jeannie Johnson, Madeline Swann, Marsha Ford, Renée Fleming, Tamara Lucas, and Veronica Abrams. Regardless of marriages, we'll always be known by those names to each other. There were others in our group. They were a part of the story, at different times, but we are the core.

This is our story—school, marriages, children, careers, divorces—connections lost and connections re-found. This is the story of African-Americans growing up in the South during an era of enormous societal transition.

SCHOOL
1956—1968

CHAPTER 1
WHERE WE MET

"While we were too young to understand, life was already presenting us with a glimpse of structural racism and white privilege."

None of us can remember the first day of school, but what we all remember is the absolute sense of peace, contentment, and normalcy that permeated our lives. We were growing up in the Eisenhower years. The war was over. Now our parents, like others across America, were benefitting in the post-World War II era. Soldiers were being thanked generously by the country through GI benefits, and those benefits also enabled some of our parents to purchase the most fundamental symbol of the American dream—a home.

While the GI benefit was available to all soldiers, few banks would finance the purchase for African-American families. Many families were trying to buy in the historically black neighborhoods in which they had always lived, but these neighborhoods had been 'redlined' by the federal government, literally marked on a city map with a red line, characterizing them as risky or undesirable for a federally-secured loan. Buying a home in a 'white' neighborhood—a 'safe' investment—was what enabled many of our parents to use the GI Bill for their home purchase. For others, the loan came directly from the current homeowner ready to flee Northside, the residential area in segregated Richmond that was now opening to black families. While we were too young to understand, life was already presenting us with a glimpse of structural racism and white privilege.

Richmond has many neighborhoods. The city was, and still is, roughly divided into four quadrants, the East End, the West End, Northside, and Southside. Northside was home to Virginia Union University, a college founded in 1865 to educate the newly freed slaves. Originally Union, as it is known, was well on the outskirts of the city, but as Richmond grew, the campus became something of a buffer between the all-white community of Northside and the black neighborhood called Jackson Ward.

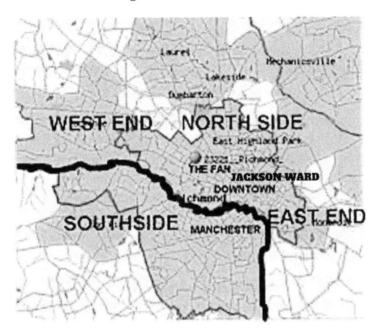

Jackson Ward had long been home to the black upper crust in Richmond. It was called the Harlem of the South and the Wall Street of Black America. At one time over 100 black-owned businesses thrived there, and the leading black entertainers of the '30s, '40s, and '50s performed there—Cab Calloway, Duke Ellington, and Ella Fitzgerald were regulars. They would perform at the True Reformer's Hall or the Hippodrome Theater both on 2nd Street, the premier business strip in Jackson Ward. After their shows, they'd take the short walk across the 'Deuce' as locals called 2nd Street and stay at one the three upscale, black-owned hotels: Eggleston's, Slaughter's or the Harris' Hotel because regardless of their fame, they could stay nowhere else.

One of Jackson Ward's most famous residents was Maggie Walker. She lived in the 100 block of Leigh Street, a block called 'Quality Row' because the substantially-sized, beautifully crafted, brick homes were of the highest quality and were the homes of the city's black leadership. Known for being the first woman to charter a bank in the United States, the St. Luke Penny Savings Bank, Maggie Walker was one of the many black entrepreneurs who called Jackson Ward home. When some white banks wouldn't even allow blacks to deposit money in their banks, African-American's would put their money in what they called "Miss Maggie's bank" And by 1920, Miss Maggie's bank had made over 600 loans to black families enabling them to buy homes.

My family owned businesses in Jackson Ward. One great aunt owned Woolfolk's Florist at 423 Leigh Street, and another a barber shop (a different type of business for a woman of her day). And even my dad had a business there when he was in his 20s. He and his business partner owned what was then called a confectionary, a snack bar in today's language, right below the most popular ballroom in Jackson Ward. This parallel, black world bustled with thriving businesses, beautiful homes, and vibrant culture, but that would soon change.

In 1942, the demarcation between black Jackson Ward and the white Northside started to crack. A teacher at Virginia Union University became the first African-American resident to purchase a home in nearby Northside. By the early 1950s, increasing numbers of blacks were moving into Northside. Whenever blacks became homeowners in any community, whites left. They didn't want to live near blacks. The reasons were multiple—a perception that crime would increase, that their property values would decline, that their families weren't safe—all stereotypes that had developed, and been reinforced, over decades. Wanting to depart, whites priced their houses low or offered to finance a loan-for-purchase themselves thereby providing blacks with an enhanced opportunity to buy homes that ordinarily most couldn't afford. At the same time the white departure was escalating, and more houses were becoming available, the historically black neighborhood of Jackson Ward was being destroyed.

The white leaders of Richmond decided that the city needed an improved north-south connector. U.S. Route 1 and Route 301 were major north-south highways. At points, however, they shared the same road and bridges into Richmond creating congestion. To alleviate this, the city fathers and state officials decided to build a new road. In 1955, financing began on the Richmond-Petersburg Turnpike. The location was chosen, one in which the residents had little power to protest. It would cut through one of the oldest and most influential black communities in Richmond, Jackson Ward. Black veterans who may have selected Jackson Ward to be home now faced a dissected and a virtually destroyed community. They turned to Northside to find homes for their young families.

So, in the early 1950s, white flight became a growing phenomenon in Richmond, Virginia. White middle-class families left Northside in record numbers. As they moved to the suburbs, they left a well-established, charming community. Unlike Jackson Ward, a neighborhood of brick row houses with tiny front yards, streets in Northside were lined with free-standing homes, a mixture of Queen Anne and American Foursquare style, alongside Arts and Crafts style bungalows. The lawns were manicured, and the trees were mature. This tranquil, beautiful setting was our neighborhood. We were the first wave of African-American families to live here.

OUR NEIGHBORHOOD

It wasn't just the neighborhood that was a peaceful reflection of 1950s Americana, it was our families, too. Like most of America in the 1950s, we grew up in two-parent families. Our fathers worked, but unlike much of white America, most of our mothers did, too. Black women didn't need the women's movement of the '70s to be liberated and enter the work world. Most black women had always worked to help support their families. The corollary to that was that many black men also didn't need a women's lib movement for them to help with the household chores. Black men could cook, buy groceries, cut the grass and repair the front steps. We grew up in two-parent families in which, for most, both parents worked inside and outside of the home. Our parents were partners long before the sharing of parenting and household responsibilities became the hip thing to do.

So, on that September day when we started school, both parents probably held our hands as they took us to our renovated and renamed school. The George Thorpe Elementary School, named after an early white colonist who came to America to found a school for American Indians, was now Albert V. Norrell Elementary School, named after an African-American educator.

It was here that our friendship began.

CHAPTER 2
EDUCATION SHAPED OUR LIVES

*"For most of our grandparents, the prospect of an
education beyond high school was a dream."*

Elementary school wasn't only where we started our education, it was where we formed friendships that would last a lifetime, learned about life and laid a foundation that has informed who we are, what we have done, and how we have done it for over half a century.

Ethel Thompson Overby was the first African-American principal in Richmond Public Schools, and she was the principal of our school when we started what was then called Junior Primary 1. We didn't know this consciously, but Mrs. Overby's stature as the head of the school was an important first lesson to a group of young girls. She was formidable, clearly in charge of all that happened in that building. We weren't afraid of her. We don't remember that she elicited fear. We respected her authority. Just as young children today don't find it remarkable that an African-American was president of the United States, we didn't note the fact that our principal, the leader of our school, was a woman and a black woman. It just was. From the beginning of our education, we were receiving a significant subliminal message on who could be a leader and on how to lead.

It's important to remember that we entered the first grade less than a century after the end of slavery, essentially just three generations removed. It was said that our school had been built on the site of Confederate military structures and fortifications. Our great-grandparents may have attended the Chimborazo School in Richmond, one of the earliest Freedmen Bureau schools established for former slaves by the federal government. Opened in 1868, it had been a hospital for Confederate soldiers. When the Chimborazo School started, it had students from age 4 to 29. It was reflective of Booker T. Washington's comment that after slavery, "a whole race was trying to go to school." Just as we weren't aware that our principal was a black woman, 80 years earlier probably none of the Chimborazo School students noticed that all their teachers were white. Most leaders were white, and these former slaves wanted to learn from anyone who would teach them. Education in any form was the premium, but the subliminal message of what a leader looked like was still there for our grandparents as it was there for us.

By the turn of the 20th century, accessing an education was still hard. The 1896 Supreme Court decision Plessy v. Ferguson declaring separate-but-equal the law0 of the land shaped our grandparents' and our parents' education. Within this environment driven by unfair federal statues, Virginia officials made it even harder for blacks to advocate for and obtain a quality education. A new state constitution that passed in 1902 required that you had to be a Civil War veteran or the son of a veteran, pay a poll tax, *and* pass a literacy test to vote in Virginia. Effectively preventing most African-Americans in Virginia from assuming one of the most important roles of an American citizen, that of voter. Our ancestors were denied the possibility of voting on many issues, including those affecting the provision of education to their children. Not only did this shape our grandparents' and our parents' access to quality education and their thirst for it, but it also shaped their understanding of the power of the vote and the importance of civic engagement, a belief that would affect all of us in the coming Civil Rights era.

But even amid what was then Jim Crow segregation, our grandparents and parents got an education, a separate and unequal one, often a paternalistic one, but an education nonetheless. Many were educated through schools started in churches. Others may have attended one of the Rosenwald schools, small schools, often just one-room, that were established across the South by Julius Rosenwald. Booker T. Washington, one of the significant black leaders in post-slavery America, had convinced Julius Rosenwald, owner of the Sears, Roebuck, and Company, to build formal schools for African-American children. Three hundred and eighty-two such schools were opened in Virginia between 1917 and 1933. The focus was primarily on the lower grades. Remarkably, even by 1918, there were only four high schools for blacks in the entire state of Virginia when a high school diploma was *the* educational goal.

For most of our grandparents, the prospect of an education beyond high school was a dream. Even though by the late 1800s, early 1900s, dozens of colleges had been established for African-American students, economic realities prevented most from attending.

Many of the colleges that were being established then were referred to as 'normal' schools, schools focused on teaching what was standard or typical for educating students to become teachers, a profession that was lauded by both blacks and whites. Having been denied an education for so long, blacks were happy to learn to be teachers. They saw this as a way to ensure that their families and all in their race received a good education. Some suggest that whites felt this was the highest profession to which blacks could, or should, attain. Regardless of the origin of the sentiment, colleges that educated educators were celebrated by both races. Hampton Normal and Agricultural Institute (now Hampton University), Saint Paul Normal and Industrial School (Saint Paul's College closed in 2013), and Virginia Normal and Collegiate Institute (now Virginia State University) started in Virginia. My paternal grandmother, Mary Smith Lucas was one of those in the early class at Hampton University. Atypically for the time, her father could afford to pay for his children to attend college. While he was uneducated, he understood the importance of education and expected his children to go to college. She did, and as was expected of her, she taught for a few years at Peabody High School, a segregated school in Petersburg, Virginia. Peabody had opened in 1870, as the state's first publicly supported black high school. Being a teacher was a highly respected profession in the African-American community, and this school was historic in Virginia.

My friend, Madeline's grandmother's story is one of how many African-Americans used their resourcefulness to get an education. Madeline's maternal great-grandparents didn't have the funds to send their daughter to college, but she was determined to go. Somehow, she found out about the Seneca Institute. Not unusually, this school had a direct connection to the church. It had been started by the Seneca River Baptist Association in South Carolina. Perhaps with a sense of trepidation, but also a desire to achieve, Madeline's grandmother, Anna Goldsmith, left her family in the Greenville, South Carolina area and went over 150 miles away to live with the Starks, the family that had founded the school. When Dr. Starks and his family left Seneca for him to become the president of Morris College, Madeline's grandmother followed them there. She graduated from Morris College in 1919 becoming the first in her family to earn a college degree. For many blacks, this was their route to an education. For Anna Goldsmith, John Jacob Stark and his wife became her extended family. Blacks have been displaced from their families for decades starting when families were separated during slavery. At least this separation was a voluntary one and one that led to academic achievements in this family for generations.

As one would expect, for our parents, the route to education differed from their parents. While most still could not afford to pay for college, by the 1940s, there was a new road to education. In 1944, Congress had passed the Serviceman's Readjustment Act. The GI Bill, as it was popularly referred to, helped to enable many of our parents to go to college as it had helped some to purchase homes.

In September 1956, as our parents took us to Albert V. Norrell Elementary School to begin our education, some of the kindergarteners' parents were in college finishing theirs or like my friend Renée's parents had graduated a few years earlier. Without family financial resources, many of our parents and their friends had to rely on a well-earned government benefit to open the door to college, but for their children, they knew that would be different. This would be the first generation of African-Americans in which many would be able to afford to pay for their children to go to college.

We didn't know it, but they did: we were going to college, and they had already started saving for it. It would not be only a dream for their children. The world was different. An African-American had been elected to the Richmond city council, the first since that disenfranchising 1902 state constitution. Brown v. Board of Education had proclaimed separate-but-equal unconstitutional, and Rosa Parks had refused to give up her seat on a Montgomery, Alabama bus launching the civil rights movement. Opportunities for African-Americans were increasing in Richmond, in

Virginia, and across the country. College would be a reality for their children, not only to become teachers but to move into whatever profession and wherever their knowledge, skills, and interests took us.

CHAPTER 3
BECOMING FRIENDS

*"Our separate-but-equal world gave us many
opportunities to interact with each other."*

At Norrell Elementary, we played in the schoolyard together and were
evenly divided between Mrs. Littlejohn's Junior Primary class and Mrs.
Anderson's. The junior primary grades, JP1 through JP4, were the
equivalent of kindergarten and first grade today. JP1 and 2 combined as
our first school year, with JP3 and 4 as our second year. As a group, we
don't have significant memories of that critical first couple of years of
school. We probably did the things five and six-year-olds typically do. We
learned our letters, shapes, and colors. We played on the jungle gym in the
school's playground, and we mastered the art of hopscotch. Family was still
our primary friendship group. But that changed somewhat two years later
when we gathered for the first time as a social group. We became Brownies.

The Girl Scouts had been established in 1912. Then two years later the
Brownies were formed to provide a service and social group for younger
girls, younger, white girls that is. It wasn't until the 1930s that troops were
started for black girls in the South. Our parents wanted us to have the
scouting experience. Maybe they were influenced by a 1952 article in *Ebony
Magazine*, a magazine started in 1945 to celebrate black life in America, in
which Girl Scouts were credited with breaking down some of the racial
taboos in the South. Or maybe our parents were listening when in 1956,
Martin Luther King, Jr. described Girl Scouts as "a force for desegregation."
Or perhaps, our parents were seeking another element of a well-rounded
child's life when they introduced us to scouting. Whatever the reason, we
became Brownies.

Separate-but-equal was still the de facto standard in Richmond,
Virginia. Our all-black Brownie troop was housed at All Souls Presbyterian

Church, two blocks from our school. The church had initially been the Overbrook Presbyterian Church until it was purchased by the all-black congregation to which Madeline's family belonged, another sign of the racial changing of Northside. Before our Brownie meetings started, Reverend Elligan would take us to explore the church. He would tell us stories of Attic Annie, a friendly spirit who lived in the church's attic. Then he'd turn us over to Mrs. Swann, Madeline's mom, and Mrs. Ballard, Ricki's mom, our troop leaders.

Ricki Laura Ballard was a part of our core group until high school when our paths separated. She left the public school system and our friendship group to attend private school. Ricki's mom and Madeline's mom were both pursuing Masters degrees, an unusual occurrence, at the time, for most Americans and certainly for African-Americans. They were enrolled at Virginia State College (later Virginia State University). One day while talking at work, they learned that they lived close to each other and were both attending State, as the school was called. They carpooled the 25 or so miles from Richmond to Petersburg where Virginia State was located. Then they discovered they both had four-year-old daughters. Upon learning this, Mrs. Ballard invited Madeline over for a tea party. Ricki's and Madeline's friendship had begun. We suppose it may have been on one of those rides to Petersburg that Mrs. Swann discussed the possibility of a Brownie troop for their young daughters and convinced Mrs. Ballard to be a part of this parenting adventure.

Ricki, Madeline, Debby, Renée, Gloria (another early member of our group who separated around college) and I were all Brownies. We had cooking projects and outdoor activities, hooked pot holders, hiked, and made 'stone' soup. We baked cookies, sold Girl Scout cookies and learned songs together, but most importantly learned to be friends. We knew we could depend on each other and knew what each other liked and didn't like. We were learning how to play together and how to work together. Being in the Brownies was an essential part of the development of our friendship.

But, our friendship didn't just revolve around Brownies. There were sleepovers. We would be invited over to someone's home. Most of us didn't have sleeping bags as children do today. We'd bring blankets and pillows to sleep in the basement or in the living room on a thick carpet. The event wasn't as orchestrated as they are now with movies and manicures. We'd play games and practice the latest dance steps, but mostly we'd talk. Giggles would rule the night as only they can for 10-year-olds. Finally, the host's mom or dad would flick the lights and announce it was time to settle down. In 1960s America, that's all it took. We'd find our spot on the floor, recall the story one more time of the most recent movie or Brownie outing and then off to sleep we'd go right beside our best friends.

And then there was dance. Several of us attended Chapman's School of Dance. The Chapmans, a white family, had opened Richmond's first dance school in 1922. In the early '50s, the school offered classes in Jackson Ward for African-Americans. Debby, Madeline, Renée, Gloria, Ricki and I took dance lessons there. While the ballet, tap, toe and jazz lessons led no one to a career as a professional dancer, it opened our eyes to the world of dance, taught us discipline and the importance of cooperation as we mastered the steps for our annual recital. The weekly dance class was another link that would connect us and further develop our friendship.

So, we took part in the Brownies together. We danced, had sleepovers, and played together. We lived in the same neighborhood and went to school together. Our separate-but-equal world gave us many opportunities to interact with each other and with our friends' parents. In our close community, one parent would pile all of us into the family car, sans today's requirement for each person to have a seatbelt and take us to whatever that day's activity was. Someone else's mom or dad would pick us up. The act of carpooling in the '50s and '60s did not differ from today, but I wonder if the children today feel that every adult is a strong parental figure? Everyone corrected us, parented us, and we took that for granted. Somehow, we knew all of these interactions and all of the adults in our lives were focused on one thing: preparing us for a world of opportunities. It wasn't just our parents who wanted us to be educated, well-rounded and ready. It was the entire black community. We couldn't have had a more extensive, more cohesive, support system.

During it all, we were becoming friends. We were sharing experiences, learning about each other, building memories. A solid education, both inside and outside of school, would prepare us for the professional and personal opportunities that awaited us. No one thought much about the development of our friendship, not us, and probably not even our parents, but the development of our friendship connections may have been even more powerful in shaping our place in the world than our formal education. Our friendship would bind us forever and give us another layer of security, strength, and support throughout our lives.

CHAPTER 4

THE ELEMENTARY YEARS

*"Family and teachers were focused on exposing us to the
world and protecting us from it."*

Albert V. Norrell Elementary was an imposing structure to a young child.
Built in 1906 as Barton Heights Public School (later named George Thorpe
Elementary), the main building was a traditional two-story red brick
schoolhouse with wooden stairs and a plain, iron banister leading up to the
massive front door.

OCT · 58

TAMARA LUCAS IN FRONT OF NORRELL ELEMENTARY SCHOOL

An enormous staircase was central on the first floor with classrooms
and administrative offices around it. The stairs led up to more classrooms
and an auditorium. In 1953, a modern one-story structure with additional

classes and a cafeteria was annexed to the original building. It was in the new annex that we started school. Our classrooms were large with lots of windows. Posters of the alphabet in print and in cursive were thumbtacked above the large blackboards. We would be expected to master penmanship, an art that seems to have vanished in today's electronic age. All the girls wore dresses or skirts and blouses with Buster Brown Oxford shoes. We sat in neat rows at wooden desks with surfaces that flipped open for storage of our lined paper, glue, blunt-tipped scissors, pencils and a box of crayons in which the 'flesh' color didn't resemble our skin tone. Richmond education officials felt we had all we needed to be ready to learn.

WHITE DOLLS

Our introduction to reading, the core of all formal education, was through the Dick and Jane readers. This series was the basis of reading instruction for over 80% of first graders—black and white—between the 1930s and the 1950s. There were the two main characters, a little boy named Dick and a little girl named Jane. Also, in the book was Mother, Father, a baby named Sally, and a dog called Spot. As the years passed, the debate around the readers centered on pedagogy. Was the whole word, repetition approach to learning to read better than the emerging emphasis on phonetics? The more prominent reality for six and seven-year-old black children was who was in the book. Every character in the book was white.

It wasn't until 1965 that any black characters were introduced, long past the time we were in elementary school. And remember, this text was part of defining what all first graders learned constituted a family, how they interacted, where they lived and what the 'average' American family looked like. And it wasn't only in readers that white figures shaped our world. For most of us, white dolls lined our beds and sat on shelves in our homes.

A study by psychologists, Dr. Mamie Phipps Clark and her husband, Dr. Kenneth Clark, both black, in the late 1930s, was revealing. They used identical dolls except one had brown skin and black hair while the other had white skin and blond hair. When asked to choose which one was good or which one was better, over half of the black children chose the white doll. Drs. Clark felt the doll test demonstrated how internalized racism was affecting the sense of self-worth and identity of young black children. Twenty years after this study, when we were young girls, there still were very few dolls being made commercially that looked like us. There were some. However, most were derogatory cloth dolls made to look like stereotypical images of young, black slaves. Only Madeline can remember having black dolls that looked like her, but then so did her mother. The women of that family had understood for decades the importance of black images.

At an age when psychologists suggest that children are shaping how they see themselves especially relative to the larger world, most of us saw white dolls and Dick and Jane as the standards. These were the images that were routinely presented to us. Fortunately, these subliminal messages were still in the context of a broader world shaped by influences from our families, our neighbors, and community leaders.

Even though we were being educated in an all-black environment, there was not an overwhelming emphasis on our history. Most of our textbooks were hand-me-downs from the white schools, and even if they had been brand new, the history texts didn't talk about our history. They focused on American history, white American history. We were left out except for the occasional mention of George Washington Carver's experiments with peanuts, Booker T. Washington's emphasis on self-help and maybe a small acknowledgment of the institution of slavery. Recognizing this deficit and the impact of not knowing about our history, Carter G. Woodson established the Association for the Study of Negro Life and History in 1915. The following year, the *Journal of Negro History* was introduced. Through these means, he encouraged black teachers to look for auxiliary texts, such as biographies, newspaper stories and information coming from his association to teach black children about their history. He did not believe there should be a separate emphasis on "Negro history," but the inclusion of information on the Negro in history, both in American history and in world history. He wanted us to know the richness of our contributions to America: in politics, in science, in the arts, in all aspects of the evolution of our country.

Our principal may not have been educated about all the accomplishments of our race, but Mrs. Overby did want to continually affirm us as a people. She did this by being the leader of our school, by encouraging the teachers to showcase information about black historical figures in our classrooms, but she also did it more actively, and perhaps most powerfully, by exposing us to the Negro National Anthem. We stood every morning to say the Pledge of Allegiance to our country and to sing the National Anthem, but it was with a very different sense of pride that we sang 'Lift Every Voice and Sing' at every assembly at all-black Norrell Elementary School. Every assembly was opened or closed with the singing of "Lift Every Voice and Sing" by James Weldon Johnson. We probably sang, by rote, the words Johnson had written in 1900 as a poem to introduce Booker T. Washington at a celebration of Lincoln's birthday. But, there was a power to the words and to the lilting melody written by his brother, Rosamund Johnson.

> "Lift every voice and sing, til' earth and Heaven ring, ring
> with the harmonies of liberty; let our rejoicing rise high as
> the list'ning skies, let it resound loud as the rolling sea."

Maybe it was the way Mrs. Overby introduced the song at the assembly, standing and saying, "Children, now we will sing the Negro National Anthem. Please stand." She said it with pride. This was our song, our anthem. Even today, most African-Americans don't know Johnson wasn't only a songwriter. He was an educator, a journalist, a lawyer, and a diplomat. His accomplishments merit his inclusion in black history, but even if we don't know these things about him, singing his song made us all proud to be Negroes.

Racial pride was inherent in our environment. All of our teachers were black. All of our administrators were black. When our parents dropped us off at school, they left us with educators in what they knew was a nurturing environment. For these women—and they were all women—teaching wasn't merely a job nor was it even just a career. It was a responsibility both understood and desired. They were teachers, entrusted with preparing an entire race to be leaders, to succeed well beyond what had been possible for their parents or for them.

Mozelle Sallee understood that when she introduced French to her third graders at Norrell. In 1959, French was not a part of the elementary school curriculum, but Mrs. Sallee was preparing her students to be citizens of a much larger world. Once a week, Mademoiselle Maxine would come to our class to teach French. This African-American woman, Maxine Page, fluent in French, gave us not only language lessons but introduced us to another culture. Encouraged by Mrs. Sallee and Mademoiselle Maxine, many parents bought us French language books so they could reinforce what was being taught at school. Our parents didn't speak French, but whatever could make us more competitive in a changing world was what they wanted. They already imagined a world in which their children would travel and interact globally, not just locally.

Berthinia Taylor understood when she was strict on my friend Debbie for not focusing on her long division and called Debbie's mom to talk to her about how they both could support Debbie to learn this important part of mathematics. Teachers engaged parents early and often. Everyone was focused on success. They knew that a time was coming when the classified ads in the newspapers wouldn't list jobs as help wanted—female (c) and help wanted—male (c) with the "c" standing for colored and the positions being primarily menial.

Ruth Chiles understood when she taught us to read the new language of computers in the fourth grade. For Madeline, Renée and me, learning the binary system and how to program computers was very much like learning another foreign language. And, like learning French with Mademoiselle Maxine, we mastered the binary language also. Little did we know that computers would change the world, but Mrs. Chiles knew this was a new technology that others were learning; so, we needed to learn it, too. We didn't realize then our computer-related submission to the science fair at Virginia Union University would be one of Madeline's early entry points into science, a field that would shape her professional identity. We didn't know, but Mrs. Chiles and all of our other teachers were working very hard to see to it we were prepared for whatever this new world of opportunity would offer for African-Americans.

Part of that preparation for the new world involved seeing it. The country was about a decade away from affordable air travel, but living in Virginia, there was much to see right in our own backyard. Elementary school was full of field trips.

We had trips in town, like the annual outing to the Richmond Symphony. It may have been one of these trips that inspired Renée, Madeline, and Debby to start playing the violin in the fourth grade.

R TO L (WITH VIOLINS), DEBBY, RENEE AND MADELINE

We also had trips out of town and recall outings to Jamestown, Williamsburg and Washington, D.C. We can remember climbing on the school bus or lining up two-by-two to get on the train. Boys would have on suits and girls would have on dresses with white collars and crinoline skirts. We wanted to look our very best, always aware—without being told—we would be representing our race. There wasn't much discussion of slavery on the trips to Jamestown and Williamsburg. Just as we didn't learn much about black history at school, we also didn't learn much about our role, the role of African-Americans, in shaping our country on these field trips either. When we toured historical locales in Virginia, we learned about colonial America and the rigors of a nation being born. But heard little about Crispus Attucks, an escaped slave who became the first to die in the American Revolutionary War. On our Washington, D.C. trip, we remember little discussion of the free black man, Benjamin Banneker who played an important role in surveying the city as it was being planned or of the many parts African-Americans had played in the building of our country. Instead, we learned more about the founding tenets of democracy, the white leaders who shaped our country, and the threats that faced the nation.

We knew about those threats. This was the time of the Cold War. At school, our teachers would take us through air raid drills, making us get on our knees, cover our heads and face the wall as we got ready for a possible missile attack or lining us up to go to the fallout shelter in the school. As children, what we didn't know was that the real threat to us wasn't only from the leader of Russia or of Cuba, it was from the leaders of our own state and country.

In 1956, the year we entered elementary school, Harry Flood Byrd, a United States senator from Virginia and former Virginia governor, was one of the 100 members of Congress who had signed the Southern Manifesto, a document intended to demonstrate southern leaders' commitment to reversing the Brown v. Board of Education decision. At home, Byrd initiated a program of massive resistance designed to galvanize Virginia politicians to fight school integration. As the leader of what was then called the Byrd Machine or the Byrd organization, Harry Byrd used his tentacles into Virginia politics to prompt the Virginia General Assembly to pass legislation denying state funds to any Virginia school that integrated. Finally, in 1959, our third-grade year at Norrell and five years after the Brown v. Board of Education decision, a federal court ordered all Virginia schools to integrate. Our parents understood the act of declaring that the schools should integrate didn't mean it would happen. It hadn't occurred in 1954, and it was unlikely in 1959, but what they knew was that it was on the horizon. They anticipated that in the not-too-distant future they would have a choice. Would their daughters continue in the segregated school system and attend all-black Baker Elementary School for the sixth grade, as was the traditional next school after Norrell, or would we go to the white school, J.E.B. Stuart Elementary, right in our neighborhood?

While our parents may have been thinking a lot during our late elementary school years about this critical decision and debating the pros and cons, this decision didn't permeate our lives. In fact, we don't remember the conversations. What we recall is ordinary family life. We all went to church on Sundays. Meals were eaten as a family. Families went out together, maybe only to the library on Saturday to check out books or to the Virginia Museum of Fine Arts on Sundays to see the Russian Imperial Easter Egg Collection. Being with family was important. Our parents seemed to have had what many seek today, work-life balance. They found time to be with their children and some of the most significant was during family vacations.

Debbie and Jeannie can remember trips to the beach. Their dad loved the ocean. By now, there were four kids in the Johnson family; so, getting in the car and driving to the beach was an easy vacation option. Veronica also remembered beach outings; recalling, as an adult, that even the beaches had at one time been segregated. Blacks in Richmond often drove to Bay Shore beach, near present-day Virginia Beach. Whites went to the adjoining Buckroe Beach. Both had concession stands, amusement park rides, and boardwalks. Separate-but-equal was the practice of the day and would still be the practice in Virginia for a few more years. Although even today Veronica recalls the reality of the separate beaches clearly, it is likely that as a young child, all she was struck by was the warmth of the sun and the fun she had playing in the ocean.

Segregation and racism often surrounded us. Our parents did all they could to protect us, but sometimes they couldn't. One instance, mentioned, that I remember was at the Broad Street train station when traveling to visit

31

relatives. Maybe what made it memorable was the look of sadness on my mother's face when she had to lead me to another part of the station.

Madeline also recalled when racism entered her world on a memorable car trip to visit family. Madeline and her parents were about 30 miles outside Richmond in Amelia County when she noticed people dressed in white robes guiding cars to a parking area. When she raised her hand to point out the oddly-dressed 'parking attendants' to her parents, she was pushed down to the floor of the car. Her parents kept their eyes focused ahead and drove on. It was only later Madeline would learn they had witnessed people gathering for a meeting of the Ku Klux Klan. This experience with whites may have been a part of the Swann's decision about which school Madeline would attend for the sixth grade once integration was an option.

Our families were secure units, and our school experience was structured and expansive. Both family and teachers were focused on exposing us to the world and protecting us from it. In the spring of 1962, the protective environment of Albert V. Norrell was about to end for us. We had been nurtured and encouraged. Now having finished the fifth grade, the last at Norrell Elementary School, it was time for us to move on. Our education would continue, but the educational environment would never be the same.

CHAPTER 5
The Sixth Grade: A Defining Year

*"A year the realities of race would for the first time
enter our consciousness."*

In 1962, Brookland Park Boulevard was the dividing line between a robust, upwardly mobile, black community to the south and a white neighborhood to the north. It was a tree-lined, vibrant commercial strip with a friendly community grocer, novelty shops and a variety of businesses in small store-front, brick buildings. Companies on Brookland Park Boulevard weren't white businesses or black businesses. They were businesses catering to both communities as they divided black Northside from white Ginter Park. Brookland Park Boulevard was both the man-made barrier that separated our community and what brought us together. Everyone got rich French vanilla ice cream at Woody's Ice Cream Parlor and filled their prescriptions at Atkinson & Howard Pharmacy. In the early 1960s, this street was a bustling demarcation between two distinct worlds.

South of Brookland Park Boulevard was called Barton Heights and north of Brookland Park Boulevard was Ginter Park. We referred to the entire area as Northside. So, while Norrell Elementary School was in the Barton Heights section and J.E.B. Stuart Elementary was in Ginter Park, they were both in Northside for us. But, Baker Elementary School was different. It was in Jackson Ward.

In retrospect, we wonder what our parents discussed as they sat at the kitchen table or in the living room that spring before our sixth-grade year. They could now send their daughters to a white school, a perceived 'better' school. They didn't know anything about J.E.B. Stuart, but they knew the black schools received the outdated textbooks, had ill-equipped science laboratories and poorer facilities overall. For some, a school in Jackson Ward would be symbolic of the past. Our families, like many middle-class black families, now lived in Northside. This was their home community, and this was where their children should go to school. For others, Baker Elementary was known. Baker was likely to be a far more nurturing environment than Stuart. Some may have even been apprehensive, thinking their children might receive a cruel or even violent, reception at Stuart. In the end, Debbie, Jeannie and I went to J.E.B. Stuart Elementary School for the sixth grade. Our other friends, Marsha, Madeline, Renée, and Debby, went to Baker. Proximity may have been the actual determinant as those whose homes were closest went to Stuart, at least all except Madeline.

During our elementary school years, Madeline's family had left Northside and moved to a new housing section for blacks called Hungary Road. Hungary Road was in adjacent Henrico County, outside of the city limits. A large tract of land had been purchased by an African-American who wanted to offer blacks land on which they could build their own homes. Many of the black upper crust of doctors and lawyers were choosing Hungary Road as the area for their families as Northside had been selected a decade earlier. Madeline's uncle bought land there as did Madeline's parents. As a brick mason, Madeline's dad had the skills necessary to build his own home, and he did just that. In 1960, Madeline moved to 1612 Hungary Road, the house her dad had built. Now, her parents had an even tougher decision: should they buy into the Richmond School System or send Madeline to Henrico County schools. They probably felt that Henrico County was out of the question due to the racism that permeated that area. They had even looked into boarding schools for Madeline. Finally, they decided Baker would offer Madeline the nurturing environment they felt was most necessary; so, since they lived outside the city, they paid for Madeline to attend a Richmond city public school. She joined the Baker Elementary School group. For her parents, culture and environment, not proximity, were the deciding factors.

You may have noticed Veronica wasn't mentioned relative to the sixth-grade school decision. Veronica, the missing member of the core group going off to Baker or Stuart, hadn't joined our group yet. In fact, we hadn't even met her. She lived in a different section of Richmond.

Veronica lived in the East End. The East End of Richmond was another historically African-American section of town. Within the African-American community, a friendly rivalry existed between those living in the East End and Northside sections of the city. Nowhere was this competition more pronounced than in the annual football game between the only two high schools in Richmond for African-Americans, Armstrong, and Walker.

Armstrong High School's history dates back to the 1870s with the establishment of the Richmond Colored Normal School through the Freedmen's Bureau. Eventually, it became a part of the Richmond Public School System, and in 1909 its name was changed to honor General Samuel Chapman Armstrong, a white Union soldier who during the Civil War led the U.S. Colored Troops. By the mid-1930s, the school's enrollment well exceeded its capacity. Richmond needed another high school for black students.

In 1938, only four years after her death, the new high school opened and was named in honor of Richmond native and Jackson Ward entrepreneur, Maggie Walker. Next to Virginia Union University, on land formerly owned by the university, Maggie Walker High School became the new school for the black elite who lived in Jackson Ward. It was proclaimed "equal in rank and dignity with any high school in Virginia" meaning any white high school in Virginia. And that same year, the tradition of the Armstrong-Walker football classic on the Saturday after Thanksgiving started.

Over time, that high school football game came to symbolize a rivalry that had cultural roots and implications. Kids in Northside were perceived as uppity or progressive while East End kids were either behind the times or more hip depending on where you lived. That perception was true throughout our high school years and may even have shaped Veronica's high school entry into our group. We were from Northside. She had come from the East End. For now, however, Veronica wasn't a part of the group, a group that for the first time was dividing.

We didn't know it, but our separation was only for one year, but that school year, September 1962—June 1963, was a definitive year for all of us, a year the realities of race would for the first time enter our consciousness.

Baker Elementary School in Jackson Ward had a deep history. It opened in 1871 and was one of the first public schools built by the city of Richmond. When the Colored Normal School was condemned and forced to close in 1908, their students came to Baker where classes were held in shifts because there were so many students. In 1918 during an epidemic of influenza, the school was closed for several months while it served as a hospital for the black residents of the city. In 1939, it was demolished to make way for what came to be known as the new Baker. Opening in 1940, the new school had 28 classrooms, a cafeteria, an auditorium and a state-of-the-art communication system. It was to this new Baker that Marsha, Debby, Renée, and Madeline went on the first day of sixth grade.

Renée and I both remember this was the first time we had had male teachers. The memories of these two men, Mr. Williams at Baker and Mr. Yearwood at Stuart are incredibly different. Mr. Williams introduced Renée to the color line. For African-Americans, until recently there has always been something called *colorism*, a preference for lighter-skinned black people. In the early 20th century that preference was manifested in the paper bag test. Is your complexion darker or lighter than a brown paper bag? For years, the lighter-skinned you were, the better you were treated not only by whites but also by some blacks. There was never a skin color hierarchy in our group, but at school, for Mr. Williams, skin color made a difference. Renée recalls he showed a distinct preference for lighter-skinned students, even moving Debby, a lighter-skinned member of our group, to a desk near his. Renée is darker skinned. Sadly, Renée remembers this as the first time skin color made a difference with an adult, but not the first time that skin color mattered.

Renée recalls a neighborhood friendship with a girl whose complexion was like her own. A lighter-skinned girl moved into the neighborhood, and Renée's friend stopped being friends with her and moved to a friendship with the new girl on the block. In Renée's mind, that friendship ended only because of the color of her skin. The specter of color had entered her world.

Maybe she had relegated it to something kids occasionally did until she faced it for the first time with an adult at Baker Elementary School.

Mr. Yearwood, my white sixth-grade teacher, made integration a non-event for me. He was a young, caring, and engaging teacher. Race didn't seem to matter to Mr. Yearwood. He was focused on performance. One day, he walked the seven blocks from the all-white neighborhood of Stuart Elementary School, across the chasm of Brookland Park Boulevard, to my all-black neighborhood. I wasn't as surprised that a white person was coming to my house as I was that a teacher was coming to my house. My parents were probably shocked Mr. Yearwood had crossed decades of culture and norms to visit our home. He was there to suggest they should allow me to skip the sixth grade and go on to seventh. After careful thought, my parents decided they wanted me to stay with the same group of girls and did not want me to skip a grade. They probably knew I needed the consistency and support of my long-term friendship group as I continued in this foreign world of integration.

And foreign it was. Although only about five miles away from Baker Elementary School, Jeannie, Debbie and I were having a much different experience than the other girls. We were attending J.E.B. Stuart Elementary, an all-white school named after a famous Confederate soldier. The Confederacy was revered in Richmond. There was the Museum of the Confederacy that opened in the late 1800s in the former White House of the Confederacy, home to the President of the Confederate States, Jefferson Davis, his wife Varina and their children. Then there was Monument Avenue.

Monument Avenue was, and is, a Parisian-style, broad, boulevard with beautiful old homes and expanse of tree-lined median strip, interrupted at almost every corner by huge statues to Civil War heroes—Robert E. Lee, Stonewall Jackson, Jefferson Davis and J.E. B. Stuart. Our school was named for one of the most well-

JEFFERSON DAVIS MONUMENT AVENUE

known and beloved soldiers of the Civil War. Interestingly, as discussions occur across the country about the many ways in which the Confederacy and its leaders are memorialized, those talks are also happening in Richmond. The renaming of J.E.B. Stuart Elementary is now part of that conversation.

As noted before, while only Brookland Park Boulevard separated the two worlds, we knew our school was in a different world. No one had to tell us. The houses looked the same. The streets were lined with the same beautiful, mature trees, but this part of the neighborhood was genuinely separate, visually equal and fully occupied by whites only. Debbie, Jeannie and I were the intruders.

I recall my mother telling me before that first day of school I must remember adults weren't always correct and everything adults said wasn't always right. I was surprised the message wasn't about respecting adults, but in hindsight, I know this was my mother's way of preparing me for racist acts or statements from the adults at Stuart. None came, at least no overt actions on the first day or during our one year at Stuart. However, my parents' instinct to focus on the adults was right. The kids were fine. No one remembers overt racism from the students, but their parents must not have been happy with this newly integrated school. In less than five years, J.E. B. Stuart went from about 700 plus white students and a handful of black students when we entered in 1962 to the 1966 statistic of 761 black students and twelve whites. The school had completely flipped racially. Whites left the urban core of Richmond for suburbia or perhaps remained in the city but applied for and received tuition grants from the state government to attend private schools. Yes, public grants to attend private schools. As part of the response to the Brown v. Board of Education decision, Virginia Governor Thomas Stanley led an effort that was called the Stanley plan. It established the Pupil Placement Boards that had the power to determine to which school all students attended and the plan provided grants for students to attend the private school of their choice. It was during the '50s and '60s that many private schools referred to as segregation academies were established across the South for white students. So, it was to the surrounding counties of Henrico and Chesterfield that many of the Stuart

Elementary School families moved or, with state funds, sent their children to private schools, many in Richmond.

It is noteworthy that the girls who had gone to the all-black Baker Elementary School were the ones who were introduced to race negatively while those at predominately white J.E.B. Stuart Elementary School experienced a 6th-grade year with no racial overtones. All of that was about to change as both groups started what is now called middle school, but what was then referred to as junior high school.

CHAPTER 6
CHANDLER JUNIOR HIGH SCHOOL

"That safe, nurturing environment we had experienced in our school lives had ended. We now lived outside the cocoon of an entirely black community."

Northside Junior High School, as it was originally named, opened in 1919 with four teachers. The pre-teen population of Northside quickly outgrew this space. A new school was built in 1926. The new imposing, white stone structure with Northside Junior High School chiseled majestically across the façade could house 1,150 students in the auditorium and contained 39 classrooms. In 1930, it became Chandler Junior High School, renamed for a long-forgotten Richmond Public School System school superintendent. Thirty years later, Chandler became the first white school in Richmond to accept black students. And, in September 1963, our Baker Elementary School girls and the Stuart Elementary School girls came together again at Chandler for junior high school, the 7th and 8th grades.

While we were focused on entering junior high school, the next transition in our lives, the country was focused on something so much bigger, the civil rights movement. Less than two weeks before we started Chandler, the March on Washington occurred in the nation's capital. On August 28, 1963, about 100 miles from Richmond, a quarter of a million people of all ages and races marched from the Washington Monument to the Lincoln Memorial in Washington, D.C. The marchers were demanding passage of the Civil Rights Act, an end to school segregation, a jobs bill, an increase in the minimum wage, and an end to the police brutality that had been seen on televisions in living rooms across the country and around the world. They also wanted representation in Congress for the primarily black residents of the District of Columbia. Numerous actions had led to this pivotal gathering. Rosa Parks' quietly defiant act in 1955 and the subsequent Montgomery, Alabama bus boycott sparked the organized civil rights movement. Martin Luther King Jr.'s eloquent *Letter from a Birmingham Jail* undergirded the movement with humanity and reason. But it was probably the actions of avowed Birmingham, Alabama segregationist Bull Connor, using powerful water hoses and vicious dogs to attack protesters not much older than we were, that truly ignited the movement, leading to the March on Washington. Of our group, only Debby Anderson's dad and brother participated. Debby had wanted to go, but no one knew how safe it would be in Washington on that Wednesday in August. Debby remembers being disappointed her parents made her stay at home.

Most of us were unaware of the momentous change happening in the country. We didn't understand segregation or civil rights or even integration. We were 12 years old. Our frame of reference was limited, as expected, and our parents protected us. Sometimes they had to go to great lengths to do so. Before a trip, they might review the Green Book, a directory first developed in the late 1930s by Victor Green. It was where African-Americans could find information on lodgings, where they could eat and even which service stations would let them use the restrooms. Our parents used this resource to shield us from negative incidents in which we might be denied service. They wanted us to only see what was possible, not what was cut off from us. They also monitored our TV viewing, shielding us from the nightly news reports of NBC's Huntley and Brinkley or of CBS's Walter Cronkite. Most of us were not exposed to the horrors, or even, the inconveniences of segregation. That was true for most, but not for all. Debby Anderson's experience was different.

Unlike all of the rest of us, Debby had older siblings, and that made a difference. While we were in junior high school, Debby's older sister, Anna, was attending Virginia Union University. Virginia Union, like college campuses across the country, then and now, was an incubator for change. In 1942 the Congress of Racial Equality, CORE, was started by a black and a white student at the University of Chicago. It was the CORE philosophy of nonviolent protests that led to the sit-ins and the Freedom Rides years later, protests that would not have had the same impact or may not have even been possible without the thousands of college students who participated. In 1960 a civil rights organization solely for students was formed. SNCC, the Student Nonviolent Coordinating Committee was established at Shaw University, the school Jeannie and Debbie Johnson would attend less than a decade later. College students across the country were taking on the mantle of the civil rights movement. Unlike adults who had the threat of retaliation through the loss of jobs, college students had the freedom to take bolder actions. They became the life's blood of the civil rights movement.

Debby listened as her dad spoke about his experience at the March on Washington and, particularly as her older sister Anna talked about the protests that were being coordinated in Richmond. Students at Virginia Union University planned and undertook the first major civil rights protest in Richmond in February 1960. Thirty-four students, the Richmond 34 as they were called, were arrested trying to be seated at the upscale Richmond Room restaurant in Thalhimer's Department Store.

There were two anchor department stores in Richmond, both on opposite corners of the south side of 7th and Broad Streets. Thalhimer's and Miller & Rhoads were at the heart of downtown Richmond. About five blocks from the Governor's Mansion and Capital Square, these two stores were the linchpins of Richmond shopping in the 1950s and '60s. Thalhimer's traced its history back to 1842 when William Thalhimer, an immigrant from Germany, started a dry goods store in Richmond. Miller & Rhoads opened in 1885, also as a small dry goods store, but by 1924, it covered an entire city block.

Blacks could shop in the stores. Thalhimer's even allowed a limited return policy for blacks which was almost unheard of and blacks could purchase food at the downstairs snack bars, but they couldn't sit down nor could they eat in the swanky upstairs restaurants, the Richmond Room in Thalhimer's or the Tea Room in Miller & Rhoads. When students from Virginia Union entered the store, sat down and demanded to be served, the police were called. Some of the students commented on their fear when they saw the police come into the store with dogs, but there was no violence like the episodes in the Deep South. Bonds were paid, the students were released, and a celebration ensued. Protesters and their supporters went to

Eggleston's Hotel on Second Street in Jackson Ward. This was still the center of black social life in Richmond so where else would such a celebration be held. The civil rights protests had come to Richmond. Blacks were happy this vital step had been taken.

Debby Anderson heard these stories, and she saw her sister leave their Northside home with her sandwich board emblazoned with protest messages. Anna was often on her way downtown to picket Loews movie theater, one of the premier white theaters in Richmond. Loews was a true movie palace having been built in 1928 at the beginning of the motion picture era. Like almost all businesses in Richmond in the late '50s and early '60s, there were parallel communities. There were the black movie theaters, and there were the white movie theaters. Going to the movies was a regular Saturday outing for the girls. We got to go for free, and we got free popcorn and sodas because my father managed one of the black movie theaters. So, it wasn't that movie viewing was denied to blacks, it was the fact that again separate was rarely equal. The black theaters received the second run movies unless it was a black film and while the facilities were adequate, none had the stately qualities of anything like the Loews Theater that Anna and her friends from Virginia Union University picketed. They picketed like students at North Carolina A&T University, my friend Marsha's future alma mater, had in 1937 when the theaters then deleted entire scenes from movies that included African-Americans when they were being shown in the South. The degree of the injustice had changed, but injustice there still was.

Debby's mother felt Debby was too young to take part with her sister in the protests, but Debby still wanted to play a role. By now, civil rights leaders understood the power of the loss of revenue. The visual image of protesters at the theaters wasn't enough. The owners had to realize they were losing money. Debby was one of the behind-the-scenes, young activists who would call the theater to ask if there were picketers that day. When told yes, she would comment, "well we won't be able to come down then." Not that this young, African-American girl would have been going anyway, but the person on the other end of the phone didn't know she was black nor that she wasn't even able to enter the theater. All they knew was they'd lost another customer.

A few months after the protests at Thalhimer's, the lunch counters were integrated for full service at most downtown Richmond stores. The demonstrations had led to the desired outcome. One year later, William B. Thalhimer and Webster Rhoads invited Richmond's leading black civil rights activists to dine with them in their respective upstairs restaurants. Soon after, the movie theaters integrated without incident. At least to us, it seemed suddenly we could go to the white theaters, but we weren't sure we were happy about it. For young girls, the magnitude of this change was not understood. All we knew was that all the adults were pleased, but now we had to pay to go to the movies and popcorn was no longer free. It wasn't until research started for this book we learned of the role our friend Debby Anderson had played. We hadn't known as kids, and if we had, we probably wouldn't have understood the importance of her actions. And we didn't understand the impact integration would have. Maybe our parents didn't either. African-Americans had so wanted the equality and opportunity that integration offered. Many may not have thoroughly thought of the potential for adverse impact on black businesses, on black communities and, on black children in schools or maybe they naturally felt the positives would outweigh those negatives.

At Chandler, integrating black students with white students wasn't going as smoothly as in downtown Richmond. The lunchroom at Chandler was a far more volatile place than the Tea Room and the Richmond Room in the downtown department stores. There were food fights. In the mornings before school started, we would gather in the basement cafeteria. The black students would migrate to one section of the room and the white students to another. We self-segregated, not as much a function of race as it was a function of friendship groups and familiarity. We sat with the people we knew and liked. We never knew what triggered it, but often there would be food fights. Sandwiches and fruit would fly from one part of the cafeteria to the other. We don't know if this was a different experience for the white students or whether periodic food fights between different cliques had happened at their schools. But for the black students, this had never happened before in any school we had attended. And what made the experience even odder, as Marsha remembers, is the failure of teachers to intervene. "It would be chaotic and confusing," recalls Marsha, "particularly because teachers would watch and not do anything." All of our previous experiences with adults were ones in which they protected us. Never were they silent observers to an event that could have escalated but, fortunately, never did. That safe, nurturing environment we had experienced in our school lives had ended. We now lived outside the cocoon of an entirely black community.

But that didn't mean there weren't nurturing teachers. Madeline remembers with great fondness, Mrs. Beaton, her chemistry teacher at Chandler. Like all of our teachers at Chandler, Mrs. Beaton was white. Madeline was in advanced chemistry. Realizing Madeline's knowledge and proficiency with the subject, Mrs. Beaton explored with Madeline the various career possibilities in chemistry. By the time Madeline left her class, she knew she wanted to be a biochemist. While Mrs. Chiles, our 4th-grade teacher, may have kindled Madeline's early interest in science, Mrs. Beaton nurtured it and honed it. Madeline believes she became a biochemist because of Mrs. Beaton at Chandler Junior High School. So, while there were white teachers, in later years, who tried to squelch our potential that was not our experience at Chandler. New possibilities were being introduced. Our world was changing.

Three months into our 7th-grade year there was an event that changed the world. The entire United States population and many around the world were shaken on November 22, 1963, when President John F. Kennedy was assassinated in Dallas, Texas. It's not clear to anyone of us, if the announcement of this tragedy was made at school on that Friday or if the news just spread throughout the school. All we can remember was talking about it in the way children do as we walked home. It was an event, but we had no idea of the magnitude of the president's death on the country and on black Americans in particular. Since his campaign and election President Kennedy had been taking actions to support the passage of the Civil Rights Act. Some of the steps were small and unknown. Such as an invitation to Richmond's own William B. Thalhimer to come to Washington with a group of business leaders to discuss civil rights or more visible actions, such as denying the Washington, D.C. football team use of the federally-owned land on which the then-named D.C. Stadium was located unless the team integrated. What the country saw was a president who was increasingly supportive of actions to provide equal rights and equal protections to African-Americans, and now that president was dead.

Most of us can remember watching the television coverage of the events over that weekend leading up to the national day of mourning on Monday, November 25th when the funeral occurred. What must our parents have thought? Did they expect a reversal in political thinking since his successor, Lyndon Johnson, was a Texan, a son of the South? As they watched the funeral, it is likely their hearts were heavy, fearing the road to the passage of the Civil Rights Act had just gotten longer, perhaps much longer.

While our parents' hearts may have been heavy, ours were still carefree. We were sad during the several days of the assassination and funeral because that was the emotion we saw all around us. While that heaviness of heart stayed with our parents for months, we were kids. We moved on, again not appreciating what had happened.

Playing was our reason for being. Marsha, both Debbies, Jeannie and I lived within about five blocks of each other. Our homes were on parallel streets—Montrose Avenue was the farthest west, then going east on the grid was Edgewood, then Griffin, then Hanes. We lived in the 2700 to the 2900 blocks; so, jumping from house to house wasn't hard and that's what we would do. We might ride our bikes to Jeannie's and Debbie's home to listen to the latest music of the day. We all had phonographs to play the 45 rpm records which were popular then. Someone had probably gotten their mom or dad to drive them to Barky's Record Store in Jackson Ward to buy the latest music. Barky's, had opened in 1956 and was a favorite spot for black teens. The best song, the most popular one, would be on one side of the 45-rpm record and sometimes a sleeper was on the other side. Berry Gordy had started Motown in 1960. That same year Chubby Checker introduced the world to the Twist. We'd do the Twist, and the Swim and then practice the newest line dance, the Madison, that was later popularized in the movie "Hairspray" about the integration experiences of Baltimore teens in 1962. We would listen to Smokey Robinson and the Miracles or Martha and the Vandellas as we'd preen in front of the mirror or thumb through the latest teen magazine; ordinary activities for the twelve and thirteen-year-old group.

The Johnson household was probably our favorite to visit. With a house becoming full with kids, the Johnsons were perhaps the most kid-friendly, but at some point, even they would be ready for this gaggle of neighborhood kids to leave their home. We'd be sent outside to play. Outside was a safe, fun place. The saying "It takes a village to raise a child" wasn't used then, but we were a part of a village. As we'd ride our bikes, we'd wave to Mrs. Morris on her porch or race our bikes along Fendall Avenue where my grandmother lived or stop and buy a candy bar at Hooper's Market, a small neighborhood convenience store near Debby Anderson's house. We thought nothing would happen to us, nor did our parents. It was the early 1960s. We were safe. And, if our parents were wondering where we were, a couple of quick phone calls would soon result in someone saying they'd seen us ride by and overheard us telling the location of our next stop. After riding around the neighborhood, maybe we'd go to my house and hula hoop in the front yard or stop by someone's house to talk, but most likely we'd head to our favorite spot, Battery Park.

Battery Park was so named because it had been home to a battery, a military unit comprising cannons and soldiers. The park area had been a part of the infrastructure for the defense of Richmond during the Civil War. Remember, our home city, Richmond, Virginia, had been the Capitol of the Confederate States of America, the states that had left the Union and formed their own "country" during the Civil War. Many vestiges of the Confederacy, both real and symbolic, like the statues on Monument Avenue, remain, but this was the only one in our specific community. If you didn't do a little research on the park's name, the Civil War wouldn't come to mind as you drove by or played in Battery Park. We never thought of it.

The park was about 2-3 blocks from our homes. It was a large urban park, the center of the Barton Heights section of Northside. It had basketball courts and swing sets, sandboxes and lovely hills to climb, something for every age group. In the summer, there were arts and crafts programs during the day, and at night there was music and dancing. But perhaps the most prominent features of Battery Park were the tennis courts. These were the courts were Richmond's native son and Wimbledon champion Arthur Ashe played as a teen. A few years older than we were, we didn't know Arthur. He had graduated from Maggie Walker High School when we attended elementary school. As a native son and an up-and-coming star in tennis, a sport not known for black achievement, we all knew who Arthur Ashe was, and many of us spent hours in the summer either taking tennis lessons or hanging out at the park.

It was probably the many hours spent just hanging out that moved us from being a loose collection of girls, friends in overlapping dyads and triads, to being a cohesive group. It was somewhere around this time we became the social club that would soon become the Valianettes.

The Valianettes emerged from another organization, a boys' club, the Valiants. The founding group of Valiants had been friends most of their lives and decided they wanted to establish a club. This boys' social club started at Graves Junior High School in the late '50s. Graves was the mid-point of the Jackson Ward neighborhood's feeder school track of Baker Elementary School, followed by Graves Junior High School and then Maggie Walker High School.

It is the nature of humans to form groups. African-Americans did it for the same reasons it has always been done—protection or enjoyment or both. The history of blacks organizing into groups dates back to the time following the Civil War. Initially, the purpose was pragmatic, not social. African-Americans knew they must band together to get anything they needed. No one person could meet his or her needs without the support, help, and involvement of a group. One of the first efforts to join forces was the establishment of burial societies. These groups, one of the earliest forms of insurance, ensured African-Americans had a fitting funeral and a final resting place in a cemetery.

It is interesting to note that in Richmond, the black cemeteries, six, all contiguous, were in the Barton Heights section of town, where we lived. The first, the Phoenix Cemetery, was established in 1815 by the Burying Ground Society of the Free People of Color of the City of Richmond. Next was the Union Burial Ground. Ebenezer Baptist Church, the church where Renée serves as a deacon, established a cemetery for its members. Other graveyards followed. By the late 1800s, not only were there six cemeteries for African-Americans, the cemetery as a locale had become a place for social gatherings. Blacks picnicked there every April as they celebrated

Negro Memorial Day, the day in 1865 when Richmond fell to Union soldiers. As time passed after the Civil War, the primary purpose and the benefits of joining together changed. Increasingly, individuals or at least families could meet their basic needs. Now, it was time for fun.

Just as the cemeteries were both places of sadness and places of joyful gatherings, the burial societies also had a dual purpose. Not only focused on death, they were also support groups. They took care of the sick and the aged. The early burial societies transformed in two ways. They became a part of the business world, becoming black insurance companies and a part of the social realm evolving into fraternal groups and social clubs.

Soon after the turn of the 20th century, one of Richmond's leading social groups was formed, the Astoria Beneficial Club. Like the burial societies of a few decades earlier, the Astoria's were focused initially on direct support of individuals. Later, they worked to benefit the African-American community. In the 1950s, for example, the club paid the requisite $1.50 poll tax for each of its members, a fee required for anyone who wanted to vote and a financial barrier to voting for many African-Americans. In 1959, a companion group to the Astoria's was established, the Astoria Wives. In today's time of women's equality, many would question why a group of women would become the Astoria Wives as opposed to a free-standing, separately-named women's club. Again, the roots of our race in bondage provide an answer. In slavery, women worked as the men did. Sadly, they felt fortunate when they could work beside their husbands or mates in the fields or in the owner's house as opposed to being separated on different plantations. After slavery, women continued to work. They worked as domestics or as seamstresses, skills that had been acquired during slavery. Some moved into teaching and other professions, but regardless of the job, most women worked to help support their families. It was not a sign of submission or subservience to a husband to be an Astoria wife, but a name filled with pride. The husband had risen to a level in society, he was an Astoria and the wife was proud to claim the role of 'wife.' Her husband had become the protector of the family, a position that black men had sought for decades.

So, it was in that tradition the Valiants and the Valianettes emerged in the mid- 20th century in Richmond.

Like most black kids of the era, they were listening to the doo-wop sounds of groups with names like the Platters, the Moonglows, and the Flamingos. As the guys sat around trying to think of a name for this new group—no one remembers where it came from, maybe the then-popular comic strip "Prince Valiant"— but somehow, they became the Valiants. Soon after forming, they decided that, like the Astoria's, they, too, wanted a companion group. The girls became the Valianettes.

The names sound hokey today, but this was the era of singing groups like the Shirelles, the Ronettes, and the Marvelettes as well as two emerging groups, the Primes and the Primettes that would later become the Temptations and the Supremes. In the early 1960s, no one thought of the names Valiants and Valianettes as odd, and no one thought it was strange for a girl's club to emerge from a boys' group. Certainly not our group of girls at Chandler Junior High School.

We were invited to the home of Janet Foster, the President of the Valianettes, as the first step in becoming the Junior Valianettes. The 'junior' group would be mentored by the older girls until we took their place as they graduated from high school. Janet was the granddaughter of Christopher French Foster, one of the original twenty-two who founded the Astoria's. In fact, the first meeting of the Astoria's was held at Christopher Foster's home 60 years earlier. So, Janet Foster's leadership of the Valianettes followed a family tradition in which the value of social clubs to the members and to the community was recognized.

Janet let us know the Valianettes had been watching our group and felt we were the right group to follow their legacy. We were stunned. The Valiants and Valianettes had a reputation and what a reputation it was. They were all high academic achievers, involved in the community, conscious of what was going on in the evolving civil rights movement, but not radicals. Their parents placed high expectations on them. They were expected to succeed. These young people would be leaders. This was the legacy we were to continue.

We were being invited to become Valianettes. We were in awe and honored.

Before becoming Junior Valianettes, we weren't a club. Not really. We didn't have a name, or at least, not one any of us can remember decades later. We were a loose collection of friends that by our regular connection referred to ourselves as a club. But, now we were an official social club with a name. We had been anointed by an older group of well-known, well-respected and well-liked girls. Not only would we follow in their footsteps, but we'd also have a brother club, a group of guys who would look out for us as we moved into high school. We would be the third generation of Valianettes and the first generation to go to the white high school, John Marshall.

All around us the world was changing.

Many, including some of our parents, had questioned whether Lyndon Baines Johnson would continue President Kennedy's path of supporting civil rights. That previous year, Kennedy had set the stage for the bill that would prevent all discrimination in public places and provide greater protection of the right to vote. The question of Johnson's position on civil rights and on supporting Kennedy's vision was quickly answered when in his first address to Congress following the assassination of President Kennedy, he said there would be no greater tribute to the former president's memory than the passage of the Civil Rights Act.

The Civil Rights Act of 1964 passed while we were in the 8th grade. None of us truly understood the magnitude of the passage of this landmark legislation. We were children. We had no idea how significant this law would be in changing our lives forever. What we knew was we already attended an integrated school. What we didn't realize was that we were among only 5% of blacks who were attending integrated schools in Virginia.

Massive resistance to integration had transitioned into passive resistance, more subtle actions, but compelling institutional racism nonetheless. What was then called the Pupil Placement Boards were supposed to assign students to schools based on where the child lived. Most Boards, however, weren't assigning black students to white schools. We didn't know that. While not the Pupil Placement Board per se, Madeline remembers a conversation with a counselor at Chandler during the summer as she was preparing to leave Baker Elementary and come to Chandler for the 7th grade. The counselor had reviewed Madeline's grades which were excellent and told her advanced placement classes were available at Chandler in math, science, and French. She asked Madeline which one she would like to take. Madeline asked if the students coming from other schools were limited to one advanced placement class. When told, "no," Madeline then calmly told the counselor she wanted all three of the advanced placement options. Our teachers—black teachers—had always had high expectations for us. They would encourage and push us to the highest level. Soon we would learn some white teachers thought we couldn't do the work even though our grades would show the opposite. Biases were there. It would take years to prove to these school administrators that the stereotypes they held were not reality. In hindsight, I wonder if only we thought we had shown that. The school administrators may have held on to these negative beliefs regardless of other indicators. Prejudices were deeply seated.

While civil rights was far too broad and almost esoteric a concept for us to understand. We did understand—pragmatically— relationships and perceptions between the races.

Renée and Madeline knew they were the only black kids taking ice skating after school. When one couldn't attend, spitballs were thrown at the other. Marsha and Debby recalled a white kid on a school bus throwing something at them as they walked home down Brookland Park Boulevard. Acceptance of blacks in a white environment was inconsistent. We were tolerated, but not embraced.

These incidents weren't only in the school environment. As our worlds started to slowly integrate, they affected our home lives and our out-of-school time also. Renée remembers her family was one of the first black families to build a home on Woodrow Avenue near Chandler Junior High. When the cement was poured for the sidewalk in front of the house, 'nigger' was written and became part of the concrete. This was the same year Dr. Martin Luther King, Jr. received the Nobel Prize for Peace, the same year the World's Fair in New York City had the theme 'peace through understanding.' We understood Dr. King, and many others were working for peaceful co-existence in our country and around the world. We knew there was the belief if the races spent more time together, there would emerge an understanding we were not that different. In Richmond, Virginia, even with the painless, i.e., nonviolent, process of school integration, there were still indications the road to co-existence might be extended, and the struggle for genuine acceptance would be even longer. The signs were all around us.

One such sign revolved around swimming. By the early '60s, the public swimming pools—for Negroes and the ones for whites—were still closed in Richmond as they had been for about a decade. In the '50s, the fear of the transmission of polio had been cited as one reason. By the early 60s, the stated explanation was often insufficient funds to make needed repairs, but many believe what caused the closures was the prospect of blacks and whites swimming together in the same pool. Swimming equality wasn't a major tenet of what blacks were fighting for. Blacks wanted access to all facilities supported with public funds. This was an essential part of being recognized as a tax-paying, equal member of American society.

Until that happened, however, the black community did what it had always done, it took care of its own. Since there were no public swimming pools for African-Americans to use to learn to swim, a local black physician—Dr. Jackson—whose Northside home included a swimming pool allowed the black YMCA to teach swimming to the neighborhood children. White children still swam in their parents' or friends' pools or at local country clubs. We didn't have as many options as whites, but, as always, our community found a solution.

But it wasn't just access to swimming facilities in the early 1960s that stood in the way of us learning to swim, it was also our hair. Over decades, most African-Americans had accepted and internalized the desirability of white standards of attractiveness. Narrow noses and lips and long, flowing, straight hair were signs of beauty in the black community, particularly the hair. These physical traits suggested there was a large pool of white genes in your family's history. That reality elevated you in the eyes of whites and of too many blacks. Because of their white ancestors, some blacks had naturally straight hair. Other blacks with coarser, curly hair achieved this straight-hair look through a laborious process. Oil applied to the hair, and a metal comb typically heated on the kitchen stove was combed through the hair, straightening out the tightness of the texture of the hair. The process worked, but the hair only remained straight if it wasn't exposed to water; therefore, most African-American women avoided swimming pools.

In the early 1900s, Garrett Morgan, a former slave, had invented a product that straightened the hair and lasted longer. However, it was a harsh chemical product that damaged the hair after multiple uses and could even burn the skin if left on the hair too long. It wasn't until the 1950s that a product was perfected by Johnson Products, a black-owned business founded in 1954, that was deemed mild enough for regular use on black women's hair. With this product, kinky hair was straightened, and water didn't cause it to immediately revert to its natural kinkiness. With the introduction of hair relaxers, as they were called, black hair had become much more manageable to retain the styles of the day. So, by the late '50s and early '60s, swimming had entered the world of black girls as an activity in which we could more easily participate. Now, with this new product and our parents' ongoing desire to raise well-rounded daughters, they wanted us to learn to swim, not only for recreational purposes, but because this skill could save our lives. So, as had always been the case, the black community took care of their kids.

Yes, the Civil Rights Act had passed, but making the mandates a reality and adjusting to that would take time. We faced multiple situations like the spitballs thrown off the bus and the separate-but-equal swimming lessons. There was a great deal of uncertainty about what the legislation would mean and how long it would take to see the impact. We were attending Chandler Junior High School, the white junior high school in Northside, so we knew the world was changing, but we were also still swimming in the segregated, 'Negro' pool. For those who had held the power position in society for so long—whites—there was a great fear of what the civil rights legislation might mean. For those of us who had had no real power, we remember these incidents. The slights as well as the successes, as a society—black and white—adjusted to a very new reality.

We remember with enormous pride when the actor Sidney Poitier, formally dressed in white tie and tails, bounded to the stage that year to receive his Academy Award. This was the first time that an African-American had won the Academy Award for Best Actor. Hattie McDaniel was the first African-American to win an Academy Award. She portrayed the servant, Mammy, in *Gone with the Wind*. While blacks, in McDaniel's time, were appropriately proud of her 'first,' Poitier was being recognized for the portrayal of a character with whom the black community could be proud of, a construction worker who helped to build a church in *Lilies of the Field*. His talent had been recognized by a primarily white community of actors. When he beamed going up on the stage, every black person watching the show on television glowed with him, proud of his talent, proud of how handsome and appropriate he looked that night and proud of the eloquence of his acceptance speech. He knew as we all did that he was representing an entire race. He did that well. This was important, up another rung—as a race—on that ladder of acceptance, white acceptance, integration.

And, this was the year the now Junior Valianettes would exhibit their talent on a much smaller stage—in the 8th-grade talent show at Chandler Junior High. By now, most of us had stopped taking dance lessons at Chapman's School of Dance, but vestiges remained. Debby and Gloria, both Chapman School alumni, choreographed our routine.

You haven't heard a lot about Gloria. Gloria Tyson Reid was a core member of our group in elementary, junior high and high school. She was a member of the Brownie troop at All Soul's Presbyterian Church and took dance lessons with us at Chapman's School of Dance. She even went to Fisk University with Ricki and Madeline; however, by marrying while a sophomore in college, her life took a different path than that of most of those in the group. In 1964, we didn't know our worlds would separate. For then, Gloria and Debby were planning our performance for the Chandler talent show.

They choreographed our act to the song 'Dance at the Gym' from *West Side Story,* a popular theatrical production (1957) and film (1961) of the time. Befitting a dance set in a gym, we wore the casual clothes of the day, blue jeans and white sweatshirts. The dance was high energy. We had all the steps, but we couldn't find an ending. We sought advice from our gym teacher. In hindsight, we wonder if she snickered after we left her office knowing the likely outcome of her suggestion. She had encouraged us to lie on our backs on the floor of the stage, with our feet toward the audience, and then quickly and theatrically throw our legs over our heads. This movement left our butts to the audience. We liked it. We thought it was dramatic. So, did the principal, John Madden, a little too dramatic. He called us into his office. First, he explained our performance had been moved from earlier in the show to be the final performance, the finale. I suspect he thought of that as the good news. Originally the Chandler cheerleaders' dance was the closing number. Now we were. However, in our unsophisticated minds, we had been moved from earlier in the show, a place of prominence, to the back—the figurative back of the bus. We thought being near the beginning of the talent show meant our performance was better than those that followed. Now we were at the end. As Mr. Madden tried to explain the ending act was deemed as the strongest, someone in our group said, "We're always at the back." We didn't understand this placement in the show was because we were good and they wanted the show to end with a bang. We thought it was because we were black. Because life had programmed us in this way, we were reacting to a perceived and anticipated insult because we were black. For us, this news was already bad. Then Principal Madden shared the really bad news. We had to change the end of the dance. This time we thought race would save us. Once we told him our white gym teacher had suggested the ending, we thought he would say we didn't have to change it. He didn't. While the finish may be perceived as somewhat mild today, in 1964 Richmond, it was too risqué by the standards of the day. Having the white teacher suggest the ending of the dance didn't make the ending good just as having the black kids develop the dance didn't make the dance bad. In fact, both were the opposite. The frame of race was always there for us. Sometimes it was more in the background as it was around our dance and sometimes it was more overt as it was when we went to buy our costumes for that dance.

We had decided to go to Woolco, a discount department store that had opened in the newest shopping area in Northside. Azalea Mall, as it was called, was the first enclosed mall in Richmond. It had upscale stores, like a branch of Thalhimer's from downtown and it also had Woolco, an early version of the big box, discount stores. Woolco was a part of the Woolworth's brand. As we strolled through the store looking at the various styles of jeans and examined the prices, we were followed around the store. Not by someone seeking to help us, but by someone who we thought was watching to ensure we did not shoplift. We knew as blacks, whites would often feel we were doing the wrong thing, the bad thing, the illegal thing. It would never have occurred to any of us to steal. We hadn't been raised that way, but in the minds of the white store clerks, their stereotype was whenever a group of black kids came into the store, they were likely there to steal.

Regardless of Mr. Madden's requirement for an ending change or the incident at Woolco, we were happy. Our performance had gone well. That night we didn't focus on race as we accepted the applause of our fellow students and family. We weren't the only African-Americans performing in the talent show. We didn't feel we were representing the entire race that night. Nonetheless, we felt a different pressure than the white performers to do well. It wasn't stage jitters. It was living up to the expectations of your parents and forebearers and overcoming the negative stereotypes of the white attendees.

There was almost continually a sense of anxiety: always waiting for the race-driven remark or reaction and thinking it would be an adverse reaction or comment. This was a part of our day-to-day reality. We always knew we had to act more appropriately, achieve at a higher standard, and dress a certain way. There was no room for doubt. We couldn't be marginal. We had to be exceptional. That understanding was part of what reinforced our friendship. We shared a common unifier—race—and a common enemy, racism. These were essential ingredients that undergirded our bond in a way we could not have identified or understood. While those were powerful components of our friendship, there was so much more than race.

Friendships emerge from many factors. *Proximity*. Many of us lived in the same area. Northside had been our home all of our lives. *Shared experiences*. We had banded together in the cafeteria at Chandler Junior High and shopped together at Woolco and Thalhimer's. We had grown up together through Norrell Elementary, swimming lessons at Dr. Jackson's pool, dancing lessons at Chapman's School of Dance, scouting and so much more. *Shared values.* We were black and middle-class. Nothing was more important than our focus on preparing ourselves for college and the world of opportunity.

We had a solid bond of friendship we would need as we entered an exciting and still racially-charged time, high school in a newly integrated school in the mid-'60s.

As I reflect on our experience at Chandler Junior High School, I realize that I can only write from my memory of that experience as a black youngster. My friends and I were bonded by our culture, by our race, by our values, and by our experiences. So, too, were the white kids into whose space we had entered. I would imagine that we were seen by many as the intruders, by some as unwanted intruders. Their world had been set, stable and peaceful and here we came. Did their parents shelter them from the news coverage of the protests in the South? Did they overhear conversations, in their homes or at their houses of worship, about Richmond's racial politics and the segregationist desires of some of the state's political leaders? Did they know anything about the civil rights movement? While even though we may not have openly discussed our race, we were surrounded by what it meant to be a Negro in America. I suspect that nothing made them think about their whiteness and what it was to be white in America. At Chandler, the black students and the white students were in parallel worlds within the same building. We had classes together. We went to school programs together, but our frames of reference were drastically different. No one discussed that, and no efforts were made to bring those worlds together. To some small degree that would change in high school, not by the school administration, not by those who enabled our education, but by the students as we moved slowly, cautiously, to understand each other.

CHAPTER 7
JOHN MARSHALL HIGH SCHOOL -
UNDERCLASSMEN

"Did we know we were straddling two worlds, trying to assimilate into a society defined by whites while maintaining our black identity? No, not consciously, but that is what we were doing."

The original high school opened in 1909 in downtown Richmond. It was built on the grounds of the garden at the home of John Marshall, the country's first Supreme Court Justice, for whom the school was named. There was a parade and a day-long dedication event when the school opened. High schools were still majestic buildings then in which students were educated toward what, for most, was their terminal degree, a high school diploma. It was with far less fanfare our school, the new John Marshall (Jayem), a sprawling modern building, opened in the Ginter Park section of Northside in September 1960. And, it was without fanfare we began high school there a few years later.

No parents held our hands as they had nine years before when we entered Norrell Elementary School. Instead, many of us walked to the corner of Brookland Park Boulevard and Fendall Avenue, two blocks from Stuart Elementary School, and got on the school bus. No one expected any of the overt racial hatred that confronted many black students as they entered white schools in the South and there was none. As we walked through the doors of John Marshall High School for the first time, there was no drama, no anticipation of violence, no fears of any confrontation. We were going to get an education, but education probably wasn't even on our minds. For us, high school was only a venue, a place for us to be popular, to have fun and to meet boys. We'd get to the education part, but on that first day, we wanted to make sure our hair was styled in the latest way, that we were wearing the right clothes and we didn't do something to embarrass ourselves. We were real teenagers, not pre-teens or even 13-year-olds. We were firmly in that delicate, delightful and dangerous space of the teen years, not adults yet, but in the highest tier of childhood. High school was the place we were supposed to make memories that would last a lifetime. These were supposed to be some of our best years. We knew it and would see to it they were. High school had begun.

It was fall, 1965. Malcolm X had been assassinated earlier in the year. August had been marked by race riots in Watts, a section of Los Angeles. President Johnson had signed the Voting Rights Act and the Immigration Act, the impact of which wouldn't be felt by people of color for years to come. The fashion of the moment for teenage girls was blouses with Peter Pan collars under cable knit sweaters with plaid skirts and knee-high socks. And the popular female singing group, the Supremes, could be heard on WANT radio, the black station then at 990 on the AM dial and at 1480 AM, WLEE, the white radio station across town.

In black homes and in white ones, families were watching a new television show that premiered the same month we entered high school. *I Spy*, debuted on TV in the fall of 1965. Starring Robert Culp and Bill Cosby, it built on the espionage craze that had its roots in both the real Cold War of the 1950s and in the fictionalized Cold War of the popular James Bond movies that had hit the movie screens. *I Spy* was an action series with Culp and Cosby playing the roles of international spies. It was the first time an African-American had had a starring role in a television series that wasn't a demeaning or subservient role. There had been other television shows over the years in which blacks were featured or even starred, but not shows in which a black person played a solid, middle-class, contributing member of society.

One of the more popular early shows with black characters had a strong connection to Richmond, Virginia. It was the 1950s *Amos 'n' Andy*, a pure caricature of black life. Two white Richmond natives, Freeman Gosden and Charles Correll initially produced and starred in the radio version. African-Americans took on the lead roles for television. The show set in an all-black community had characters that were dim-witted, conniving, and ignorant.

The men were weak, and the women were domineering, all images that fed into many of the racial stereotypes of the time. It will seem entirely incongruous for many that we watched *Amos 'n' Andy* in our upwardly mobile, politically-sensitive homes. The reality is that the show was funny and that's why we and many others in the black community watched it. We suspect it may not have been viewed by its white producers as a parody, but for us, that is precisely what it was, a parody not unlike *All in the Family* years later or the sketches on *Saturday Night Live* today. There weren't people like this in our worlds. We laughed at the comedy and at the characters knowing they were not real depictions of our society. As African-Americans became more sensitive to the impact of whites, possibly/probably, viewing this show and thinking it an authentic portrayal of blacks, it was important that the show come off the air, and it did in the early 1960s. White America had very limited direct interactions with black people. Much of their perception of who we were, came as it still does from the media. We didn't want the white world to think of us as Amos and Andy.

Just as it was vital to remove a negative image off of television, it was monumental that *I Spy*, a show with a black lead character presenting a positive image, was introduced. The show was about two top, undercover agents of the United States government, who fought bad guys all over the world as they pretended to be a tennis pro and his trainer. When people were talking about Arthur Ashe and his prowess in tennis, it is interesting to note that sport provided the backdrop for this show. Art was adapting—something positive—from real life. Although the show was a drama, there were many funny moments. Cosby's comedy was sophisticated and urbane, not the country bumpkin buffoonery of *Amos 'n' Andy*. This was the first show with a black character we as African-Americans could be proud of. We wanted whites to see blacks in the image of Bill Cosby's character, smart, educated, competent—more than competent, skilled. He was Robert Culp's equal. This was the image we wanted to portray. We wanted our character, the black character, to be a black Robert Culp. We wanted to be seen as no different from whites.

These were the realities of the time. Did we know we were straddling two worlds, like the Supremes or Bill Cosby's television character, trying to assimilate into a society defined by whites while maintaining our black identity? No, not consciously, but that is what we were doing. If you asked us what we were thinking about, as 14-year-olds, it wasn't about the racial implications of television shows, it was just one thing, having fun.

L TO R -- GLORIA TYSON REID, MARSHA FORD WARE, JEANNIE JOHNSON PETTIES, TAMARA LUCAS COPELAND, DEBBY ANDERSON SMITH, DEBBIE JOHNSON RIDDICK

Family was no longer the center of our worlds. Like most teenagers, friends had become our focus. We now had activities as a club. The Junior Valianettes met monthly at one of the member's home. The first part of the meeting was focused on planning an upcoming activity. One year we planned Christmas caroling with our brother club, the Junior Valiants. Occasionally, the event would be a service project, like a visit to a nursing home, but more typically it was a social one for us. Then, we'd have a lovely lunch prepared by one of our moms and proceed to hang out together for the rest of the afternoon.

Since it was September, the school year just starting, we knew what the plan would be: the Virginia State Fair. It was a much-awaited event in Richmond in the '60s. Cotton candy, crazy carnival rides, corn dogs, candied apples and sideshow barkers urging you to come in to see whatever human condition was being mocked and exploited that year would all be parts of this magical world for us. We would save up to go to the fair, sometimes selling glass bottles back to stores, an early form of environmentally-friendly recycling, to get the penny deposits so we'd have extra spending money. We would worry it would rain because it always did for part of the week the fair was in town. We would want that perfect crisp fall day so we could go to the State Fair. The State Fair was big business. School would close a half-day early for one day. Often, we went twice to the fair, once during the day and once at night, but no matter what we went at least once every year. A couple of parents would drive us to the fairgrounds and tell us what time and where to be to be picked up. No one worried anything would happen to us at the fair. We were in a group. We were safe. We'd giggle if we saw a boy from school, but mostly we'd focus on roaming around the fair, seeing everything, eating foods we could get only at the fair and trying not to get sick on the rides that swung us from right to left and then up and down. We loved the fair. Maybe it was because we had freedom there or perhaps that it was a much-anticipated once-a-year event. But for whatever reason, this was a significant part of our teen years and another way we bonded as friends.

We don't remember ever thinking of the fair as a white event, but it was. The attendants at every carnival game were white. The ride operators were white. African-American farmers weren't submitting pumpkins or hogs for fair contests, and we knew no one who entered the apple pie or peach jam competitions. We didn't notice blacks weren't a part of the economy of the State Fair. Our parents probably didn't see that either.

Pursuing opportunities for blacks in this once-a-year, agriculturally-focused, event was not a priority. Our parents were far more focused on the recently passed Voting Rights Act and its impact on garnering power for African-Americans in Richmond. They knew economic opportunities at the State Fair would flow from a much broader power base for blacks. Most thought power rested squarely in the realm of politics.

The month before we started high school, President Lyndon Johnson had signed the Voting Rights Act of 1965 which allowed the federal government to oversee voter registration and elections in situations where discrimination might be suspected. It also banned literacy tests. Our parents understood this as one more necessary step in ensuring the right to vote for African-Americans. This was another step in a long line of actions that traced their roots back to 1865's 13th Amendment to the United States Constitution that abolished slavery. And the 14th Amendment that declared any man over age 21 born or naturalized in the U.S. was a U.S. citizen. The subsequent 15th Amendment specifically said no citizen could be denied the right to vote based on his race, color or former condition of servitude. All of those laws had been passed along with others, but still, blacks were denied the right to vote in many states, particularly in the South. So, there was considerable hope the Voting Rights Act of 1965 would correct all of the inequities that had not been "fixed" by previous statutes.

In Richmond, an organization had formed in 1956 to register blacks to vote. The Crusade for Voters, as it was named by Astoria club founder Christopher Foster, grew from a racially-mixed group called the Committee to Save Public Schools. Some whites continued to work to stop the integration of public schools in Richmond. There was a referendum on the November ballot to block this backward step. There was the expectation blacks would vote in large numbers to support the referendum. However, on the day of the vote, the turnout by African-Americans was meager. This situation showed black city leaders they needed to focus on educating blacks on issues coming up for a vote and why voting was so critical. And then get them registered to vote. Thus, the Crusade for Voters was born.

When the Crusade started, only 19 percent of eligible black voters in Richmond were registered. By the time we entered high school nine years later, that number had almost doubled to 35 percent. The Crusade-endorsed candidates and worked for their election. We heard about which candidates the Crusade had supported when we went to church on Sundays and on election days when cars with loudspeakers mounted on top would drive through black neighborhoods announcing the names of the Crusade-endorsed candidates and urging you to vote. Marsha and several others in our group recall their parents awaiting the Crusade's analysis of the candidates and endorsement decision as a crucial ingredient in determining their vote. By 1962, the Crusade for Voters and the black vote itself had been recognized as power players in Richmond. Seven of the nine candidates for the Richmond city council who were backed by the Crusade for Voters that year were elected. The power of black voters was being demonstrated.

When we entered high school, the work of the Crusade for Voters and the importance of bloc voting was often dinner table conversation for most of us. We weren't ready to use the bloc voting concept, but we heard about it, we recognized the pride with which our parents discussed it and subliminally it was making a substantial impression on us as we developed into politically-aware adults. In today's vernacular, the Crusade for Voters was an important part of the village that raised us to be politically informed and engaged teenagers, knowledgeable of the issues that faced our race as we went about the everyday world of attending a white high school.

In our freshman year, we lived in two racial worlds: the primarily white world of school and the mostly black world of all the other parts of our lives. These worlds clashed when we attended our first high school pep rally. We were confronted by how difficult it is to try to straddle two racial worlds. We'd had pep rallies at Chandler Junior High School, but they were nothing like this. The energy was higher, the students' enthusiasm was greater, and the music was louder. As the students streamed into the gym for our first high school pep rally, people were clapping and cheering and singing happily and boisterously, "I wish I was in the land of cotton, good times there are not forgotten, look away, look away, look away Dixieland." Yes, 'Dixie' was the fight song for John Marshall High School. We were fourteen-year-old kids, excited to be at our first high school pep rally, committed to integration and assimilation like our parents; so, what did we do? We stomped our feet in the bleachers like everyone else because the energy was contagious. We knew the words. How could we not, growing up in the former capital of the Confederacy. But something about singing them didn't feel right. Everyone was singing though, "In Dixieland, I'll take my stand to live and die in Dixie, away, away, away down South in Dixie, away, away, away down South in Dixie." Did the school administration consciously choose a song that lauded a time in history when blacks were enslaved? Probably not, they were the sons and daughters of the South. They had grown up hearing this song as a rallying cry to unite, to move forward toward victory. It was a fight song and using this song as the football team's fight song probably dated back to early in the history of John Marshall High School. Did we think about the fact we were cheering to a song that celebrated a time when our ancestors were enslaved? No, probably not consciously that first time at the rally. We were young, trying to fit in at the school, and we were caught up in the moment. It was freshman year, our first pep rally. The bleachers in the gym literally rocked with incredible energy. However, that period of mindless enthusiasm with 'Dixie' playing as the foundation of this joy would be very, very short-lived.

At home during freshman year, our parents still talked about the recent election of Benjamin "B.A." Cephas to the Richmond city council. This was the second African-American to be elected to the city council in the 20th century. The first had been Oliver Hill, one of the principal attorneys in the Brown v. Board of Education Supreme Court case and the dad of one of the few, black upperclassmen at our high school. Hill served on the council from 1948-1950, losing his re-election bid by less than 50 votes according to the *Afro-American*, the black newspaper. Remarkably, but not surprisingly, it had taken twelve years for another African-American to be elected to the Richmond city council. It was with pride and a sense of power our parents were glorying in their voting bloc outcome and because once again there was someone on city council who looked like them and who directly understood their issues.

At Madeline's home, her parents were talking about the recently filed, legal case of her uncle, Darius Swann. Having just returned to North Carolina from India where they were Presbyterian missionaries, Rev. Swann, and his wife Vera had enrolled their six-year-old son, James, into the nearest school. It was a white school. On the first day of school, James came home with a note from the principal saying he had been enrolled in the wrong school. According to the principal, he needed to go to the black school and then apply for a transfer to the white one closer to his home. Even after Brown v. Board of Education and a 1965 desegregation plan for the school district, real integration was slow in coming to the North Carolina community where James lived. His parents decided this incident demonstrated more was needed to make inclusion successful. They began a journey, for them and for the country, that would end in the landmark U.S. Supreme Court case of Swann v. Charlotte-Mecklenburg Board of Education, the case that would, almost a decade later, lead to mandatory busing.

Protests, like the Swanns', were happening in courtrooms and in streets across the South. And wherever there were protests, there was always one constant. Protesters—black and white—would sing 'We Shall Overcome.' This powerful anthem of the civil rights movement took its lyrics from Charles Tindley's 1900 gospel song, "We Shall Overcome Some Day," but the music is thought to have come from Gustavus Pike's 1873 song, 'No More Auction Block for Me' based on earlier slave songs. While 'We Shall Overcome' had a mournful melody, its words, "Deep in my heart, I do believe, we shall overcome someday," spoke of what was to come in a way that was nurturing and moving.

While 'We Shall Overcome' was the soundtrack for the civil rights movement, inspiring actions across the South, at John Marshall High School, we were cheering on our football team to the sounds of 'Dixie.' The irony of this didn't strike us at first. We had been raised to be proud of our race, but that pride resided within the context of wanting to prosper. Most blacks wanted to get along with whites because we saw that as our route to succeeding in their world. We wanted to be a part of their school and to fit in, like every other teenager. So, we did the things to fit in and to be successful. We yelled enthusiastically at the pep rallies, went to our classes and became the exceptional Negroes we were expected to be.

We excelled in our classes. We studied and studied. As we researched certain papers for school, I wonder if we even noticed how excluded we were not just from the history books but also reference books. For example, if we used U.S. census data for a paper, that data only referenced white and non-white as racial identifiers. No mention of Negroes, and not of black or of African-Americans. In 1965 America, the standard, for everything, was still white. Like most blacks, unconsciously we accepted that reality. We wanted to get along.

Even though the black students ate in one cafeteria, while the white students ate in another, we got along. Now into our third year of being with white students, or for some of us our fourth year, we were becoming friendlier. We weren't going to each other's homes, but we were saying more than "hi" as we passed each other in the hall or got our books out of our lockers. We would joke or talk about some assignment a teacher had

67

given—friendly conversation, but not friends. Our friends were still the black students, and our closest friends were the other Junior Valianettes and the Junior Valiants. It was with this group we were looking forward to spending the summer between freshman and sophomore year. We'd made it through that critical first year. We had succeeded in the white world, serving as proxies for our race. Now, in our minds, it was time to play.

While fun was to be the main feature of the summer, there was one requirement for some of us. We had to learn to type. At this time in our country's history, many girls learned to type. It was a skill that prepared them for the clerical positions that were available to women. For our parents, learning to type was not to prepare us for a secretarial job. It was to help us develop term papers in high school and to make us ready to meet the demands of college. We attended a morning typing class for the first part of the summer in 1966, so, our break from school wasn't unstructured and free.

It was in this class Veronica entered our world. Veronica had been attending Mosby Junior High School in the East End section of Richmond where she lived, but her parents had recently built a home in the Hungary Road area where Madeline and Ricki lived. Like most of the kids in this new, black, upper-income housing development, Veronica would attend John Marshall. As a part of her transition to the school, her parents enrolled her that summer in the typing class at Jayem, and it was there Marsha met Veronica. They hit it off immediately, spending time at each other's homes and going to the movies together. Marsha introduced Veronica to our group, and it was through Marsha's advocacy that Veronica would, in the fall, become a part of the Valianettes. Veronica would be one of the few Valianettes who hadn't spent most of her early life with the group. Would this make it harder for her to become a part of the group? Having been together for almost a decade, our connections were strong. Veronica would not be entering that loose configuration of friends from a few years earlier, we were a club now, and she would have to prove she fit in.

Veronica and Marsha didn't complain about having to take typing, nor did the rest of us. It was only for a few hours a day and only for a month.

The mid-1960s was still a time when children, and our group especially, did what their parents told them to do without question and without complaining. Taking this short class was fine. We knew we still had most of the summer to focus on our priority, having fun.

One of our favorite places to go that summer for fun was Pocahontas State Park. We loved to go swimming and horseback riding in this state park in Chesterfield County, a county that abutted the city of Richmond, probably only about 20 miles from our homes. We weren't allowed to date yet, but we could go out in groups; so, we were excited to go to the park because we could go with the Valiants, our brother club. Remember our community—the African-American community in Northside—was still relatively small. While our parents didn't have as much interaction with the parents of the Valiants as they did with the parents of the other Valianettes, they knew them. The father of one boy was among the first black police officers in Richmond. Another was a plumber who had done work in our homes, and one had worked with Madeline's dad as a brick mason. They were a known part of the black world that had the shared value of working to succeed. Our parents were comfortable with us being with the Valiants.

Our parents were also pleased we could go to Pocahontas State Park, but for a much different reason than we were. They knew one more racial barrier had been overcome. We didn't realize it, but it wasn't until after the passage of the Civil Rights Act in 1964 that African-Americans could go to this park. From 1936, when the Virginia State Park System opened, until 1950 with the establishment of the Prince Edward State Park for Negroes, African-Americans were not allowed in the Virginia State Park System. The creation of that one park for blacks only happened following a lawsuit arguing Virginia was not upholding the separate-but-equal doctrine. After the Brown v. the Board of Education decision that separate was in fact not equal, some Virginia parks were leased out making them quasi-private facilities. The park operators could then determine who was allowed in or out, i.e., keeping African-Americans out of these now private parks. At one point, the Governor of Virginia, fearing he would be forced to integrate, suggested the state should not have any public parks, a reaction not unlike the closing of the public swimming pools.

It was only through federal legislation that African-Americans could do something as simple as go horseback riding at Pocahontas State Park. Without the legislation, the Valiants and the Valianettes would have been turned away from the park. Once again, our parents had shielded us.

AT POCAHONTAS STATE PARK

We naturally thought we could now go to Pocahontas State Park because we were old enough for this outing. We didn't wonder why our parents hadn't brought us to this fun place when we were younger even though it was so near to home. We were protected and insulated by our parents from overt, structural racism and discrimination. They would never have taken us to a place from which they knew we would be turned away. They never wanted us to feel inferior or to know our options were limited. By shielding us from such racial barriers, we grew up feeling empowered and capable even though society would have given us very different cues if allowed to. In the mid-1960s, in a southern city, it didn't occur to us, as teenagers, that there were everyday things we couldn't do. A clear-cut example that our parents had succeeded.

And, as it didn't occur to us there was something we couldn't do, it didn't occur to the Richmond city fathers there was anything THEY couldn't do. They were developing a plan some would label malicious and racist. At its center sat Chesterfield County, where Pocahontas State Park was located. Unlike many parts of the country, cities are not part of counties in Virginia. They are entirely separate jurisdictions. In the mid-1960s, white power brokers took a drastic action to dilute the growing political power of African-Americans in Richmond city. The white leaders of Richmond and Chesterfield County met in what was characterized as secret meetings. The demographics of our region were like many parts of the country, urban areas, cities were becoming blacker as adjoining suburbs grew whiter. Chesterfield County was a predominately white area. By 1966, in Richmond, African-Americans made up 52% of the population, close to that tipping point at which sheer numbers might have power.

The influence, if not the power, of blacks, had been demonstrated when Winfred Mundle, my next-door neighbor, was not only elected to city council, along with Henry Marsh and a second term for B.A. Cephas, he was chosen Richmond's vice-mayor. Chosen, not elected, because, at the time, the mayor and the vice-mayor of Richmond were selected by their colleagues on the council, not elected by the citizenry. Mr. Mundle's selection as vice-mayor was taken as an acknowledgment that Richmond was becoming increasingly black and that that reality must be recognized in increasingly visible ways. Power was shifting, incrementally, but moving. Even though Mr. Mundle was seen as the more palatable choice over the longer-tenured Cephus who some viewed as militant, he was still a black man in the second highest position in the city, a place where no black man had sat before. Some white leaders saw the annexation of several square miles of an abutting, primarily white area as the solution to this power shift. So, as hundreds, if not thousands, of white families, moved to adjacent counties to escape the growing number of African-Americans in Richmond, their own white leaders were seeking to bring them back into Richmond's geographic boundaries by annexing one area to which they had moved. Whites in Chesterfield County fought this action for years. And, under the Voting Rights Act of 1965, blacks also opposed the annexation as an effort to dilute their power. Years later, the U. S. Supreme Court refused to invalidate this action. With the annexation of 23 square miles of Chesterfield County, 47,262 whites became residents of Richmond along with 555 blacks. Literally, overnight, the population of Richmond dropped from 52% African-American to 42%, a substantial demonstration of white power and of structural racism

This was not the first time whites had taken drastic action to respond to a new racial reality. A very similar, extreme action had occurred a little over six decades earlier. In 1902, the state of Virginia adopted a new state constitution. Changing a state's constitution is a significant action taking a majority vote of the members of both houses of the General Assembly for two consecutive years, and then it must pass on a general ballot, but the desire for the change was high, and passage proved easy. The state leaders wanted to limit the power of the freed slaves who actively exercised their new powers and freedom in the period called Reconstruction. The new state constitution changed the definition of who could vote in Virginia and caused the number of registered black voters to drop from 147,000 in 1901 to less than 5,000 in 1905. Now, in what was viewed as a far more progressive era, the white power brokers in the region had again demonstrated their power. The nexus of power was back solidly with the white race in the newly expanded city of Richmond.

We heard our parents and other adults talk about the machinations of the political leaders in Richmond and Chesterfield County that made this happen, but it was background noise in our teenage world, and there was a lot of this 'noise.' This was a time of high political involvement as blacks entered the political arena locally and across the country. Newspaper headlines routinely reported political activity that would affect us not only in Virginia but in other parts of the country. We heard about the recent election of Edward Brooke (R-MA) as the first African-American in the United States Senate since Reconstruction. We also heard about the statement he made following his election, "I do not intend to be a national leader of the Negro people." Our parents were talking about this at our kitchen tables. They were proud of his election, but they were concerned by his statement. Influential voices were needed for African-Americans. They were disappointed by such a public stance not to represent his race. The nuances of Brooke's comment and the intricacies of the local legal maneuverings were far too complicated for us to understand. Significant milestones in the liberation of black people swirled around us, but we didn't think about them, talk about them, or perhaps even entirely comprehend they were happening. We were living life as middle-class, teenagers in Richmond, primarily in still segregated, black Richmond, but during the school year, in white Richmond, too.

It was time for us to again focus on school. We had made a name for ourselves freshman year. We were smart, actively participating in class discussions, raising our hands to be acknowledged for the many answers we knew. We had school spirit. We loved going to the basketball and football games. Some of the Valiants were on the junior varsity teams. We enjoyed cheering for them. We fitted into the culture of John Marshall or at least we thought we did.

What would Harry Flood Byrd think? Remember, he was the senator from Virginia who about 10 years earlier had led the congressional action for massive resistance to school integration, not just in Virginia, but across the South. He died on October 20, 1966, the beginning of our sophomore year at John Marshall High School. By then, we were acclimated to Jayem. We were engaged in school activities. We were Marshallites.

We joined clubs. Madeline, Renée and I were in the Young Americans Club focused on national pride, patriotism, and good citizenship. Madeline and Renée were also in the German Club. Debbie, Jeannie, and Gloria were in the Spanish Club. Debby was in the Russian Club. Veronica chose Future Homemakers of America and Marsha joined DECA, the Distributive Education Club of America which focused on retail and wholesale businesses and public relations.

With several other Jayem students, both black and white, Madeline, Renée and I also participated in the Junior Achievement program. While our parents wanted us to be prepared for college and professional career opportunities, they may have been more attuned than most to the need to also expose us to entrepreneurial options. Many black businesses had thrived during segregation, but with integration, blacks became more reliant on whites for employment. My father would often comment integration was the best thing that had happened to black people, and it was the worst thing. It opened many doors but closed others. Black customers frequented the white-owned cleaners or the white-owned florist.

To some degree, it was because they wanted to exercise their fought-for options. In other ways, it was because blacks had internalized what they had heard for so many years that, "white is better." Therefore, following integration, many black businesses closed forcing blacks to move from their own companies into other corporate or employment areas. In those venues, whites were in charge and controlled who got the jobs. Our parents were determined we would always have a backup plan, a plan we controlled; so, we were in Junior Achievement. We learned how to research business ideas, develop a prototype if there was a product, market the idea or product and determine what the profit margin might be. Junior Achievement was another resource in the arsenal to prepare us for life.

Back at school, we screamed and cheered at the bonfire before the homecoming game, but this year we weren't as enthusiastic about the playing of 'Dixie.' In fact, we chose not to join in the cheering when it was played. Instead, we had our own cheer, "Ungh, ungawa, Justices got the power." No one knows for sure how it became the foot stomping chant it did, but it wasn't only at John Marshall High School for our team, the Jayem Justices. It became an expression black kids were using. The derivation of the term is interesting. Some suggest it was rooted in the west coast. 'Ungawa' seems to be a term made up by MGM movie staff who had lunch on Gower Street. Somehow 'on gower' evolved into 'ungawa' and was one of the primary "terms" used by Tarzan to communicate with animals in the Tarzan movies of the 1930s and '40s. Over time 'ungawa' seemed to have many meanings in those movies, some racist and others benign. Urban legend says in the '60s the term was co-opted by black teens on the west coast to suggest black power. We don't know how this word or the chant made its way to Richmond, Virginia, but we did know in 1967, it was a part of our response to the playing of 'Dixie.' It almost had a call-and-response rhythm. The white students would sing 'Dixie,' and then the black students would respond with "Ungh, ungawa justices got the power." There was no malice in the actions, just a recognition of differing perspectives, differing cultural vantage points, as both groups actively supported our school's sports team. We still didn't know how else to show our disapproval of 'Dixie.' If we had talked with our parents, they would have offered many ideas, but we didn't ask them. We were teenagers. We could handle it. We had our way. On some subconscious level, we didn't want to rock the boat too much. We still worked to fit into the student body.

We got a sign we were succeeding when we were acknowledged by the student body. I was the first in our group to win a school-wide honor. I was voted onto May Court. The May Court was an annual rite of springtime at Richmond high schools, maybe even at many schools across the South. Girls would be elected to the May Court, a collection of royal ladies-in-waiting, so to speak, to the May Queen. Some believe this celebration of spring had pagan roots, but it definitely dated back to villages in ancient England. At John Marshall, five girls from each class would be elected to represent their class. They would wear formal gowns in pastel colors and would wind pastel-colored ribbons around a pole like a flagpole, but dubbed the Maypole for this occasion, to signify the beginning of spring. All kinds of gymnastics events would be featured on that day. The cadet band would play, and the student body would come out to watch the activities, very much like a village festival. I was one of the sophomore class attendants to the May Court. That year five African-Americans girls were in the May Court. The story of this event was proudly covered by the *Richmond Afro-American*, the black newspaper in town. This was another first, the first time black girls were voted onto the May Court, another sign we were being accepted into the white world of John Marshall High School.

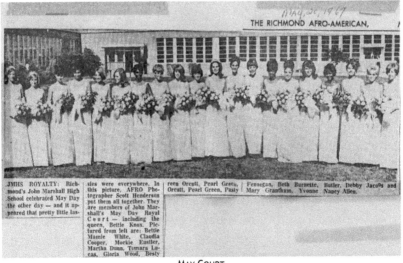

THE RICHMOND AFRO-AMERICAN,

JMHS ROYALTY: Rich-mond's John Marshall High School celebrated May Day the other day — and it appeared that pretty little lassies were everywhere. In this picture, AFRO Photographer Scott Henderson put them all together. They are members of John Marshall's May Day Royal Court — including the queen, Bettie Knox. Pictured from left are: Bettie Mamie White, Claudia Cooper, Mockie Eustler, Martha Dunn, Temara Lucas, Gloria Wood, Besty Orcutt, Pearl Green, Pasty Orcutt, Pearl Green, Pasty Green, Fennegan, Beth Burnette, Butler, Debby Jacobs and Mary Grantham, Yvonne Nancy Allen.

MAY COURT

75

While there weren't any violent or school-wide overt acts of racism, all wasn't as rosy as the pastoral scene at May Court suggested. In sophomore year, several students came to John Marshall from all-black junior high schools. These schools included 7th, 8th and 9th grades; so, it was in the ninth grade they and their parents, with guidance from the black school administrators, had to decide if they would move into a black high school or into a white one. Madeline can remember a French teacher in sophomore year publicly saying the black students who were entering John Marshall from Mosby Junior High in the East End, where Veronica had attended, and from Graves Junior High in Jackson Ward wouldn't be doing well at John Marshall because the Negro education system was inferior. We can remember some in that group of kids didn't do well. While there is never the occasion when everyone does equally as well, we wonder if they internalized that negative prophecy of their futures. Not expected to do well, they didn't. Madeline also recalls her parents having to come to school that year to advocate for her when she received a grade of C after the first six weeks in Honors English even though everyone knew she had the highest marks in the class. The teacher refused to change the grade even when faced with evidence of her error. Like Madeline's Honors English teacher, discrimination existed in pockets, individual-by-individual, but not rampantly or as destructively as it did in some parts of the country. Our parents had to be vigilant always and vocal from time to time, but all-in-all, sophomore year ended with nothing louder than a whimper. The fireworks would come in our junior year.

For now, the summer between our sophomore and junior years would be calm. We probably thought of it as the last summer before we were upperclassmen, almost adults in our eyes. We were all turning sweet sixteen. We could get driver's licenses, and soon we could date. This would be a great summer.

The Valianettes had planned our summer adventures before school ended. One of our big treats for the year would be a pool party at my aunt's house. Aunt Lois, my mom's sister, had built a home in the Hungary Road section of Henrico County, the black part where Madeline, Veronica, and Ricki lived, and she had a swimming pool. Swimming pools were still a novelty in black communities. For us, swimming pools meant two-piece bathing suits, not real bikinis, but something sexier than the bathing suits of our earlier years. We were probably divided, half wanting to show off the curves beginning to emerge and the others well aware their bodies had none of the shapes they saw in the teen magazines. For both groups, body consciousness was starting, and all of us had to look right for this party.

Two-piece bathing suits were in vogue, having gained acceptability after they were worn in the squeaky-clean, beach party movies featuring Disney teen stars Annette Funicello and Frankie Avalon. Two-piece bathing suits, Motown music, relaxed hair, and boys—and not just the Valiants—our friendship group of boys was growing. We had a party and what a party it was. We danced to 'I Heard It Through the Grapevine' by Gladys Knight and the Pips and Aretha Franklin's 'R-E-S-P-E-C-T.' Girls feigned anger as they were thrown into the pool by boys trying to get their attention. We were connecting with boys in that flirty, but innocent, way of 15-year olds. My parents and Aunt Lois grilled hot dogs and hamburgers. We had sodas and chips. The societal acknowledgment of healthy foods hadn't started and, if the eating disorders of anorexia or bulimia were affecting other teenagers, those maladies weren't affecting us. We ate. We danced. We swam. We had a great time. The summer between our sophomore and junior year was getting off to a bang.

Although not stated or even thought about, the pool party was only for black kids. Our world was still separate-but-equal. We weren't socializing with the white teens from school or finding out what they were doing over the summer. Our world was black. Our music was soul music, black music. Our friends were black. We never thought about it. The white kids were acquaintances but weren't our friends. We wanted the opportunities they had, but we hadn't started thinking about intertwining our two worlds. That phase of integration would come much, much later for us.

That summer, however, integration struck my world in a rather odd way. My Dad had worked for Lichtman Theaters for about 15 years in progressively responsible roles. By this summer, he had been the manager of the Gem Theater in Petersburg for almost 10 years. In the late '20s, Abe Lichtman, a white man, had purchased what would come to be called Negro theaters. He owned several in Washington, D.C., and Virginia, including the Hippodrome, the Walker, the East End and the Booker T theaters in Richmond and the Gem Theater in Petersburg, a city about 30 miles from Richmond and home to a large black population due to black Virginia State University being located there. With integration, attendance at the black movie houses had declined, and the neighborhoods in which the theaters were located had changed. Middle-class blacks could move to different areas of town, and they did. By the mid-60s, the Lichtman company changed its movie selections in several of their theaters in black neighborhoods to X-rated movies, trying to find a new niche these movie houses could fill. Even though my dad had been with that company for some time, he left not wanting to work in that entertainment environment.

His entrepreneurial spirit took over, and he studied to become a real estate agent. Blacks were becoming mobile, the housing market was strong, and he knew many people through his days at the theaters. We can all remember him reading his real estate books as he would wait in the car for us when it was his turn to pick us up from whatever event we were attending. While we couldn't appreciate his desire to go into real estate or understand the magnitude of his desire to be self-employed and only rely on his own business decisions, we could identify with the fact that like us, he had to study, to achieve his next goal.

CHAPTER 8
JOHN MARSHALL HIGH SCHOOL - UPPERCLASSMEN

"We had moved into a sharp recognition of who we were as a people. No longer a darker version of the lighter race. We were becoming black."

1967-68 was our junior year. This year was a momentous one for America and for us. While our underclassman years had been relatively quiet as we acculturated into John Marshall High School, the 1967-69 period was full of fireworks for us and for the country.

Thurgood Marshall, one of the African-American lawyers in the Brown v. Board of Education Supreme Court case, would now sit on the U.S. Supreme Court having been named to the bench by President Lyndon Johnson. Again, so much was swirling around us we could not fully understand. So many doors were opening for our race. Some were doors we didn't even know had ever been closed. Then there were other doors for which the enormity of their opening was incomprehensible to us as they were to most teens. We could not understand or appreciate the significance of these actions.

In our minds, Thurgood Marshall being named to the Supreme Court was somewhat akin to Winfred Mundle being named vice-mayor of Richmond. We knew they both marked a milestone in black history, but we didn't understand the relative importance of either. We heard about the election of Carl Stokes to become the mayor of Cleveland and of Richard Hatcher's election to the mayoral position in Gary, Indiana. The latter's relevance we understood a little bit, but in an entirely different context. The Jackson 5 singing group was from Gary so we could put Hatcher's election within a teenager's frame of reference, not one of historical relevance, merely geographic location. We heard our parents talk about these actions as critical civil rights accomplishments. We may even have read about them in the local newspapers. While we didn't understand what it all meant, somewhere undergirding all of this, we were being empowered. We were learning about the power of the vote and the enormous power of a group identifying a goal and working as a collective unit toward that goal. These were practical lessons we were about to put into action.

In our junior year at John Marshall, the black students began organizing. We had identified two goals that were very important to us: the cessation of 'Dixie' being played as the school's fight song and the election of a black homecoming queen.

While some of the black student activists had spoken with Mr. Madden, the white principal, about the playing of 'Dixie, the song continued to be played. The black students wanted it to stop. Unbeknownst to the entire student body or even to all of the black students, a small group of black students—all members of the band—had come up with an idea around the school fight song. They weren't going to play it. On this particular day, we entered the gymnasium as usual for the pep rally before the football game. When it was time to go into the expected rousing rendition of 'Dixie,' the black band members played other songs—not one song, different songs. Cacophony ruled. At first, no one knew what was happening. The band director quieted the musicians and called for the song to start again. The same thing occurred. In the gym stands everyone was confused. Then, the black students were the first to understand and roared our support. The white students were baffled. No third attempt was made to play 'Dixie' that day. The program went on without the fight song.

No one remembers what punishment was earned that day by those who refused to play 'Dixie.' It is likely that given the racial overtones of the song, the heightened sensitivity to racial issues, and the relatively benign nature of the student's protest, a simple warning may have been all that was given by the principal to those who were involved. Now the school administration understood the magnitude of our disdain for that song. It signified all of the degradation, servitude, and pain the civil rights movement was fighting against. A select group of students had organized a response. They had figured out a way to demonstrate frustration and antipathy in a nonviolent, public, and compelling way. They had understood and emulated the lessons of Dr. King. After this incident, 'Dixie' would never again be played as the fight song at John Marshall High School. No one recalls a formal announcement being made. It just happened, and school life went back to the basic day-to-day of classes, book reports, and presentations. At least, it did until it was time for homecoming.

Several of the seniors had crafted a solid strategy to nominate and elect a black homecoming queen and now it was time to act. The homecoming game against Thomas Jefferson High School was the last game of the season and was where the homecoming queen would be announced.

The strategy that had been chosen was one we'd heard about almost all of our lives. We heard about it at our dinner tables and from the church pulpit. It was the strategy promulgated and utilized by the Crusade for Voters: bloc voting. We knew by 1967, the black population at the school was high, probably around 40%, and we knew if there was only one black candidate and we all voted for her while the white students divided their votes among the multiple white candidates, our candidate had a great chance of winning. Zenobia Johnson became our candidate. She was smart, and she was popular. We thought we might even get a few white votes. All of the black students got behind her when it was time to nominate candidates for homecoming queen; ensuring her nomination as the first, black, homecoming queen nominee at John Marshall. She was the only black candidate, and there were four or five white candidates.

The black teenagers were excited. The strategy had worked. Now we had to all vote for her and hope the white vote was dispersed across multiple candidates. Just as the buzz around her candidacy heightened among the black students, talk about her also escalated among the white students. Someone said they had seen a note passed among the white students that they had heard we would vote in a bloc so they would do the same thing. They had chosen one candidate to support. For the first time during our time at Jayem, racial tension was high. Black students were discussing what they would do if Zenobia wasn't elected homecoming queen. While these conversations were going on, the white students were coordinating their strategy to ensure she wouldn't be the 1968 homecoming queen. The voting occurred, but no one would know the results until the announcement later in the week at the homecoming game.

The night of the homecoming game, the team went out on the field and played fiercely. While they were still a team and played as one, tensions were high between the black and white players. Black team captain Warren Winston remembered when the team came into the locker room at halftime, the black players went to one area, the white players to another. Out of the team's hearing, now was the time when the homecoming queen was being announced on the field. The black players threatened to walk off the field if Zenobia wasn't the homecoming queen when they returned. Before the game, Warren had been asked and had agreed, to help dissipate any tensions that might arise that night. Warren encouraged the players to act as a team representing John Marshall regardless of what happened. When they returned the field, Peggy Ramos, a white senior, had been named the '67-'68 Miss Justice, the homecoming queen. No one walked off the field. Tempers may have simmered, but they didn't boil over. The game went on. The students cheered the players.

The Jayem homecoming victory of 21-6 that night didn't help to lift the spirits of the black students. Even with what was then an emotionally crushing blow, Jayem students didn't riot. We didn't fight. We didn't leave our classrooms on Monday morning and protest in the halls as some had suggested. That wasn't the style of most of the black students attending the school. We were disappointed, but we didn't allow our disappointment to turn to anger. As Warren Winston remembered, he had already been accepted, on early decision, to attend the College of William and Mary, and wanted nothing to prevent this from happening. Warren, like most of the black students, was focused on the same thing we all had since the beginning of our education: academic success. While fighting for civil rights was the primary mission of some, this was a secondary goal for most of us. With help from our parents, we came to see we had achieved a victory around homecoming. We had organized. We had presented a viable candidate, and we had lifted her up to a platform never held by a black person. Our parents reminded us that winning took many forms. Our victory had been an incremental step, but a critically important one for the next black Miss Justice candidate. This effort had demonstrated our growing power to the entire school and to us. It had also alerted the school administration to the potential for other coordinated efforts among both the black and the white students.

Once again, after a monumental effort, school life went back to normal, but this school year, boys were a much bigger part of our day-to-day world. That attraction had started over the summer and been reinforced during the dances after the football games. Boys were increasingly on our minds. Junior year seems to have been the year hormones were flowing wildly. It wasn't just the African-American boys we were noticing. It was the white ones as well. No one talked about it, but flirty little comments were being tossed back and forth occasionally. We understood the racial taboos. The thought of interracial dating may not even have consciously crossed our mind. This was Virginia, the state in which a white man and a black woman who were legally married had been arrested in the middle of the night in 1958. The Lovings—Mildred and Richard—had grown up as neighbors, not far from Richmond, in Caroline County, Virginia. Interracial dating was quietly accepted in their small rural community, but when they went out of state to marry, they started a firestorm of legal issues. Anti-miscegenation laws, laws forbidding the marriage of people of different races, were enforced in Virginia. It was not until 1967, the beginning of our junior year, that the U.S. Supreme Court declared these laws unconstitutional. Most of us don't recall if we even knew any of this. As black girls what we knew was we had been warned by our mothers, white boys might view us stereotypically as sexually loose—easy—and they might try to take advantage of us. No one in our group remembers that happening. What we hadn't been prepared for was rumbling somewhere in our own psyche's that that blond-haired, blue-eyed, football player was really cute or the red-headed senior who always wore that blue, button-down shirt and loafers had the greatest dimples and what a sense of humor. Yes, some of us were attracted to the white boys in our school, and we remember signs those innocent, teenage feelings were probably mutual, but no one—no one—acted on them in 1967.

In our community, it wasn't yet time to focus on anything interracial on a personal level, but we were engaged in efforts to promote a more positive interracial atmosphere at school. Even as we worked to eliminate the playing of 'Dixie' and actively pursued a black homecoming queen, we still sought racial harmony. Celebrating our race and eliminating illusions about racial stereotypes did not mean we didn't want to get along with the white students in the school and work with them toward a shared understanding. In fact, we wanted them to understand why the playing of 'Dixie' was offensive to us and why we felt a black girl could as aptly represent the beauty of the girls of our school as could a white girl. Toward this goal of racial understanding, Debby and I served on the Superintendent's Student Advisory Group. We gathered with black and white high school students from across the Richmond Public School System. Our task was to identify areas of racial tension and then to forge positive connections across races. This work was directly aligned with the original Valianettes' philosophy of working for the success of our race, but not taking a radical approach.

While we were proud of what the black students at John Marshall were doing to change our school environment, our parents also worked for change, but at a much higher level. They were strategizing and planning for the election of an African-American to serve in the Virginia General Assembly, the state legislature. It had to be the right candidate, and the black community had identified such a person. That fall, Dr. Ferguson Reid, a surgeon from Richmond, would become the first black elected to the Virginia General Assembly in the 20th century. Vetted and endorsed by the Crusade for Voters, this clean-cut, upper-middle-class, extremely well-educated member of the black community was the prototype of the right candidate for this honor, the honor of being first. Once again, our credentials, our demeanor, and our overall look had to be of a particular kind to make us acceptable to the white world. And, agreeable to the white community was a necessary consideration. While we would vote in a bloc for this candidate, blacks were not in the majority and did not have the sole power to elect. White voters were needed to select Reid and Fergie Reid, as he was called, had it all—looks, charisma, and the academic credentials—all of the characteristics many felt could appeal to some subset of white voters. In November 1967, he became the first black elected to the Virginia General Assembly since Reconstruction.

That 'since Reconstruction' clause was a statement of derision in my household. Whenever that phrase was used, and it often was, many felt it suggested that while blacks had been elected to public offices in the late 1800s, it was only through post-Civil War confusion and unethical actions. And that those officials weren't representatives of the people. My paternal great-grandfather had been one of those who had been elected.

His name was Henry David Smith. Born a slave in 1834, he was a self-educated farmer and a distiller. He garnered sufficient wealth to purchase the 900 plus acre estate, "Merry Oaks," the home of his former owner and even loaned funds to Greenville County, his home community when it was in financial distress. H.D., as he was called, had three wives and seventeen children, including my paternal grandmother, Mary Smith Lucas.

H.D. SMITH

While lacking the educational credentials Ferguson Reid had, H.D. was well-respected, charming and a stalwart member of his community. In 1879, he was elected to the Virginia House of Delegates. His service to the Commonwealth of Virginia was recognized in 2012 by the Virginia General Assembly through Senate Joint Resolution 13 introduced by African-American state senator and former Richmond Mayor, Henry Marsh. My family is proud of his service. So, when my dad would hear Dr. Reid referred to as the first African-American elected to the Virginia House of Delegates, he would often quietly add, "in the 20th century." Remarkably, however, it wasn't until after my dad's death I would learn about his grandfather. Until then, I thought he was bemoaning historical inaccuracy.

Like my daddy, Madeline's father, Edwin Swann was a quiet, reserved, proud man. He, too, didn't share his hurts, physical or mental, even with his family. They knew he had been wounded in Italy during World War II.

Both his mother and sister had died while he was away in the war. He hadn't been able to be with them which caused him great sadness. He'd also suffered physical injuries that had weakened his body. In the fall of 1967, Madeline's father died from complications related to that war-time injury.

This was the first time that mortality had affected our group. Before Mr. Swann's death, it probably hadn't occurred to any of us that a parent could die. Not only did we not understand death, but it also doesn't seem we understood compassion either. While I can vaguely remember calling Madeline to say I was sorry her father had died, that action had been prompted by my parents. We had never encountered death. We didn't know what to do and didn't understand its impact on our friend. Remarkably none of us can remember attending Mr. Swann's services. Our parents did, but we didn't. While we girls didn't support Madeline during this tragedy, we know many of our families did.

My parents and the Swanns had become close. While they saw each other at those school events, it might have been a health scare that cemented their friendship. There was an occasion during elementary school when Madeline had been sick for several days and didn't seem to get better. Mrs. Swann asked my mom who was a registered nurse to come over to their home to check on Madeline. She did and assured Mrs. Swann that Madeline would be okay and she was. Over the years, the mothers visited with each other, shared sewing techniques since they both were expert seamstresses and played pinochle together. They even banded together later that year to meet with the John Marshall High School principal over concern about interpreting a critical test score for either SATs or National Merit Scholars. Mrs. Swann and my mom met, like we did, during our elementary school years and, like us remained friends all of their lives.

It was with great sadness that, after Mr. Swann's death, Mrs. Swann continued with plans for Madeline to be a debutante the following spring. Preparation had already started for the Sigma Gamma Rho sorority's annual debutante ball. In 1953, the sorority hosted the first debutante ball for African-American girls in Richmond. While the balls started out in the black community, as they had in the white, as a visible announcement the participants were now ready for marriage, over time they had evolved into charitable events. In our year, 1968, twenty-nine girls would be formally introduced to black Richmond society via the spring debutante ball and seven of them were Valianettes. While the ball was the culminating event, we participated in multiple charitable projects over the six months leading up to the ball. None of the activities left enough of an impression for us to remember. What we recall was all of the preparation. We had almost weekly rehearsals at the park house, a meeting facility in Battery Park near our homes. Just as the park was the center of summer recreational activities, it was also the central location for many community gatherings as it was for this event, too. We practiced every part of our formal introduction to society from the curtsy to the dance with our fathers and the very formal, patterned dance we would do with our teenage escorts. What we would wear also demanded much preparation. Multiple shopping trips led to the selection of the right white, cream or ecru evening gown with matching long evening gloves. Even though only the toe of the shoes was seen, they, too, had to be just as elegant as the gown and be comfortable for a night of dancing. This was a dress rehearsal for the weddings that were hoped would ensue after college.

The event was primarily for the immediate and extended family along with the adult friends of the debutantes' families. The only young people who were invited were the post-debs, the collection of young women who had been debutantes the previous year and their escorts along with the sub-debs, the group that was a year younger who were likely to be debutantes the following year. In May 1968, the debutante ball was held at the Mosque Ballroom. The Mosque was a regular location for significant events in the city. It had opened in 1927 primarily as a meeting place for Shriners. Modeled after a Muslim temple, it was a spectacular building with an elaborate gold dome and intricate tile work. In the 1940s, it was purchased by the city of Richmond. Ever since then, the Mosque had become the preferred venue for city events ranging from high school graduations to performances by world-famous entertainers and activities like our debutante ball.

That night as the lights dimmed and the Dave Williams Orchestra played, we were each individually introduced. With trepidation, we smiled demurely as our dads escorted us out onto the ballroom floor. A curtsy we had practiced endlessly followed the formal introduction. For all of us, this was the first time we had been on the arm of our dads. Their role wasn't so much as 'dad the protector' or as 'dad the provider' for the family. Instead, this evening, our dads were more of a formal escort. We felt almost like adults as we danced the opening waltz with our fathers. Everything was perfect. Well almost everything, it must have been a bittersweet moment for Madeline and for her mom as her uncle, not her dad, escorted her on that singular evening. Madeline smiled throughout the dance and must have made peace with this touching moment. After that special dance, our dads turned us over to our teenage escorts. The spotlight shone on the ballroom's dance floor as we nervously danced the elaborately choreographed figure dance we had been practicing for months. It was a magical moment. The music was perfect. We were in the arms of some young man special to us. We felt we were girls entering young womanhood as the ball signified. Another rite of passage.

Because it was a charity event, the person who raised the most money for the sorority's designated charity was the queen of the ball. Imagine our surprise, when the debutante queen was announced, and she was a member of our group. I was named the queen of the Fifteenth Annual Sigma Gamma Rho Debutante Ball. My mother had made what I thought was an exquisite and sophisticated gown for me to wear on this special evening. I loved it. I was ready to assume the central position that night among Richmond's black debutantes. Like everyone, I beamed as Scott Henderson, a well-known, local photographer, took the obligatory group picture. This would be the featured photo on the Society Page in the next issue of the *Afro-American* newspaper.

Some have asked about our jealousies of what each other had or achieved. Maybe teens were different in the '60s, or maybe it was black teens that were different. There was a group mentality. Yes, we were teens, and some of the "me" mentality of the '80s even existed back then, but before we thought of ourselves as teens, we thought of ourselves as black. We were proud of what anyone in our group or in our community achieved.

MAKE DEBUT: These smiling young ladies were presented at the Fifteenth Annual Debutante Ball sponsored by Iota Sigma Chapter of Sigma Gamma Rho Sorority. The debutantes, including Tamara Olivia Lucas who reigned over the affair as queen, are (front row, from left) Queen Burnett, Mae Harrison, Roslyn Brown, Brenda Hubbard, Miss Lucas, Linda Smith, Madeline Swann, Deborah Smith, (second row) Veronica Dungee, Roxanne White, Donna Jones, Cheryl Simpson, Jacquelyn Cherry, Gloria Tyson, Cynthia Spencer, Peggy Jackson, Peggy Robinson, (third row) Shelia Byrd, Bernadette Giles, Jean Johnson, Zena Herring, Patricia Perry, Jean Cabbia, Debra Johnson, Rene Morgan, Janice Jackson and Effra Jackson. Not shown are Gail Harvey and Celestine Gray, who were also presented.

DEBUTANTES - MAY 1968

No one remembers being jealous I was named debutante queen. I felt everyone was happy for me. No one in our group was jealous Debby Anderson was in the May Court in junior year. We were delighted for her. We were pleased when Gloria, Madeline, Renée and I were inducted into the National Honor Society. Maybe we weren't jealous because, within our community, everyone had the same goal—success for people in our race—and everyone had the same things. We all had the clothes that others were wearing. No one was overly focused on labels. In fact, Debby remembers the joy of hand-me-downs. Her sister was eight years older; so, when Debby was looking for gowns to wear to the prom, she only had to look to her sister who was at the age to be regularly asked to be a bridesmaid. Bridesmaid's gowns adapted well to prom dresses. Debby always looked great. No one knew they were Anna's dresses, and if we had, it's unlikely we would have cared. We would have thought it was cool to have an at-home selection of dresses from which to choose your next special outfit. It would not have been seen in any different light than the fact Madeline's and my mom made a lot of our clothes. No difference at all.

We didn't know the occupations of most of our parents. Many knew my dad had changed to real estate only because they saw him studying for his license, but no one thought about what that meant for his income or about income period. There was no financial hierarchy. Because we all lived primarily in the same area, we didn't think a lot about someone having more or less than we did. Part of that was a function of being a teen and partly, perhaps, the function of being a part of a relatively homogeneous population. We knew the Hungary Road section of Richmond had become the home to more of the black upper crust of professionals and we knew parts of East End was home to public housing where people who were poorer lived. We knew this, and we knew people who lived in both places, but the concepts of wealth and poverty were too abstract for us to comprehend. While we were paying attention to what the other girls were wearing, we definitely were not thinking about what it might have cost. We merely had fun.

We were all smiles and giddiness that night, but a little less than two weeks earlier a deep sadness had come over most of our homes. It was Thursday evening, April 4th. We were looking forward to the weekend. We still had things to do to get ready for the ball. For some of us, we didn't know what evening wrap we would wear with our gowns. The weather forecasters were saying April 15th, the night of the ball was likely to be chilly; so, we needed to make provisions. We were focused on using the upcoming weekend to finish everything for the ball. We had come home from school, finished our homework and had dinner. Now, we needed our mom's attention to help us finalize plans, but they were focused on the news. Walter Cronkite, the news anchor of the *CBS Evening News*, had just reported Martin Luther King, Jr. had been assassinated in Memphis, Tennessee.

There were only three television stations, ABC, CBS, and NBC. All of the news anchors had learned of the shooting and King's subsequent death during the 7 p.m. to 7:30 p.m. national news time slot. Each of the three stations interrupted their regular programming to feature as much information as was available on the assassination and to cover President Lyndon Johnson's message to the nation. Marsha remembers that even with her father's belief that King was too passive in his approach to civil rights, her household filled with sadness with the news. She can clearly remember her grandmother crying openly as she watched the television coverage of the tragedy of his death, the riots that followed in major cities across the country, and his funeral.

Dr. King's funeral was on April 9th, a Tuesday, a school day for us. On the day before, some students had requested the televisions in classrooms across the school be turned to the services. We were told this would be a regular school day. Students could not watch the funeral. But, it wasn't an ordinary school day. This wasn't a regular day for any African-American nor for many whites. This was a day to pay homage to the leadership of a great American who had been killed trying to lead our country to a new level of racial understanding. The school administration knew that, and so did the students, both black and white. On the morning of the funeral, as students arrived and went to the cafeteria as usual to await the opening bell, it seemed an almost spontaneous decision was made to have a silent protest. The black students walked throughout the school, floor-by-floor, en masse, to both honor Dr. King's memory and protest the school administration's decision. Nothing was said. In hindsight, this nonviolent response was the most fitting response we could have made as our testament to Dr. King's legacy. No proclamations or demands were made; just a quiet, civil action was taken. When the funeral aired later that day, televisions were on across the school allowing students to watch the services.

Many would think to live through events of such magnitude in the history of the country and in the history of African-Americans, we would form clear memories of both the events and of our feelings around them. We can remember significant occurrences like the 'Dixie' protest, or our march through the school in honor of Dr. King, but often our memories are vague or have to be triggered by a comment from another member of the group. Maybe our lack of memory is due to the number of years passed since the event occurred. We don't think so. We have now come to realize we have teenage memories, age-appropriate memories of what was most important to us. We knew these events were important. Our parents' reactions and comments told us that, but we were still teens focused primarily on enjoying our high school years.

While we can't remember much about the momentous events of the time, we can all remember what was memorable—even if mundane—to us. Like Laura Thornton's car. Laura was a black senior at John Marshall High, and she drove a Mustang to school. Now that's a clear memory. Why do we remember that so vividly? Because we only had a car when our parents loaned us theirs for a few hours or when my dad broke his arm and couldn't drive for a month or so, but Laura had her own, all of the time. She had freedom from reliance on her parents to take her places. A car meant freedom, so we remember a lot surrounding them. We remember the time six of us were riding back from a party in the Southside of Richmond in Mr. Johnson's deuce and a quarter (Buick Electra 225). Debbie Johnson was probably driving. We were stopped at a red light when out of nowhere came an 11 or 12-year-old kid running full speed as he was chased by a wildly snapping dog. The boy jumped on the hood of the car and stayed there until the dog went away. Then, he hopped off the hood and went along his way. We remember the time we were driving to school—probably in my dad's car—with the radio blasting. A song came on that we liked, we stopped the car, jumped out and danced in the street—teenagers totally caught up in our own world.

We remember the pay parties in my backyard, in Renée's and in Jeannie and Debbie's yard we would charge our friends and acquaintances to attend so we could raise money for whatever the Valianettes wanted to do next. We remember going to see the Supremes at the Mosque, singing along to all of the songs while thinking Diana Ross, Mary Wilson, and Florence Ballard were beautiful and oh so elegant. These are the occurrences we remember, events of little or no consequence to black history or to the goal of racial equality and parity, that strengthened our friendship and bond. We were teenagers, and these are our memories.

Later we would realize the monumental events happening around us that would ultimately open doors for us as black Americans were the present, the now, for our parents and would later become their memories.

They had a context in which to recognize the import of these occurrences. They knew what the world had been like for African-Americans. They fully understood history was being made and they tried to share with us their understanding of the impact of that history. Like teenagers throughout time, we didn't listen. We probably sat patiently while they talked about Martin Luther King's legacy or the importance of the passage of the Fair Housing Act, but we weren't really listening, and we didn't have the historical frame of reference to truly understand. We were probably more affected by the emotion we saw in our parents' reactions to events than by their actual comments about those events. We knew we were supposed to feel proud or happy, afraid or sorrowful. We saw it in our parents' eyes and heard it in their voices, but these were adult emotions backed by adult understanding and adult experiences. We were seventeen, on the cusp of adulthood, but still kids.

Seventeen was that magical time between being a girl and being a young woman. As girls, we had played with paper dolls, designing clothes for them and dressing them. As we got older, we still loved clothes. We followed the latest styles and looked at the models in the teen magazines. In 1968, when we were seventeen, we didn't see very many people in those magazines who looked like us. It would, in fact, be three more years before the first African-American model would be on the cover of *Seventeen Magazine*. It came as something of a surprise when in the month following the end of my junior year, I was called to the Miller & Rhodes department store for an interview to be a model on their Teen Board. I had applied, so it wasn't a total surprise, but I sure didn't know if I had a chance. My parents had encouraged me as had my aunt who worked in the signage department of the store. Miller & Rhodes had selected twenty girls from twenty high schools—public and private schools—in the Richmond area to serve on what they called the Teen Board. They would do in-store modeling and newspaper ads. In an era when the standard of beauty was still primarily defined by white women, this was another sign times were changing. I am not light-skinned with straight hair. I think of myself as a visual bridge between the lighter-skinned black women who had defined beauty for decades and the darker skinned ones who would soon be accepted as the beauties they were. Over the course of my senior year, I appeared in the *Richmond News Leader*, the principal newspaper for the city, several times as a Miller and Rhodes model. And I participated in monthly runway fashion shows in the Richmond Tea Room, the restaurant the Virginia Union University students had picketed to integrate less than a decade earlier. Change was coming to Richmond and to the entire country, and we were a part of that transformation.

TAMARA LUCAS

While I still saw myself as a *Negro* teen model, soul singer, James Brown, had released a new song in August 1968, "Say it Loud, I'm Black, and I'm Proud." And not only had he released the song, but he had also visually demonstrated his new sense of self by abandoning his relaxed—chemically straightened—hairstyle in favor of the newly emerging afro or natural hairstyle. The previous year Stokely Carmichael had also signaled a new era in the civil rights movement when he talked about "black power." The Black Panther political party had been established. Blacks across the country were moving on from wanting to get along with whites on their terms and moving away, albeit slowly, from the white standard of beauty. We wanted whites to understand and appreciate who we were—not merely white people with brown skin. We wanted white people to appreciate our beauty as black people. We also wanted them to understand black people had a rich history—our history, and we wanted them to understand our sense of self—black people who were the equal of white people. This was no longer an era in which we wanted Bill Cosby on the television show *I Spy* to be a brown version of Robert Culp. We had moved into a sharp recognition of who we were as a people. No longer a darker version of the lighter race. We were becoming black.

We also wanted our white fellow students to appreciate our intellect was comparable to theirs. We wanted them to understand we were their intellectual equals. Madeline, Renée, Gloria and I were proud of being named semi-finalists for the National Merit Scholarship, but we didn't want to be segregated as being in the 'special competition for Negroes.' We wanted to be judged by the same standards as whites. We didn't want separate-but-equal. We didn't want society to literally or figuratively paint the white dolls brown, as was the first way of creating what some thought were black dolls. That was the way we had initially been seen and probably was our goal at one time, but no more. Many in our race wanted to be clear we were black, and we were proud of being black.

While blacks on the west coast and in some of the major cities across the country were wearing afros as a sign of growing racial pride, it would be a few years before that hairstyle would be regularly seen in Richmond. For now, by white Richmonders, and by most black Richmonders as well, it was viewed as radical and militant. And that perspective was undoubtedly held in 1968 by the Valianettes and by our parents. No one talked about it, but none of us was wearing an afro either. Our role model was more Shirley Chisholm, who had just been elected as the first African-American woman in the U.S. House of Representatives, than Stokely Carmichael. Racial pride and success were a part of our makeup, but we didn't show our black power through hairstyles or clenched fists, at least not then.

Our black power was focused on the strength of succeeding at school and in the community on all levels. Not only did we want to learn from these experiences, we understood the value of being involved in multiple activities as colleges looked at our applications. We were earning the grades. We were in all of the clubs. By now, I was in the Chinese Club. John Marshall was one of the few public schools in the state to teach Chinese. I was also secretary of the Student Cooperative Association, the school's student government, was on the yearbook and newsletter staff and had been named to the Quill and Scroll, an honorary society for high school journalists. Renée and Madeline had both joined the newsletter staff and were also in the German Club. Debby Anderson was a library aide and would soon be named Best Personality (girl) for the school. Madeline had also been appointed to represent the school in Boys and Girls State, the only black participant from Jayem that year at this mock portrayal of government. Debby Johnson was in the Junior Red Cross, and both she and her sister Jeannie were in the talent show. Marsha and Veronica had also been in the talent show, and Marsha was a part of the Orientation Commission while Veronica was the only athlete in the group participating in gymnastics. By senior year, we were engaged, in some form, in most of what the school had to offer both academically and civically, but we were still often a minority in any venue.

That was not the case in athletics. Blacks had been succeeding in integrated athletic arenas for some time now, with Jackie Robinson leading the way in professional baseball, followed by basketball and then football. Even though athletic prowess had been demonstrated by many, the coveted quarterback position on the football team was still typically held by whites. It was just this year that the first African-American had started as a professional league quarterback, Marlin Briscoe with the Denver Broncos. Some whites commented that blacks didn't have the intellectual savvy to think on their feet and lead the team as a quarterback must. But, at Jayem, even that stereotype had been shattered when an African-American, Ivan Stovall, was named quarterback and led the team to its best season in a quarter of a century. We were being accepted into the school environment on multiple levels. We were smart, we were sociable, and we were athletic, but were we pretty enough to be the girl representing the school?

We still wanted an African-American to be named Miss Justice, John Marshall's homecoming queen. We had tried the previous year unsuccessfully. We had been voted onto the May Court for several years now, but no black girl had been named Miss Justice, *the* young woman who would be the representative of the entire female population of the school. In 1968-69, there was no coordinated effort to support one black candidate.

Nine girls received sufficient votes to be nominated for this honor. Three of them were African-American and two of the three, Jeannie Johnson and Debby Anderson, were Valianettes. Was this progress or were we being lulled into thinking we had received a level of acceptance in which people were being judged as Dr. King had hoped, "by the content of their character, not by the color of their skin?" We didn't know, but we were happy for the nominations. Jeannie and Debby were attractive, outgoing and smart. They would be ideal representatives of the school.

Remarkably while we expected the white students to vote based on the character of the nominees, we still voted by the color of their skin. We were concerned the black students' votes would be divided across three candidates. We probably didn't think about the fact the white students' votes were split among six candidates. We merely wanted a black candidate to win to demonstrate a black girl could be seen as a beauty queen and could represent our school.

For the first time ever, all of the candidates were asked to speak at a student assembly on why they wanted to be Miss Justice. In the past, Miss Justice had been chosen purely by appearance and personality. In no small measure, it was a popularity contest. This year, the principal, Mr. Madden, wanted the candidates judged more broadly on how they would represent the school. An assembly was held for all of the candidates to state their platforms. As the principal introduced the nominees, he reminded us we should listen to each candidate and vote for who we felt gave the best answer. He cautioned the students that bloc voting would not be tolerated. Only a small few knew after the previous year's coordinated effort; the principal had considered not even having a Miss Justice for the '68-'69 school year. There are at least two perspectives on why he took that position. Some think he felt this contest might further divide the school along racial lines as opposed to bringing the school together. Others suggest Mr. Madden didn't want to crown a black Miss Justice. There may be validity to both views. Some white students recall community meetings years earlier in which John Madden had expressed concern, as did many other white leaders, about integration. He spoke against integrating the schools. Perhaps he continued to be one of those adults who resisted this change. The students, however, were ready for a change. Remarkably after the tension that surrounded the previous year's contest, none seemed to be present as the student body listened politely to the comments from all nine candidates. Over forty years later no one can remember what their individual comments were, but undoubtedly all of the candidates were nervous as they took to the stage for the culminating event on the way to being named Miss Justice.

Like all high school homecomings, John Marshall's was a big event. All of the school clubs had elaborately decorated cars or floats in the homecoming parade. John Marshall was playing our archrival, Thomas Jefferson High School. We dominated the game throughout so there wasn't much suspense on the football field, but there was on the homecoming queen's float as all the candidates waited for the announcement. The voting had occurred earlier in the week, but no one knew the outcome. Mr. and Mrs. Johnson, Jeannie's parents, were in the audience as were Debby's folks, Mr. and Mrs. Anderson, and her older brother and sister. With great suspense, Mr. Madden walked to the microphone to announce the new homecoming queen. There was absolute silence as we all waited to hear the outcome. The entire stadium went wild when Jeannie Johnson was named the 1968-1969 homecoming queen.

JEANNIE - MISS JUSTICE

Not only was Jeannie the first black Miss Justice, but she was also the first black homecoming queen at any predominantly white school in

Richmond. While her breakthrough was lauded in the *Afro-American* newspaper and in the *Richmond Times-Dispatch,* it is noteworthy it was not celebrated in the usual manner at our school. As was the tradition, the principal always congratulated the homecoming queen in his morning message to the student body on Monday following homecoming. This was our fourth John Marshall homecoming; so, we knew the routine. We were surprised and hurt that Mr. Madden didn't acknowledge Jeannie's new title. Jeannie had won. She had been elected to this position by the votes of white students and of blacks. She deserved all of the kudos that attended to the honor. It hadn't occurred to us that that wouldn't happen, but it didn't. It was one of Jeannie's competitors and fellow Valianette, Debby Anderson, who was so outdone by this action she went to the principal's office to ask him why he hadn't congratulated Jeannie. Debby's exploit, a seventeen-year-old taking on the school principal, took gumption and a well-developed sense of right and wrong. That's why, even then, she was the closest our group had to a militant member. It's unlikely any other Valianette would have confronted the principal in the manner Debby did. He told her it was an oversight, but Debby felt it was much more than that and she was probably right. In our naiveté, we thought Jeannie would receive all of the recognition of any other Miss Justice. Just one more lesson: both white and black students had elected Jeannie, and both seemed pleased by her victory. There were no overt, harmful actions taken by students because she won, but the older generation, as typified by the principal, didn't seem as ready to accept this change in racial balance.

While we still had classes to take and final exams to pass, the homecoming activities seemed to symbolize the end of high school for us. Now, it was time to focus on college. I remember traveling to Hampton Institute (later University), Fisk University, North Carolina Central and Duke to see what those schools were like. Veronica, Madeline, and Ricki also considered Fisk. Debbie and Jeannie remember being encouraged to consider college options by their parents, but also by their dad's sister, their Aunt Martha. We were all surprised to learn Marsha had taken a year off. She was going to what was called a finishing school. Everyone else, however, knew they were going to college. It was no different than moving from junior high to high school. Our next step would be college. While our parents were focused on our college ambitions, that wasn't as true of our guidance counselors. Regardless of the academic accolades we had received during our high school experience, we were still told by counselors we wouldn't be accepted by school X, or we shouldn't even consider school Y. Once again, some of the white adults in the school administration either didn't believe in the capacity we had clearly demonstrated or perhaps they wanted to limit our options and our opportunities.

Nonetheless, we soared. Madeline graduated ninth in the senior class, the first African-American, and the only that year, to graduate in the top 10. Renée and I graduated in the next five, at either 12th and 13th or 14th and 15th out of a class of almost 400. Debby Anderson remembers she was #29 and, the rest of the Valianettes were sprinkled throughout. We had families, and a healthy community always telling us we could do anything we wanted to do, and we believed them. The college acceptance letters started coming in. We'd done it. No drugs. No alcohol. No tragic car accidents. No pregnancies—that never would have happened in 1969. We'd successfully negotiated that dangerous space of the teen years. We'd proven ourselves academically, and we'd demonstrated the content of our character. We were ready for college. There was one more culminating event.

On June 12, 1969, our graduation ceremony was held at the Mosque, the location of the debutante ball. We were all dressed in white caps and gowns, and everyone's parents and family were in the audience. Mr. Madden was appropriately all smiles as he awarded each person—black or white—his or her high school diploma. We aren't sure what we were thinking of that night. Were we happy to have graduated? Probably so, but there was no question we would. Did we think about college? Probably not, even though we were all going to college that was three months away, forever in the life of a teenager. We were still only seventeen or eighteen years old. We were in the moment, enjoying this *the* latest rite of passage in childhood.

In four years, Debbie Johnson, Debby Anderson, Jeannie Johnson, Madeline Swann, Marsha Ford, Renée Fleming, Tamara Lucas and Veronica Dungee had transitioned from somewhat shy, young Negro girls to poised, self-assured, young Negro women. We weren't black yet. We hadn't fully adopted the psyche of the black power movement, but we fully understood and celebrated the self-actualization of everyone in our race. We were middle-class Negroes. Our lives had been sheltered and somewhat privileged within the context of the black race. Our friendship had blossomed and grown. We had lived, perhaps obliviously, through a period of incredible change in the opportunities for blacks from that September morning when we entered Albert V. Norrell Elementary School until that June night when we graduated from John Marshall High School. Soon our views of ourselves, of our race, and our connections to each other would change tremendously. We were off to college. Adulthood was the next threshold, and we were ready.

For twelve years, we'd been together at least five days a week. We went to school together. We took classes outside of school together. We went to parties together. Some of us vacationed together. Some of us went to church together. Now all of this was ending. Our lives were about to go into eight different directions. We were so caught up that we probably thought nothing about the fact we were about to leave the comfort of our families, the loyalty of our friends, and the constancy of our school, our city, and everything familiar. For the next twenty years, while our lives would intertwine periodically, we no longer functioned as Valianettes. We were not a part of a group. We weren't even duos and trios anymore. We were individuals off to make our own way in the world. The civil rights movement had opened many doors for us, and the fledgling women's liberation movement would do the same. Now, we had to walk through those doors and make our parents and our communities proud. So many had contributed to nourish us and to see to it we were ready for all the world offered to young black women. We were prepared. All of us were off to take that next important step.

THE YEARS BETWEEN 1969– 1994

CHAPTER 9
COLLEGE—MAKING A DECISION

"Even though racial considerations were a driver for the college choices made by some, race was probably the last thing on our minds."

We never thought much about going to college. We always knew we would go. Just as junior high followed elementary school and high school followed junior high, college was the next step. We didn't think about how proud our parents were that they could provide us with a college education, something most of their parents hadn't been able to afford. We didn't think about how much our parents must have planned and budgeted for this day. And we didn't consider not going. Ever since slavery, education had been seen as the way to a better life for African-Americans. All of us knew we would go to college.

Well, that would be all of us, except Marsha. Marsha wasn't sure what she would do about college. In our junior year when the conversation moved toward college, Marsha had stayed on the periphery. She listened but didn't take part. She knew it was expected, but she wasn't having a great time in high school. To her, college sounded like a continuation—the 13th, 14th, 15th and 16th grades so to speak. If she wasn't enjoying the experience now, nothing led her to think it would get better.

Then, the Julia Gibson Career College team came to our high school for career day. Marsha had found her college. It would not be a traditional, liberal arts education. She would be specially trained for a career in fashion and interior design. It was almost as if she would skip most of the college courses she wasn't looking forward to anyway and go right into learning her trade, her career.

For the rest of us, the path was straight. We were headed into what Marsha thought of as grade 13 at a liberal arts college. The question was which one. This was our decision, and we could decide where to apply.

Up until now, all of our education decisions had been made for us. Either our parents chose our schools, or a segregated educational system did. Now, we had been given permission, even encouraged, to make this decision, the most important decision of our lives up to that point. Our parents had provided parameters, probably financial, perhaps geographic, but then they had told us to choose. The college choices of our friends, the values, and perspectives of our families and the education we had received through Richmond Public Schools shaped our decision about where we applied.

Several were adamant they would go to a black school, what is now called an HBCU, a historically black college or university. For different reasons, Madeline, Debby, Veronica, and Debbie all knew they had had enough of an integrated educational experience. They longed for a black one.

Madeline: "I always knew I wanted to attend a black university. I wanted to attend a school where race was not important. I wanted to focus on my studies and not be rewarded or penalized for anything other than performance. Focusing on race was a distraction I didn't want to have."

Debby: "I'd grown up seeing my sister, Anna, involved with the civil rights protests when she was a student at Virginia Union University. Anna had talked about her responsibility to stand up for what she believed in. I knew blacks had been kept down. I wanted to be a part of the lifting up of my race. I didn't think that could happen anywhere except at a black school."

Veronica: "To me, racism was blatant at John Marshall [high school]. I wanted a nurturing environment and, let's be honest, I wanted to be a majorette and find a husband. I wasn't going to do those things at a white school. I was going to a black college."

Debbie: "I'm not sure why, but I always knew I wanted to go to a black school. I may have thought more about it after being a debutante and seeing the sisterhood of the Sigma Gamma Rho sorority. I'm not sure, but it just wasn't a question."

If it wasn't a question for Debbie, it definitely wasn't for her younger sister, Jeannie either. They were a package, always had been. When 13-month younger Jeannie was skipped a grade in elementary school, she and her older sister became classmates, and they would remain classmates through college.

For Renée and me, factors other than race shaped our decision. Through sheer coincidence, no planning or discussion, we both ended up on the very white campus of the College of William and Mary. The college is about an hour from Richmond, on a beautiful site, in the heart of Colonial Williamsburg, an area restored in the 1920s to appear as it had in the 1700s. William and Mary, founded in 1693 by then reigning monarchs of England, King William III, and Queen Mary II, is one anchor of this colonial village. When you are on campus, you definitely get the feel of old England with its castles and manor houses and, as we all know, there weren't many black people in England back then. When our freshman class entered the university in 1969, Renée and I helped to ensure a solid black enrollment of less than 1% for the entire university.

Renée decided on William and Mary because she was determined to get out of the shadow of her father. As then-vice president of Consolidated Bank and Trust, the black bank that had evolved from Maggie Walker's Penny Savings Bank, Mr. Fleming was a leader in the black community. Renée was always seen as Jesse Fleming's daughter. She wanted to be her own person. So, when her dad told her she would have to attend a state school, she immediately rejected Virginia State College, the alma mater of both of her parents. Then she also dismissed Norfolk State, the other black, Virginia, state school. Even though her parents hadn't gone to school there, they would be well-known there. So, as she considered other schools, she met with the guidance counselor. He tried to push her toward black schools and specifically told her it was unlikely she would be accepted at William and Mary. "You know, at the time, I don't think racism came to mind. It was more about pride. I knew I had what it took to get into this school or most any other for that matter," Renée said.

With outstanding grades, involvement in multiple activities in the community and in the school, there was every reason for any rational person to see Renée as an ideal applicant for a school that liked to think of itself as the Ivy League of the South. The only reason for this white counselor to steer Renée away from William and Mary was racial prejudice—the only reason. Intending to prove him wrong, she applied. "Not only was I accepted on early admission," she recalled happily, "I received one of the first Martin Luther King scholarships that had been initiated the previous year." She had proven the guidance counselor wrong. The College of William and Mary would be her academic home for the next four years.

I was in love and not motivated by academic credentials. I was guided there by the high school quarterback, my boyfriend. My parents suggested North Carolina Central because my father's cousin headed the English Department there. I applied there and also to Hampton Institute because my grandmother had attended school there.

I applied to a lot of schools for different, random, teenage reasons. Radcliffe College, the sister school to Harvard, because another black John Marshall High graduate went there, Fisk because several friends were considering this school, Duke because the same guidance counselor that steered Renée away from W&M, told me, for the same racist reasons I suspect, that I couldn't get into Duke. I did. But I chose William and Mary for the most basic, naive teenage-girl reason.

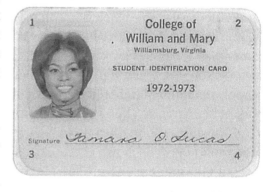

College of William and Mary
Williamsburg, Virginia

STUDENT IDENTIFICATION CARD

1972-1973

Signature *Tamara O. Lucas*

My boyfriend got a full football scholarship there. If he was going there, I was too. Unlike Renée's Dad who was pleased by her choice, my parents had mixed feelings. They did not approve of my high school boyfriend, but they recognized the outstanding reputation of William and Mary and that I would receive an exceptional education.

College had started. Even though racial considerations were a driver for the college choices made by some, race was probably the last thing on our minds in September 1969. It was scary and exciting. We were leaving home. For most of us, this was for the first time.

CHAPTER 10
THE COLLEGE EXPERIENCE

"The bottom line was we all wanted to be accepted and fit in. Our lives had revolved around school, not racial equality. Naively, we thought race no longer mattered."

"Brucie, I know I said you could have white lab mice, but I'm sorry, really I am, but I've changed my mind. I just can't live here with mice in the house," said Mrs. Swann to her disappointed 12-year old daughter, Madeline.

But when her mother added, "Let's get guinea pigs instead," Madeline's sad face transformed to beaming immediately. Her mother knew how important these animals were for Madeline, her junior scientist.

Ever since Madeline, 'Brucie' to her family, had been a little girl, she'd loved science.

"I think it was that Christmas, in elementary school when the chemistry set was more of a hit than the beautiful doll and dollhouse that mama knew she wasn't going to have a girlie girl for a daughter," Madeline recalled.

The world of science would be her daughter's love; so, it was no surprise to anyone that Madeline entered Fisk University knowing science—chemistry—would be her major.

Madeline expected to have to work hard, and she was ready to start right away. Then to her complete surprise, race entered in a way that put her studies on hold.

Madeline reminisced, "It's funny. Fisk had been founded just a little over a century earlier with the specific purpose of supporting students who were poor and who had been slaves. Even to me, just a freshman, it seemed the school had forgotten its roots."

Fisk students were protesting the lack of black studies programs and what they perceived as an inappropriate separation of the university from the community in which it was located, the proverbial town and gown distinction faced by many college communities. The students were questioning whether the school had forgotten its roots. Their protest shut Fisk down only a couple of months into Madeline's freshman year as the administration thought through the challenge and the implications.

Some might be surprised that at a black school, students would have to demand a black studies program, but they did. For decades, schools—black and white—had denied or ignored the existence of black history. Blacks had internalized this aspect of societal racism taking for granted the parameters of American history as it had been taught for decades. It took the vision of college students to sensitize administrators at Fisk, and at other colleges across the country, to the importance of teaching black history. It also took the vision of the students to suggest that Fisk, again like other universities across the country, was a gilded oasis within an economically disadvantaged neighborhood. Ultimately the school understood and valued the students' demands. They added African-American studies to the history and sociology curricula and started tutoring and mentoring programs for neighborhood kids. So, even though Madeline had come to Fisk to avoid issues of race, the overlay of race, with the addition of class, still permeated her world.

Jeannie also didn't expect race to be a factor when she went off with her sister, Debbie, to Shaw, a black university in Raleigh, North Carolina. She had spent the first few months getting into a rhythm of going across town to white North Carolina State University. The two schools were partnering to provide physical therapy majors with the array of courses they needed. The mix of the black school environment with that of the white school wasn't a problem for Jeannie. Her issue wasn't so much cultural as it was logistical. This 17-year old wasn't ready to negotiate the back-and-forth of the somewhat inadequate public transportation system between the two schools. So, once she accepted this and changed her major to physical education, one that could be accommodated fully at Shaw, she could focus more on the reality of her new school. That's when the issue of race arose.

109

Jeannie recalled, "At first I felt I wasn't being challenged academically. I had even started to think of some of my classmates as slackers. Then I realized they weren't goofing off. Unlike me, some of them were struggling with the class material. This caused me to think. 'Were the rigors of my white high school greater than those of my black university?'"

She came to realize that wasn't the case. The answer was both more complicated, but still somewhat fundamental.

"I didn't realize it fully at first, but then I figured it out. The college preparatory track at John Marshall High School had done exactly what it was supposed to do. It had prepared me for college, and it had prepared me well. For some of my classmates, their college preparation hadn't been as solid," Jeannie finally understood.

But, then she noticed something else she felt was revealing about the difference between a black academic environment and a white one. The faculty members at Shaw were there for her. When she was trying to navigate between Shaw and N.C. State and being distressed at having to change her major, the faculty and staff helped her to think through her choices and decide. As had been the case at all-black Norrell Elementary School, every faculty member wanted the students to do well, and they were prepared to do whatever it took to see to it their students reached their goals. Everyone who wanted to would succeed at Shaw. To Jeannie, Shaw was a family and then a school. Predominantly white, John Marshall High had only been a school.

Like Jeannie and Madeline, Marsha had a significant adjustment early in her college enrollment. The Julia Gibson Career College went out of business. It happened as she was getting into the rhythm of the school with her three roommates. They didn't live in a dorm but in a lovely, old apartment building in an upscale section of northwest Washington, D.C. The doorman greeted them every morning as they left to walk the short distance to school. She loved learning about textiles and fabrics during the day and then hanging out with the students from Howard University at night. Life was good. Then the Julia Gibson Career College went bankrupt. Even though the school placed its students in another local career college, it didn't feel right to Marsha. She left and enrolled in a traditional four-year institution as her parents had hoped. A black school, North Carolina A&T, became her new college home.

Upon arriving at the Greensboro, North Carolina campus, Marsha recalled the joy of seeing black people everywhere.

"There were Muslims in bow ties selling bean pies. I'd never seen this before. And, I'd never been a part of a community of all vibrant, young, black people. I loved it. I didn't realize until then this was what I had needed. I immediately felt completely at home. This was where I was supposed to be," Marsha smiled as she remembered.

The student activism led by North Carolina A&T students at the Woolworth's lunch counter in 1960 was only a campus memory when Marsha arrived in 1971.

"I sure wasn't thinking about race or civil rights," said Marsha remembering that time. "I was thinking about all the guys. I was a true social butterfly, flitting from group to group and guy to guy, first dating the cute guy from New York, then the fun guy from Florida and finally the smart jock from right there in Greensboro."

For Marsha, dating was an essential part of the college experience, and she wasn't alone in enjoying this new freedom.

Renée and I were thinking about dating, too. With a dearth of black guys at William and Mary, we looked seriously at the white guys on campus. When comparing these college dating experiences later in life, Renée and I both realized that it didn't feel like we were crossing a taboo. It was natural to spend time with someone whose company you enjoyed, whose interests were similar and who you saw in class or at the student union. It happened that most of those guys were white. Did it feel awkward? No. Well, maybe only a little when they wanted to listen to James Taylor and Creedence Clearwater Revival, and we wanted to listen to Tyrone Davis and Earth, Wind and Fire. The more significant issue of race never emerged. We were young adults going to the movies or to a fraternity party. If someone stared as we walked across the campus together, we didn't notice. We were about having fun. We weren't finding a life's mate but our Valianette friend, Veronica, was determined to do just that.

Veronica's mom definitely saw college as a place to find a husband, a suitable one.

"Ronnie, it is just as easy to fall in love with a rich man as it is to fall in love with a poor one," Mrs. Dungee told her as they talked about the possibility of Veronica attending Fisk University, a school near Meharry Medical College, both black institutions in Nashville.

Veronica wasn't so sure she was looking for a husband. She already had a steady boyfriend in Richmond. He was cute, kind and loving. He was going into the military, and he wanted Veronica to marry him. Veronica was torn. Her mother had married after one year of college and had then depended upon Veronica's dad to send her back to school. It had worked out eventually, but Veronica wasn't sure this was the path she wanted to follow. She saw her mother's lengthy struggle to achieve her goal. Even though the objectives of the then emerging women's liberation movement weren't core to Veronica, she knew she didn't want to be connected to her husband for her financial well-being. She wanted a college degree first and then the husband. Maybe she could keep the high school boyfriend by attending a school closer to home since college didn't seem to be in his immediate future. So, she applied to Fisk, in Tennessee, as her mother wanted and to a school only 60 miles from Richmond, Hampton Institute (now Hampton University), the alma mater of her paternal grandfather. Then fate intervened when a friend of her parents casually commented over dinner one evening that with Ronnie's grades, a scholarship to Virginia State College, Veronica's dad's alma mater might be possible. It was, and Veronica was off to college in Petersburg, only 25 miles from Richmond.

"I fell in love with Virginia State. The girls in the dorm were friendly, and I liked them, but the boys were friendlier. I liked that, too. There was a group of boys who would follow me around. I asked them to stop, telling them I had a boyfriend at home, but secretly I was happy both the guys and the girls liked me," Veronica recalled.

Veronica didn't want to have a boyfriend at home. She didn't like being close to Richmond and how he would show up on campus and then fret because she had things to do or question her because, in his words, she was "too dressed up." She had a new life. She didn't want to be tied to the past. She liked her newfound freedom. Would she call herself a liberated woman in the emerging vernacular of the day? Probably not, but as she was emotionally leaving her old views of marriage to a sensible guy, the true love of her life, Tony Abrams, stepped in.

"He was tall and sexy, a football player. We flirted back and forth for a while, both minimizing the attraction by reminding the other we had a boyfriend/girlfriend at home, but soon it was clear. We were inseparable," remembered Veronica, as she thought back fondly on her freshman and sophomore years at Virginia State.

"You know, I was Miss ROTC and Miss Omega Mardi Gras," Veronica continued, remembering more of her fun times in college beyond her budding relationship with Tony and her pleasure at finally being the majorette she had wanted to be since before coming to John Marshall High School.

It was interesting that a year earlier we had all worked—really worked—to get a black homecoming queen, now the beauty titles were coming without a lot of effort. Veronica was winning them at Virginia State as was Jeannie at Shaw.

When Jeannie, the first black Miss Justice, our high school homecoming queen, went to Shaw University, she was quickly named Miss Omega, Miss Delta, and Miss PE, gaining recognition for her beauty and personality from the guys and girls on campus and from the physical education department, her major. In fact, every year, she was asked to hold the title of queen for some organization or group on campus. Jeannie was even nominated to be Miss Shaw, homecoming queen for the university; however, after a nasty comment was written on one of her publicity photos and remembering the financial strain on her family caused by her high school homecoming candidacy, she withdrew, but nonetheless, she had been nominated.

113

Veronica and Jeannie were cute, flirty and outgoing, so it wasn't a big surprise they were both immediately popular in college, and they would win recognition at their new schools. The surprise was me.

During freshman year, I was among several girls who were nominated to be one of the two freshman homecoming princesses. I was flattered to have received enough votes to be nominated. Then I was shocked when I was chosen. My fellow freshmen, 99% of whom were white, had elected me to the homecoming court. Then, it happened again in my sophomore year and once more in junior year. For three consecutive years, I was one of two girls chosen to represent my respective class in the homecoming court.

While not outgoing like Veronica and Jeannie, I was friendly. I wasn't, however, one of those girls who everyone yelled greetings to as she walked across campus. I was the person who people smiled at, and I genuinely returned their smile, but not the back-to-back, chit-chatty conversation of the truly popular as they walked from class to class. I didn't overthink it, but in hindsight, I wondered why I had been chosen. I asked someone who had observed this event up close.

HOMECOMING COURT

Joyce Van Winkle Soria and I roomed together freshman year in a college-owned apartment building along with five others and then again sophomore year. She is the only one of my roommates with whom I have maintained a connection since college. Joyce is white as were all of my roommates. She was, and is, funny and generous, a kind, warm-hearted person who leaned toward being a hippie when we were in college. I immediately liked her. While I thought through the homecoming court question, I asked Joyce what she thought.

114

"I think you are underestimating your popularity," she said. "We were all in awe of you because you were so beautiful and you knew how to dress really well."

But the real crux of my place at William and Mary was probably reflected in the last part of her insightful response.

She continued, "I think some of your popularity was because you were a novelty—a beautiful, black teenager who was poised and willing to do all of the freshman things with the rest of us, including wearing those silly beanies that looked great on you."

A novelty. That is probably the right term. Not unlike my experience at John Marshall High School, it was unlikely that most of my fellow W&M students had ever spent any significant amount of time with a black person. I had been around white students for over a decade by this time. I was comfortable. I knew how to interact with them and didn't present to them as scary or intimidating. I wore the beanie hat, as Joyce noted, and thought I looked as goofy as everyone else did. I danced with the white guys who asked me to dance at the freshman socials and went out to the deli late at night with my roommates.

Since most probably hadn't had significant prior experiences with black people, I am sure I was novel to many of the white students, at first, but over time they discovered we were all slightly different, but still virtually the same—worried about fitting in at college and homesick. That is the magic of spending time with people from different races, different religions or different cultures. You discover that you're all different, but ultimately the same. Part of my role and Renée's, at William and Mary was to fit in. To show the white faculty, staff, and students, we could intellectually meet their academic standards and socially blend into the student mix. Inherently, Renée and I understood that. That was the way it had been all of our lives. It was that way when we dressed in our best to board the train to go to Washington, D.C. with our elementary class or when we prepared assignments at Chandler Junior High or John Marshall High School. We knew the expectation was we couldn't fit in, we didn't have the brain power, or we didn't know how to act in social situations; so, we as African-

Americans have always felt we had to go above and beyond. The standard for black people in a white world was, and is, consistently higher. So, unlike the other Valianettes who were attending black schools, Renée and I still played a role in the movement toward racial acceptance. We weren't consciously aware of it, but it existed. Our job was to move from being seen as novel to being accepted as ordinary.

The bottom line was we all wanted to be accepted and fit in. While we were quietly, and somewhat unconsciously, working for acceptance at William and Mary, our friends also sought to fit in at their schools. One approach, for most of us, for forming a firm, nurturing friendship group was to join a sorority, another circle of women, like the Valianettes. All who attended black schools, except Debby Anderson, pledged Delta Sigma Theta Sorority, a sorority with a rich history in the black community having been founded in 1913 at Howard University. Debby Anderson, the Valianette who was the most like a rebel, was the only one to never join a sorority.

Renée and I, the ones at a white college, joined sororities, too, just not Delta, at least not then. William and Mary had a full complement of fraternities and sororities, but none of them were black; so, Delta Sigma Theta wasn't an option for us. Renée and I were both recruited by and joined white sororities. Renée joined Kappa Alpha Theta, the first Greek-letter fraternity for women, having been established in 1870 and I joined Pi Beta Phi. Renée's connection to the sorority lasted throughout her time at William and Mary. Mine, however, only lasted a year. While the group was welcoming and very warm, they weren't the Valianettes. While I didn't think I was seeking a sisterhood, in hindsight, I know this sorority wasn't my real from-the-heart community. We would not to listen to the same music, talk about the same television shows or experience the world in enough of the same way for this to feel like "home." That was what I unconsciously wanted. I deactivated my Pi Phi membership.

But, college wasn't just pageants and sororities. We did the work, all of us. We were in college to get an education, and we all did. Madeline competed for and won her first federal grant. She did her own research on organic compounds, not following the steps in a lab book that someone else had developed. Debbie successfully student taught in a majority white school in Raleigh to prepare for completing her elementary education degree as did Debby in Hampton. And Renée and I discovered we had entered an environment of overachievers. We both finished William and Mary a semester early, but we didn't end back-to-back in the top 15 as we had in high school. Here, we truly were academically average, ordinary.

Even though some were the first college graduates in their families, we all completed college without too much familial pomp and circumstance. This was what was expected. John Marshall High School had prepared us well. With 77% of the nation's 1969 high school class finishing college, our year remains the peak for college graduation. Since then, college completion rates across the country have declined. Remarkably, and then maybe it isn't, we had all made it through college without any major hiccups. Our parents had prepared us, along with many other adults in our lives, to succeed. And, once again, we had met their clear expectation. Now we were ready or thought we were, to move on to the next phase of our lives.

What we hadn't considered was how much the world was ready for us. It had changed while we were in college, particularly for black Americans. Our lives had revolved around school, not racial equality. Events happened we may not have even known had occurred, and if we did, we probably didn't think much about their impact on our lives. Naively, we thought race no longer mattered. We had prepared ourselves to enter the work world, but we had given no thought to how the world had been transformed during our college years. It was ready to receive us in a very different way after four years.

It is unlikely we noted two crucial occurrences in our sophomore year. President Jimmy Carter named February as Black History Month that year and the Congressional Black Caucus was established. We no longer had just the week that Carter G. Woodson and the Association for the Study of Negro Life and History had worked for in the late 1920s. We now had a whole month. While we might not have even known this had happened, in hindsight the importance of this four-fold increase in a designated time to emphasize contributions of African-Americans to this country cannot be minimized. Not only was there a higher chance of whites learning about our accomplishments and recognizing what blacks had contributed to the nation, but there was also a higher chance we would better understand our own history. We had all been denied this aspect of our country's history. Carter's action changed that.

But it wasn't just our history that would impact our lives, it was also our present. History was being made, and doors were opening all around us.

By establishing the Congressional Black Caucus (CBC), the African-American members of Congress were establishing themselves as a voting bloc as the Crusade for Voters had done for the black Richmond community decades earlier and as the black students at John Marshall High School had tried to do to elect a black homecoming queen. We didn't notice. It was 1971. We were entrenched in the college atmosphere, and we probably thought we already had all the rights and protections. In our minds, we knew Martin Luther King had worked for and gained the necessary laws. What else would the CBC do?

For those of us who attended a traditionally white university, this view was being reinforced, to a certain degree, by what was then called the counterculture. The hippies who were the mainstay of this cultural phenomenon were active proponents of free love, peace, and harmony. We were living in a college bubble not only of tolerance but of acceptance. At least that's what we saw overtly. By this time, we falsely believed the color of our skin no longer mattered. If we even noticed, we were probably agnostic about the establishment of the CBC, perhaps feeling such racially-driven coordination and activism was no longer needed. Few of us were astute enough to focus on the fact this movement was called the counterculture, an explicit acknowledgment that their actions did not represent the views of mainstream America. They were counter to the prevailing norms of the day.

For those at black colleges with less regular contact with large numbers of whites, they may not have known of the shifting dynamic between college-age whites and blacks. As many of the Valianettes had said, they actually sought less of an emphasis on race and race relations when they decided to attend an HBCU.

In our junior year, Shirley Chisholm became the first African-American woman to run for president. She actively sought the nomination of the Democratic Party, campaigning in several states. I have wondered how many of us even knew about her campaign. We no longer had the day-to-day conversations with our parents to tie us into critical societal events, but New York Congresswoman Shirley Chisholm's 1972 candidacy played in the background noise of what was possible in our lives. Even if we didn't focus on the boldness of her action, subconsciously we had to have internalized her activity as something else that was possible.

I wonder if we noticed Beverly Johnson was on the cover of *Glamour Magazine* that same year. She was the first African-American to be on the cover of a major fashion magazine. For us as young women, that the standard of beauty was beginning to include African-American women went unnoticed. Maybe we saw the publication but didn't think much about the importance of the cover. We probably thought there must have been others. This was 1972 for goodness sake. By now, everyone knew beauty came in all colors, or at least that's what we were likely to have thought. There was so much happening that would impact our ability to move into society swiftly and at a level unavailable to those a few years before us.

CHAPTER 11
AFTER COLLEGE

"We had given no thought to how the world had been transformed during our college years. It was ready to receive us in a very different way after four years."

In today's world, in which over half of the population has a college degree, it is easy to think this has always been the reality. However, in 1969, the year we graduated from high school, only 47% of the high school senior class in the country went on to college. One hundred percent of the Valianettes did. Then, of those graduating from college in the early '70s, a college degree was often seen as the culmination of formal education, as a high school diploma had been for many of those in our parents' generation. That was not the case for the Valianettes. Most of us have advanced degrees. Only Madeline and Renée started this journey directly from undergraduate school.

It was not surprising that Madeline was off to grad school immediately to go deeper into the study of chemistry, biochemistry specifically. She had chosen Howard University in Washington, D.C., one of the premiere black schools in the country. It didn't take her long to blend the roles of student and teacher. She was on the fast track to move into the world of work.

Madeline had always been an outstanding student; so, when Mississippi Valley State College reached out to Howard University for a faculty member for their chemistry program, many thought of Madeline. While she hadn't yet earned her Ph.D., she was adequately credentialed. Madeline was ready for this opportunity, and the school wanted her. She knew she was prepared to teach chemistry. She thought she was ready for the environment of a small campus, but what she wasn't prepared for was a small town in the Deep South.

With her mother, Madeline drove from Washington, D.C. to the Mississippi Delta. As she entered the state, she noted the massive Welcome to Mississippi sign. Instantly, she recalled the rhyme "M-I, crooked letter, crooked letter, I crooked letter, crooked letter I, humpback, humpback, I" that had been the prompt in elementary school to help young students learn to spell this state's name. Her mind was drifting back to Norrell Elementary School as her eyes were seeing farmland alongside the highway. All kinds of crops were growing, most of which she couldn't identify, but she could recognize the cotton. The sight of it took her even further back to the 1800s thinking about slavery and her ancestors and then she saw the sign.

"What was that?" she asked her mother.

"What?" replied Mrs. Swann who had been drifting off to sleep riding in the car on what was a hot day. Even though she had grown up in the South, she had forgotten her early South Carolina days and the oppressive heat. Even Virginia wasn't this bad. The drive with her daughter was bringing back lots of memories of the South for her too as she drifted to sleep.

"That big sign we just passed," Madeline replied incredulously. "It said that we are entering some plantation."

"Yes, Brucie, land owned by one person or one family is still often referred to as plantations in parts of the South. It's archaic, I know, but many still use the term," she replied knowledgeably and impassioned, "those signs are offensive and should come down."

"Plantations, are you kidding me?" Madeline almost yelled, not at her mother, but at the ridiculousness of still using a term that brought back to life such horrible images."

"Plantations," she still mumbled as they drove onto the campus of Mississippi Valley State College, a small black school, about a mile outside of the small Mississippi town of Itta Bena. Madeline knew about Itta Bena because it was where D.C.'s newly-elected mayor Marion Berry had been born. Barry had already had a visible and illustrious political career in the city were Madeline attended graduate school, and he was an alumnus of her undergraduate school, Fisk University; she knew about Barry and a little about Itta Bena.

While the use of the term, "plantation" was startling, Madeline's Mississippi Valley State experience of race in the South was just beginning. After a few weeks, she learned that the local grocery stores were segregated, not by law, but by practice. When her closest grocer—in the "black part" of town—didn't have an ingredient that Madeline needed for dinner one evening, she went across town to the other grocer. As she entered the store, she was confronted not by words, but by harsh stares and silence. She knew she had crossed a line that few blacks in this small town had crossed. No one commented, but tension was in the air. She didn't dwell on this incident, bought her items and returned to school.

The culminating event for Madeline, however, was her attempt to visit the post office on a November day. Police cars were everywhere. In fact, the town square was so dense with police cars she turned around and went back to campus. When she asked what had happened, she learned that this show of police force was precautionary. It was election day. Two of the candidates were black. The local officials thought there might be trouble. The police were there to prevent any incident while also being ready for any violence that might break out. That was enough for Madeline. While she found the college community welcoming and the students focused and capable, she wasn't ready to stay in Itta Bena. She knew why native son B.B. King had left and she knew what had influenced his blues music. Madeline left Itta Bena, never returning to the South, at least not for any period longer than a short vacation.

Madeline's time in Itta Bena, however, was broken by one significant bright spot. Her longtime Valianette buddy, Renée Fleming, came to visit. Renée and Madeline had been friends for as long as they could remember. Madeline thought their connection might go back to elementary school when the practice was to line students up by height as they walked to the cafeteria. Renée and Madeline had always been two of the tallest in the class. They were put together early, and soon they discovered that it wasn't just height they had in common, they liked each other. When you said Renée, you said Madeline. Theirs was one of the Valianette duos that continued after high school. No longer a Valianette connection per se, they were now merely good friends. And Madeline knew for sure because Renée had come to Itta Bena. Only the closest friend would do that.

When Renée went to visit, she was a graduate intern with the National Institute on Drug Abuse. She was working in her discipline training substance abuse counselors across the state of Missouri while also working on her Ed.D degree from Laurence University in California—student and teacher, like Madeline. Within the context of race, however, Renée had a very different experience from her friend. Madeline was working in a black, academic enclave. Renée often found herself as the only black person in a setting where she had to train a white audience. Having been a student at predominately white William and Mary, she discovered that this racial ratio was not uncomfortable for her. While she was comfortable, others weren't always. She had Madeline laughing when she told her about her experience with her white roommate at the University of Florida.

After college, Renée had gone even farther into the South than Madeline had. She had decided to attend the University of Florida. The location hadn't been a factor in her decision. She had chosen the school because it had the degree program she was seeking and because it operated on a quarter system. Since Renée had finished college a semester early, she could go straight into graduate school, entering the master's program in rehabilitative counseling. She wasn't exactly sure what she wanted to do, but she thought this degree would take her in the right direction. Then there was her father. Like all of our parents, Mr. Fleming appreciated education. He knew it was through ongoing learning he had risen from a bank teller to become president of Consolidated Bank & Trust. He even wrote his master's thesis on the history of Consolidated Bank within the broader context of black banking. So, Renée was not surprised by her educationally focused and fiscally responsible dad's guidance.

"My dad had told me that if I went straight from college to grad school, he would pay for it; so that's just what I did," Renée recalled.

The University of Florida was, and is, a large university in Gainesville, Florida. Gainesville is a college town with the median age of 25 in the city driven by its college residents. Not only is it a college town, but it's also a college town in the South. Much like Madeline, Renée hadn't thought a lot about what that might mean. She hadn't experienced overt racism at William and Mary, another southern college in a small southern town.

"Can you believe it," she told Madeline as they were sitting in Madeline's small apartment in Itta Bena, "my roommate, my white roommate, would ask me to leave the room whenever her parents were visiting."

"What, you've got to be kidding?" Madeline asked with exasperation.

"Yeah, she didn't know how her parents would react if they knew her roommate was black; so, she thought that would just be easier," Renée responded.

"Easier for her maybe, but what about you?" asked Madeline.

"Well, you know, I really didn't think too much about it. We got along okay, and I knew the situation might cause her problems. I really didn't mind that much," remembered Renée.

1973 and a "relationship" with a black person, even one in graduate school, still caused an issue. Was Renée so accustomed to accommodating the needs of white people, perhaps unconsciously, that she didn't mind leaving her room for this brief period of time or was she merely thoughtfully avoiding a needless confrontation? Maybe a little bit of both. Staying in the room to make the point she had every right to be there wasn't worth the potential aggravation. We may have thought we had overcome, but many white people were still uncomfortable with being around or were disdainful of blacks.

No one else in our group other than Renée and Madeline went immediately into graduate school. For the rest of us, education continued in different ways.

Jeannie took another course, off campus, to round out her education. Of our group, she seems to have been the one who was the most affected by the Vietnam War, a war that had divided the country. Soldiers were returning home without fanfare and without limbs. Many of them needed rehabilitation. Corrective therapy was a field that had emerged after World War II to address the therapeutic needs of soldiers coming home after that war. While the country didn't embrace the returning Vietnam veterans as they had the WWII soldiers, Jeannie did. She appreciated their service to the country and felt compassion for them. She also had a free semester and had graduated a semester early, but unlike Renée, she wasn't sure what to do with her time until she heard about a unique program back in Virginia.

"From the beginning of college, I had wanted to major in physical therapy. That wasn't possible because Shaw didn't offer what I needed," Jeannie recalled. "Now, with this extra semester, so to speak, I decided I would follow that dream. I had heard about a one-semester course at Hampton Institute on corrective therapy. I applied and was happy when I was accepted. This was the kind of work I wanted to do."

The course offered jointly by the Veteran's Administration Hospital and Hampton Institute was ideal, meeting her professional interests, giving her an additional credential, and only about 50 miles from home. So, for Jeannie, college didn't stop after meeting Shaw University's requirements for graduation. She was now off to Hampton.

Valianette Debby Anderson was at Hampton Institute, too, finishing up her senior year, but she and Jeannie never connected during this time. It is ironic that we had all been so close for twelve years of our lives, but once we were in college, even those of us in the same school didn't connect. We were making new friends, establishing new communities, and going in different directions.

Much of Debby's time was focused on Kenneth who would become her fiancé while in college. She and Kenneth had started dating while she was a junior and he a senior at John Marshall High School. They had continued an exclusive dating relationship throughout their years at Hampton Institute and become engaged before he graduated. She knew, however, that before she got married, she wanted to find a job. And before the marriage, she would have a little fun and maybe expand her education a little more, too.

One of her professors in one of the many art history classes she took at Hampton was a nun whose religious order supported a scholarship to study for six weeks in Europe. Debby applied for and was accepted to be a part of the 1973 program; so, she boarded her first airplane and went off to Italy. She loved Venice and Florence. She loved the adventure of meeting new people and making new friends, of exploring Italy and she loved the art. A new country and freedom before settling into marriage and work, this was the perfect sojourn between college and her post-college, personal and professional life.

I was taking a different path. Unlike my friends Renée and Madeline or Debby and Jeannie who were all still studying, I thought I was moving directly into the work world. I would make the world better for poor children and families. I didn't see my year after college as a learning year. It was the beginning of my working, adult life. It ended up being so much more than that.

"Do you know 'E.P.'?" asked the caseworker on the phone, naming someone listed in one of my case files.

When I received this call, I had only been working for the Richmond Department of Welfare for a short period. With a degree in sociology and as the daughter of a nurse, working with people who needed support seemed the right path for me. On my caseload was a young girl who had been in foster care all of her 15-year life. 'E.P.' was her mother.

"Yes, I know the name," I responded. "Her daughter is one of my clients, but I've never met her. There's been no contact."

There was an uncomfortable silence as the other caseworker did not respond.

"Do you know her," I asked, wondering why the mother's name was coming up after years.

After what seemed to be an inordinate pause, the caseworker said, "Yes, she is a foster parent here."

126

Through a series of tragic events, this mother had been placed in a juvenile detention facility for girls when she was a teenager. Her crime? Truancy. While there, at what was euphemistically called a reform school, she became pregnant and gave birth to my client. The child was taken from her at birth and placed in foster care. When the mother was released at age 18, she tried to find her baby. Black, poor, uneducated, and alone, she faced a bureaucracy that refused to help her and one that ultimately told her, incorrectly, she had signed papers releasing her baby for adoption. This young girl eventually went on with her life, married and had a family. Her way of always remembering and honoring the child she never knew was to become a foster mother herself, hoping the adoptive mother who mothered her child had been as kind and caring to her daughter as she was to the children placed in her care. Once that story came together, the agency responded they couldn't put the mother and child in contact because it would make the organization look bad. For me, this was a powerful lesson in injustice. I ignored the agency's position and connected the two. Was that the right thing to do? Yes. Were mother and daughter well prepared for this meeting? No, I had the correct sense of right and wrong, but not the skills to facilitate such an emotional meeting. I don't know what happened to that family. I left the agency soon after their first meeting. I hope it was the right thing to do—for them. It was definitely the right thing to do for me. It was a life-changing event.

Their situation had provided me with first-hand experience of injustice, no textbook examination of a historical event, nothing hypothetical. This was real. This was now. My efforts may have righted a wrong for one family, but I suspected there were many other situations in the child welfare system, and in other systems that needed to be corrected. Having thirty plus kids on my caseload, knowing their stories and those of their foster parents and biological parents, even with my limited experience, I could see the problems of this system could not be addressed one child at a time. I thought broad policy change was needed and I would be a part of fixing this broken system; so, off I went to the School of Social Work at Virginia Commonwealth University in Richmond to study community organizing and social planning. Graduate school hadn't been a part of my plan when I finished William and Mary, but I could tell I needed more skills and advanced credentials to have the impact I wanted to.

One evening in graduate school I looked up at the black professor and suddenly realized I had not had a black teacher, instructor or professor since I was in elementary school at Albert V. Norrell. While I don't remember the specifics of the test I took that evening, I recall the last question was one of those open-ended questions, "tell me all you know" about something or the other in social welfare. When I looked up in response to the professor calling my name, I realized it was just the professor and me in the room. Everyone else had turned in their papers and left for the evening. I was so engrossed in telling him "all I knew" that I hadn't noticed.

"I think you can stop writing now," he said. "Clearly, you know a lot about the subject."

"I do," I responded and laughed, stopped writing and turned in my paper. The subject was interesting, so I'd read a lot about it and studied to prepare for the test.

As we were walking out of the classroom, I thought about the racial identity of all who had been my teachers. For the last eleven years of my schooling, all of my structured education had come from white people. Reflecting on this now, I wonder what the impact of this was on me. Did I see them as more knowledgeable than blacks? I don't think so. My roots and connections to the black community were strong and deep. Throughout my life, I had been around black people in positions of authority and responsibility, neighbors who were professors at black colleges, family members who owned their own businesses, or family friends who were community activists or government officials. I didn't see black people as powerless or not as people from whom I could learn. They were my teachers, be that explicitly or implicitly. Nonetheless, the lack of black educators in my life must have had an impact on me subconsciously.

Equally, it must have had an impact on my white peers to not have had black neighbors, family members or family friends they routinely saw as knowledgeable and as leaders. Their view of the races was being shaped by their experience just as mine was. What they saw most was likely to have been negative images of black people as the media often focused more on the bad news of the day and on the perception of my race as takers from, not contributors to, society. I had a firm and extensive footing in both worlds. They typically didn't. Like me, their view was shaped by their reality.

CHAPTER 12
SEPARATE BUT LINKED BY RACE

"We were continuously affected by the rapidly changing racial paradigm in the United States regardless of if we knew or understood the magnitude of the events."

For a little over two decades, we were apart.

The Valianettes wouldn't be pivotal in our development during this time, but race always would be whether or not we were consciously aware of it. We were no longer that single friendship group. We were, however, still black. We were continuously affected by the rapidly changing racial paradigm in the United States regardless of if we focused on it or even knew or understood the magnitude of the events.

These were crucial decades of opportunity. As African-American women, we thought we could do it all—careers and families. That's what we wanted, and that's what we would have. Black people were in vogue. Women were being recognized as the new voiceless minority. On the television show *All in the Family*, the lead character, Archie Bunker, was saying with bigotry and clarity "I'm white, I'm male, I'm protestant. Where's the law to protect me?"

We saw some African-American 'firsts.' These milestones were less nuanced, and their relevance was even clear to us, even as young adults. For example, we noticed in 1977 when civil rights lawyer Henry Marsh was elected, by his fellow council members, as Richmond's first African-American mayor. The mayor and vice-mayor of Richmond were chosen by their peers on the city council. While not a city-wide acknowledgment of the leadership skills of an African-American, it was still a notable nod to the growing number of African-Americans in the city and the respect Henry Marsh had earned among his peers during his decade-long tenure on that body. Max Robinson, a Richmond native, also got our attention and that of blacks across the country when in 1978 he became the first African-American to anchor the national news on *World News Tonight* on ABC. And none of us could help but notice when President Ronald Reagan signed the bill in 1983 designating Martin Luther King's birthday as a national holiday. Even we knew this recognition of Dr. King had taken over a decade and that this wasn't a recognition fully embraced by the president or by all in Congress. This was important. Martin Luther King, Jr. was *the* symbol of the black race. Acknowledging him for a national holiday was a capstone to admitting we were now a part of America. We understood this.

President Reagan may have had little choice but to sign the bill, but in our home state of Virginia, leaders were determined not to enact it. Just as Virginia and other southern states had done many times before when a national action, legal or otherwise, did not align with cultural heritage, Virginia leaders decided to "honor" this decision in their own unique way. They changed the long-standing Lee-Jackson state holiday to Lee-Jackson-King Day.

Ever since 1889, the Commonwealth of Virginia had honored the President of the Confederacy Robert E. Lee. In 1904, that recognition had been expanded to include Confederate General Stonewall Jackson. Remarkably, Virginia had been acknowledging King's birthday since 1978 by celebrating it on New Year's Day making it a virtual non-recognition. With the passage of the federal measure, the Virginia General Assembly moved its recognition of Dr. King to the already established Lee-Jackson day creating what many saw as a travesty with the ill-suited Lee-Jackson-King Day coupling. With this decision in 1983, the Valianettes and all other adult African-Americans in Richmond and throughout Virginia were reminded harshly that Virginia was a state still more committed to the vision and culture of the Confederacy than to the idea of multi-racial acceptance espoused by Martin Luther King, Jr.

While this action in the early '80s reflected a state moderately tolerant of change, but not widely accepting of it, a few years later Virginia would rise to a place in history no one would expect given its racial history. On November 8, 1989, Lawrence Douglas Wilder became the first African-

American elected to governor of any state in the United States. P.B.S. Pinchbeck, an African-American, had served as governor of Louisiana for 35 days, but only due to the circumstance of the sitting governor having to step down due to an impeachment process. As lieutenant governor, Pinchbeck served out the remainder of his term. Not by a circumstantial fluke, but by savvy political skills, a keen understanding of the needs of the state and a charming southern gentleman demeanor, Wilder had won. When the population of Virginia was 77.5% white, a victory would not have been possible without an overwhelming belief by whites that Wilder was the candidate better capable of leading Virginia. However, his victory was so slim that a recount was immediately called for by his opponent. Just as African-Americans nationwide had celebrated Pinchbeck in 1872, we celebrated Wilder in 1990. As the circumstances of Pinchbeck becoming governor were irrelevant, so to was Wilder's margin of victory. African-American across Virginia and across the country called friends and family as the votes came in and cheered madly as the announcement was made, but not one Valianette can remember calling another that night. We weren't friends again yet.

We didn't chatter on the phone about the 1991 hearings to confirm Clarence Thomas as the 2nd African-American to serve on the United States Supreme Court. We didn't go as a group to see Spike Lee's 1992 movie *Malcolm X* even though we all saw it and years later commented that Denzel Washington should have won the Academy Award for his performance. And we didn't get in touch when African-American Rodney King was beaten by Los Angeles police officers that same year triggering huge race riots. These potent reminders of the overlay of race in the country were happening without the Valianettes reaching out to each other. Only Madeline knew this was the year Renée would earn her Ph.D. We weren't reconnected yet. AJ hadn't been born (you'll meet him a bit later), but this was the year Marsha first reached out to me, the year that put us back on the path to reconnect.

CHAPTER 13
THE ADULT WORLD

"Professional doors were open for us in the 1970s that never had been open before to blacks and to women."

What was happening all around us in the early to mid-'70s shaped what we thought we could become and what others thought of blacks. Every time a black person gained an audience of whites in a positive setting, the sense of who we were and what we could do was likely to change. That transformation happened incrementally, in countless positive one-on-one daily encounters, but it changed in a significant—broader societal—way when Texas Congresswoman Barbara Jordan, for example, delivered the keynote address at the 1976 Democratic National Convention. An intelligent, poised, articulate, well-dressed black woman stood on a national platform and demonstrated that a black person could not just hold that spotlight, but could command it with her knowledge, insight, and vision. That was powerful for the country and for us.

Now, it wasn't only the civil rights movement that was affording us opportunities. It was also the women's movement also. We were coming of age in the midst of what was later called the second wave of the women's movement. The first wave at the turn of the century in 1900 had focused on women's suffrage. Women were demanding the vote. By the second wave, women were concentrated on sexism, the paternal—often patronizing—nature of men deciding for them and denying them opportunities. It was into this world we began our careers. The timing could not have been better for African-American women starting up the career ladder. We were black, and we were women. Professional doors were open for us in the 1970s that never had been open before to blacks and to women.

We all benefited from Shirley Chisholm, Beverly Johnson, and Barbara Jordan. They showed us what was possible for black women in America. Just as Mrs. Overby had served as an example of what was possible when we were in elementary school so, too, did other black women as we moved into adulthood. We absorbed all of this subconsciously as our array of opportunities and possibilities continued to expand as women and as black women.

This was the time in which we were no longer Valianettes, and we hadn't yet become the group called Divas. We were finishing our educations, forming new friendships, establishing our own families and pursuing our careers. The events of, this period can't be told as one story. No longer was there one, intertwined story of eight girls. We were living separate lives as we moved into adulthood.

DEBBIE

Debbie Johnson Riddick is the oldest in the group by a few months. That distinction has been significant. Debbie is also the oldest of six children born to St. Elmo and Clara Johnson, three girls and three boys. She is the divorced mom of two adult daughters and now Gigi (grandmother) to three.

Debbie was the first of our group to move solidly into her profession. After college, she returned to Richmond with her degree in elementary education and looked for a job. In 1973, the country was in a recession. Many were looking for jobs; so, for a right-out-of-college teacher, it might take a while, and it had. Debbie hadn't been successful until a family member suggested she talk with Herbert Crockett, a member of her church, who was the principal of Highland Park Elementary School. Mr. Crockett knew the family and had watched Debbie grow up. He knew her values, trusted her educational experience. He needed another third-grade teacher. Debbie was right for the team he was creating. She was hired.

In 1974, Debbie went to work at Highland Park Elementary School, in a neighborhood that abutted Northside where most of us had grown up. When we were growing up there in the '50s and '60s, Highland Park was predominantly white. By the time Debbie taught this was a low-income black community with challenges. While Debbie, as idealistic and self-assured as most recent college graduates, felt she could teach any kids. She felt more prepared for this community, more dedicated to enhancing the potential of these kids and more comfortable in this setting than she might have in an integrated or predominantly white environment.

"I started a few weeks into the school year," Debbie recalled, "But instead of having a classroom with randomly chosen students, the principal asked each teacher to send me, the new teacher, five students from their over-enrolled classes."

Human nature being what it is, the teachers sent from their classrooms the students who presented the most significant educational or behavioral challenges. This caused Debbie, the first-year teacher, to have a class of students who needed particular attention.

"I wasn't happy. I had a classroom full of what most would have called the 'bad' kids. Their parents weren't happy either. They had met their children's teachers, and now they were being told an untested, first-year teacher would be their teacher," remarked Debbie as she thought back on this early year in her career.

While the situation wasn't ideal, this year was pivotal in preparing Debbie for the hundreds of parents and students she would have throughout her teaching career. She made it through that year successfully. The parents ultimately liked her. Their children learned, and they adored her, too.

Four years after Debbie started teaching there, the students of Highland Park Elementary School left the building that had been the school for young children in this community since 1914 to go to a new school. Ironically, the new school was named Overby-Sheppard Elementary after Ethel Thompson Overby, the black woman who had been the principal of Albert V. Norrell Elementary when we attended there in the late 1950s and Eleanor Sheppard, a white woman and the first woman to be mayor of Richmond. Symbolically, if unintentionally, this naming joined the civil rights and the women's rights movements.

Debbie had met Bob Riddick while her sister, Jeannie was taking courses at Hampton Institute. Bob knew Jeannie and thought she was cute and fun, but with Debbie, he felt something special. She did, too. They had chemistry. They married on July 7, 1979.

In 1981, Debbie and Bob's first daughter, Katrina Joi, was born. Three years later, Bob and Debbie had another daughter, Jennifer Carrie. "I didn't want more children than that," Debbie commented. "Even though I was from a big family of six kids, I was happy with my two girls and so was Bob."

They were the all-American family. They bought a house, got a dog and took family vacations to Disney World. Like most young families, their world revolved around their children, their careers, and their extended families. Bob had always been a sports enthusiast. He loved watching and playing a variety of sports and encouraging others to play. He had landed a job with the Department of Recreation in Henrico County, a community right next to Richmond. This was ideal for him. Debbie was establishing herself as a reliable teacher, learning how to engage the kids and how to involve parents in their children's education. Their nuclear family was healthy.

Debbie's siblings also married and started their own families. The connections for Debbie were definitely family-centered as new relationships emerged with sisters-in-law and brothers-in-law. Clara and Elmo Johnson, Debbie's parents, were shifting into the grandparent role. Debbie's family was evolving and growing. Friendships also changed. Neighbors on the block where they lived or the parents of their children's friends became the people who they saw the most. These were the people with whom they now had the most in common, and they became their primary friends. While there might be an occasional phone call or a chance running into someone at the shopping mall, the Valianettes as a group... was the past. Life had evolved into new duos and trios, robust new family connections and children whose passions for tennis or dance or going on sleepovers now controlled all of Debbie's spare time. Her family was complete. Her life was fulfilled. She was looking to the future, not to the past.

Ever the steadfast, practical one, eventually Debbie divorced, realizing that Bob wasn't the right choice, but teaching was. She retired after teaching in the Richmond, Virginia public school system for over 35 years.

DEBBY

Debby Anderson Smith is the youngest of three children born to Winston and Leader Anderson. She wasn't as successful with her teaching degree as the other Debbie. After college, she found a job quickly with the public school system in Washington D.C. where she had moved and where her sister Anna worked.

"I just wasn't cut out to be a teacher, at least not that kind of teacher. I quit after a year. A friend of Anna's was leaving her job with the American Cancer Society and thought that I would be a good fit. I got the job and became a health educator. I loved it. That was my niche," said Debby recalling the difficulty of those early career years.

In her job with the American Cancer Society, Debby could use her education training since she was in schools teaching kids from elementary age through college about the dangers of smoking and how to stop if they had already started. She also taught adults about the importance of early detection for certain cancers. Debby loved this teaching, enjoyed the flexibility of this workplace, and felt passionate about the impact of smoking and the devastation it was having on the black community, in particular. She had found a position that spoke to her social justice roots.

Debby was the first of our group to get married. And as we were all expected to attend college and start our careers, we were also supposed to marry and start families. Regardless of the women's liberation movement messages prominent in the 1970s, 21 was still the median age for women to marry in 1973 when we graduated from college. Many young women earned their BA degrees and their MRS 'credential' in the same year.

For our group, Debby was the only one who fell into this statistic. In this, she was following tradition, but there was nothing traditional about her wedding. Debby's sister Anna was engaged at the same time. Debby knew Anna was planning a large, traditional wedding the following year, so she and Kenny decided they would be different. Not only did they elope, it was on the spur of the moment in November following Debby's graduation.

"I wore a knee-length, red knit dress, fitted at the waist with a V-neck and long sleeves and I covered my short 'fro with a beautiful white lace mantilla. I thought I looked good," Debby chuckled as she remembered. "Oh, yes, I forgot the shoes. Black platform shoes. I was bad."

Wearing red on her wedding day is so Debby. Remember, she's the Valianette most likely to be called militant. She's the rebel. White would have been far too traditional. Unlikely to be even considered. A pastel color would have been too mellow and meek. Black would have been over-the-top non-conformist and not celebratory as she genuinely felt. Debby wore red, a power color, a happy color, and an in-your-face-I'm-a-bit-of-a-rebel color.

"Kenneth looked pretty good, too. He had on a sharp burgundy suit. The pants had pleats in the front giving them a baggy look, and he had on black platform shoes, too. You couldn't tell us anything. We were sharp," noted Debby with humor as she recalled the day. No one could tell then that a little over a decade and two children later this marriage would end.

Kenneth had gotten a job with IBM, a hallmark company. If you worked for IBM, you were thought to be smart and successful. So, when Kenneth left IBM to sell mega computers to governments and corporations, his background was the good housekeeping seal of approval. He was personable, and his sales technique was excellent. He was named salesman of the year four years in a row. But as personal computing increased and competition grew, the pressures on Kenneth to stay ahead grew more intense, and he became less capable of managing his volatility.

Debby had always known Kenneth was volatile. Initially, she had thought of this as passion. He felt strongly about issues and about her, and he was ready to fight for what he believed in. His commitment to social justice and racial equality may even have been a contributor to her own passion for these issues. And, what she came to see as Kenneth's possessiveness of her, had felt protective and comforting initially. But, as the children came—Kenneth, Jr (Kenny) in 1977 and Aaron in 1980—the pressures on Kenneth, Sr. to take care of his family combined with the stresses of the job created a difficult situation for the family.

"Kenneth became dependent on drugs. In hindsight, I think he may have been self-medicating to correct an undiagnosed mental illness, but all I knew was his substance abuse, and his periodic bouts of rage could not be tolerated. I would not raise my boys in such an unhealthy environment, and I didn't want to be unhappy either," Debby commented regretfully. She left Kenneth and subsequently divorced.

Now, a grandmother to six, Debby lives in Washington, D.C. She has taught school and held many direct service positions with an emphasis on health services and on helping the homeless and those with mental health conditions.

JEANNIE

Jean Johnson Petties, Debbie Johnson Riddick's sister, is the flirty, bold one.

For Jeannie, there wasn't a family member or a family friend to serve as a bridge into the work world. But with her bachelor's degree in physical education and her corrective therapy knowledge, she felt there was one place where she'd be sure to find a job: Walter Reed Army Hospital in Washington, D.C. With so many soldiers returning from the Vietnam War with injuries necessitating Jeannie's skills, she knew she'd have no problem finding a job.

"I went into the interview with high energy and made sure they knew how much I wanted to work there," Jeannie recalled. "The interviewers were all smiles, telling me I was a great candidate and they would be in touch VERY, their emphasis, soon. But no follow up call came. The federal government had enacted a hiring freeze. My dream job was gone. I was devastated. I really didn't know what to do."

Jeannie returned to Richmond. With relative ease, she found a position as a physical therapist at a nursing home in Richmond. This type of job wasn't hoped for, but it used her training. Like everything Jeannie did, she went into it with as positive an attitude as she could.

"The job was okay. I connected with the seniors easily, but I quickly became concerned about the way many of them were being treated," Jeannie said. "Food would be brought to them and just left, even before those who couldn't feed themselves very well. I pointed this out to my supervisor who told me in clear terms the residents were well cared for. I didn't think they were. I wasn't happy there. I had to decide what my next steps would be."

It would take Jeannie a few years, different positions, and a halted wedding to send her to Atlanta where her professional life would start and quickly blossom.

Jeannie had been moving through life, taking the steps in a logical order. She had done high school, college, and was trying to start her career. She knew marriage and then beginning a family was the expected next steps.

Her route to the altar took a different course than that of her sister Debbie. Always friendly and outgoing, dating had never been an issue. She had dates, lots of them. Then, one day coming home from work, she saw a guy in her apartment complex who looked familiar.

"I was parking my car, and Norman was standing on the curb and smiling," Jeannie remembered. He had been a year behind us in high school but hadn't been on Jeannie's radar screen then. She was pretty, well-liked and had been voted homecoming queen. He would have had to stand in line behind far more popular seniors and college guys to have gotten a date. But when she turned into her apartment complex that day and saw Norman, a friendship began that quickly moved into a romance. He was gentle, kind, fun loving and in love with Jeannie. She thought she was in love with him, too, so when he proposed, she accepted. Wedding planning started in high gear with Mrs. Johnson, Jeannie's mom and her mom's sisters moving at a lightning pace. They were so excited.

"One day, I realized everyone was really into this wedding planning, that is everyone except me," Jeannie commented. "I was a bystander, and it wasn't just that I was watching the process. I discovered I really wasn't interested. I called off the wedding."

"I didn't know what to do then. The family thing wasn't working out too well, and I really wasn't happy in my job," said Jeannie. "I had a friend in Atlanta, so I decided to go there and take one week to find a job and maybe a new life."

This was in the early days of Atlanta being a hot spot for both the up-and-coming black professionals and for those who had already "arrived." Atlanta was so different from staid, traditional Richmond. Jeannie liked it, but unfortunately, the job search wasn't going well at least not until her last day there. Unexpectedly, she got a call back from a health care facility and was offered a position. Atlanta was now home. She loved it. The city was dynamic. She liked her job and the people who she worked with. Brenda, the friend who had drawn her to Atlanta, was introducing her around. Everything was falling into place. She'd been raised as a regular churchgoer, so now she had to find a church home. The non-denominational Hillside Church led by Dr. Barbara King was the spiritual home she was seeking. She became active in the church working with the youth groups and helping to plan special events. So, it was a typical Sunday when she walked down the aisle to find her usual pew. Her spot was taken, so she walked back toward the rear of the church to a bench in front of where her friend Jim was seated. When it came time for fellowship and greetings of congregants, Jeannie turned and held out her hand to the person sitting beside Jim. Tall, dark and handsome Andre Petties smiled back. That was October 1981. Engaged by December, they married the following August. "Life was good," Jeannie recalled. "Andre was with the Marriott Corporation in the mid-'80s when he was invited to play a vital role in a new venture in Birmingham Alabama. The Birmingham Turf Club was opening. It would be the first thoroughbred racing horse venue in the Deep South. Investors were coming in from all over the country. The prospects were good; so, Andre moved first, and then I came."

Their first child Jake was born there in 1987 and then daughter Noelle two years later. The Birmingham Turf Club didn't survive, but Andre had established himself in the business community in Birmingham and Jeannie was becoming a part of the helping community through her work in the Red Cross. She hadn't been so sure about moving from Atlanta to the Deep South, but when they moved in a mostly white neighborhood and were welcomed warmly, Jeannie felt her apprehensions were unfounded. At least that's how she felt until she took her young child to a city-referred child care center one day. After confirming by phone that a slot was available for the day, Jeannie was stopped at the door, and the manager said: "I'm not allowed to keep colored children here." This event in the late '80s in Birmingham was a powerful reminder that race was still a factor in our country.

Jeannie is now divorced with a son, a daughter, and one grandchild. She is a management consultant in Alabama.

MARSHA

Marsha Ford Ware is the older of two daughters born to Lloyd and Doris Ford. Marsha is the funny one, the real comic of our group.

Like Jeannie, Marsha would ultimately have to change cities to move into her ultimate career path. After college, she returned to Richmond trying to figure out her first professional steps. She had a degree in clothing, textiles and related arts. While the notion of interior design had interested her years ago, she didn't think this was where she wanted to be.

"I had absolutely no idea of what I would do," Marsha remembers. "Veronica became my connection to an industry I'd never thought of—insurance. She'd started working at Aetna Insurance Company after she got her master's degree because she still couldn't find a teaching position in Richmond. Just like I had introduced her to the Valianettes years ago, she introduced me to the hiring folks at Aetna. I got the job and started out as a claims adjustor. I never would have guessed I would stay there for 12 years."

Insurance certainly wasn't a passion or a calling for Marsha, like teaching was for Debbie or rehabilitation was for Jeannie, but it fit her nonetheless. It wasn't until she married and moved that her calling would become apparent.

Like me (I'll get to it at the end of this chapter), Marsha married a 'smart jock' who she had met during her college years. They had dated off and on in college, but Marsha finally called it off when she felt he was hanging out with the wrong folks.

"He called me once in the early '80s as he was passing through Richmond. I knew he had married. I didn't return that call," Marsha recalled. But when he called again, after his divorce, they connected. It seemed he couldn't get Marsha out of his mind. She felt a strong connection to him, too. In December 1987, Marsha married and moved to the western part of Virginia. Her husband had relocated there when offered a position. He was going to be the breadwinner; so instead of looking for a job immediately, Marsha thought she'd use some of the skills she had learned at the Julia Gibson Career College over a decade earlier. She was going to create a home for her new family, not intended to be a showcase, house beautiful, but a cozy, warm home that reflected who they were as a young couple.

Unfortunately, once again just like at the Gibson school, Marsha's dream was incredibly short-lived. By January 1988, she already felt the marriage was a mistake. She was seeing some of the behavior that had led her away from her husband when they were in college. She knew she was in trouble when one day she started to cry while out shopping in a small boutique, still working to create the perfect home. Marsha remembers the empathetic store clerk who took her into a back room at the store, made her a cup of tea and talked and talked. While Marsha couldn't stop the tears from flowing, she wasn't ready to share the whole truth of what was going on in her life with this stranger. She disclosed she had just married and moved to her new home and was having trouble adjusting to the new city. The clerk said she had experienced the same adjustment problem when she was new to the city and encouraged Marsha not to isolate herself by staying at home, to go out and get a job.

Marsha followed that advice and went back to her professional roots—insurance. She found a job with a third-party administrator who was just moving to the area. It was perfect—a small office representing many insurers. She could focus her energies on helping to develop this new business. From 9:00 a.m. to 5:00 p.m. her mind was occupied, and she didn't have time to focus on what was going on at home. But after 5, she had to go home and to an unhappy environment. She had finally put a name on the situation – substance abuse. Her husband was drinking excessively. His drinking was destroying this young family before it even had time to form. Marsha knew it was time to leave the marriage and she did.

Marsha is an actively engaged aunt to her sister's two children and great aunt to one. Her work with an international nonprofit organization causes Marsha to travel the world as she focuses on substance abuse, a problem that devastates so many families. She lives in Virginia Beach, Virginia.

RENÉE

Renée Fleming Mills is the older of two daughters born to Jesse and Aliceann Fleming. Renée is the self-described seeker, always looking for the next challenge. She came home from the University of Florida thinking she had a calling. Her internship in Florida had her counseling substance abusers. She had enjoyed that work, so she applied for a position with Project Jump Street, a substance abuse treatment program in Richmond.

"It was really only on paper that I was right for the work they had me doing at Project Jump Street," Renée remembered. "I wasn't twenty-five years old, and they were sending me to the prison to talk with inmates about why selling drugs was wrong. I was supposed to convince them a minimum wage job was preferable to the higher money found in the drug world. Fat chance I could do that. I believed the drug world was wrong, but I didn't have enough life experience to counsel them about their options."

That's when Renée applied for the National Institute for Drug Abuse's Minority Internship Program, the program in which she was a part of when she visited Madeline in Itta Bena.

"That program was intense," Renée remembers. "Eighteen months of practice in Missouri training medical doctors, nurses and substance abuse counselors about Fetal Alcohol Syndrome while also being a student in the Ed.D program at Laurence University in California. I ultimately dropped out of the Ed.D program when I learned the university wasn't accredited on the east coast where I knew I planned to live. I think church kept me sane throughout this crazy time. I attended the only black church in Jefferson City. That community became my family. It was through church connections that I decided to join the alumni chapter of Delta Sigma Theta. Now I had a church family and a sisterhood."

Renée came back to Virginia knowing substance abuse wasn't her calling as she had thought when she graduated from the University of Florida. She applied and was hired for the position of Assistant Director of Career Planning and Placement at the University of Virginia, the school from which her younger sister had graduated. The fact there was a consent decree requiring the university to hire minorities was an additional incentive for the university to hire someone black and with the extensive credentials Renée had. This work in human resources would be the foundation for her ultimate career path.

As Marsha was accepting the inevitability of her marriage ending, Renée was starting hers. Her relationship with Albert Mills had started years before. It had weathered the natural ups and downs of relationships, including distance, but somehow Albert remained constant.

"I was always learning something, and I was focused on achievement. Both my mom and my dad had seen to that," Renée commented. "So, while my career soared, my love life really didn't. I didn't have the best of records for choosing men. They were all tall like me and probably nice looking and popular, but loyalty and fidelity weren't usually among their qualities. Albert was different."

In 1987, Renée married Albert in a small, private ceremony. Then all of her friends, the group she had met while working at Project Jump Street and the Valianettes all smiled as we gathered for the reception at the venerable Jefferson Hotel in Richmond to toast Renée and Albert.

Renée is still married to Albert, an active stepmom to three and Grandma Née Née to a granddaughter and three grandsons. She lives in Richmond where she is Director of Human Resources for the Supreme Court of Virginia and has also worked in the private and nonprofit sectors.

MADELINE

Madeline Bruce Swann is the only child of Edwin and Ruth Swann. She is the gentle one. It took Madeline a little longer than most of us to enter the work world. While she had that brief episode at Mississippi Valley State College, it wasn't until age 29 when she finished her Ph.D. in chemistry that she got her first real job, starting a long-term, employment relationship with the United States Army.

For most of us, we would think by 1980 the Cold War was over, but it wasn't. The United States was still prepared for attacks from the Soviet Union. It was in this arena Madeline began her career. "I had thought I would work on the eradication of human diseases, but that wasn't meant to be. The U.S. Army had another plan for me," Madeline recalled.

She went to work for the Materials, Fuels and Lubricants Division of the Research, Development and Engineering Center at Fort Belvoir outside of Washington, D.C. Her job was to determine how to make diesel fuel flow in icy weather when the fuel can readily crystallize. When that happens, the vehicles and equipment become inoperable. If the United States had to fight in cold Siberian Russian, we would be ready. Madeline's task wasn't focused on saving lives in the way she had earlier envisioned it. But her research and subsequently written guide on warming fuel lines and the additives necessary to keep the fuel liquid undoubtedly saved hundreds, if not thousands, of soldiers' lives. Not in Russia, but in other cold climates across the globe in which American soldiers were fighting. "I had assorted jobs with the Department of the Army," Madeline told me as I gathered material for this book, "including working on psychological research at the Army Research Laboratory, Human Research and Engineering Directorate where I worked on issues directly affecting soldiers and the stress of war. This was the closest I came to doing work to directly affect people as I thought I would when I finished Howard. But, you know, Tamara,"

Madeline said sadly, "no matter how much experience I had or the Ph.D. after my name when I walked into a room full of high ranking leaders more often than not, I was stereotypically taken to be the clerical support for the meeting." Madeline B. Swann, Ph.D.—a black woman in a white man's world. Some things had changed, but others remained very much the same.

She retired after 30 years as a civilian employee of the U.S. Department of the Army.

VERONICA

Veronica Dungee Abrams is the only child of Winfred and Margaret Dungee. And she is the artsy-craftsy one.

Like me, she had thought after college, she would move straight into the work world in Richmond, but fate shifted that a bit. She hadn't felt she would have a problem finding a job. In fact, she had thought her mother's position as the president of the black teachers' association might have been an advantage. It wasn't.

"I couldn't get a job anywhere in Richmond," Veronica recalls. "Being Margaret Dungee's daughter was a hindrance more than a help. Mom was working with her counterpart at the white teachers' association. Together they were fighting for teachers' rights. No one seemed to want to hire the daughter of what they perceived as a rabble-rouser. I guess they thought I'd come in and make waves, too."

So, it was off to Lynchburg, Virginia in the western part of the state she went. She'd been hired to teach at Rustburg High School, a school in a community of a little over a thousand people in a rural area near Lynchburg, a relatively large city in the state.

"I was surprised they pursued me aggressively even meeting my demand that I not be expected to stoke the little wood burning stove that provided heat for the cottage, separate from the school building, that housed my classroom in the home economics department. When I asked why they were so accommodating? The school officials said they wanted positive black role models for their students and thought I was just what they needed," Veronica commented, incredulous at the progressive thinking of the administrators in this rural area.

It started out as a great year. She used her college majorette skills to sponsor and choreograph a dance troupe that won prizes throughout the region. Also, she taught cooking, sewing, home decorating, and personal care to her students. While these skills were the fundamentals of the job she had been hired to do, she felt she also must build a bridge between the black and white students. She thought she did that until one day when a white student said, "You make us white students do all of our work, and you let those n@#%&*%'s do whatever they want."

On the surface, Veronica had gotten the students to talk to each other and to work on projects in which the teams were racially integrated, but with this one comment, she realized her successes were superficial. They had worked together because she made them. And even though she was not favoring the black students over the white ones, at least not consciously, the white students thought she was, or at least one particularly verbal student did. And a word Veronica knew as one filled with venom, hatred, and ignorance still seemed to be acceptable to say out loud in this small, rural, predominantly white community. She didn't have the impact she had thought.

She had received news she had been awarded a scholarship to enter the master's program in education at Virginia State College. She had done what she could as a young educator in Rustburg and was ready to leave. And being an administrator at a school was more comfortable for her than direct teaching anyway. To get to that level, she needed the additional academic credential; so back to Petersburg, Virginia she went. Virginia State would be her home once again.

Veronica—the high school majorette—had also married a football hero, in 1975. There wouldn't be a Meharry College doctor as she and her mother had thought initially, but with an accounting degree and high ambition, career opportunities were popping up for Tony. With her solid education credentials, Veronica was getting offers, too. Positions took them to Charlotte, North Carolina, then Atlanta and finally back to northern Virginia, near Tony's hometown of Washington, D.C. That would be home.

Desiree (Desi), their first child, had been born in North Carolina in 1981. Veronica recalled she had hoped to remain near Valianette Debbie Johnson Riddick and her children, that they could grow up together as their mothers had. "That was hard with the distance between North Carolina and Richmond. Even with the closer proximity of roughly 100 miles between northern Virginia and Richmond when Tony and I moved back, distance remained too much of a factor for our two families to become close."

Soon it became apparent that a large part of their family's friends were connected to their involvement with Jack and Jill, a social and educational connection that had emerged because of Desi. The Jack and Jill club was a cornerstone of the African-American community. It had been founded in 1938 by a group of African-American women in Philadelphia. These mothers wanted to ensure their children had specific cultural and leadership opportunities and to create a network with children and youth from similarly upwardly mobile, black families.

Veronica had entered the Jack and Jill community kicking and screaming. Her outside impression of Jack and Jill was it was a snobby gathering of professional women, social climbers. This was a group she didn't want to be a part of. In hindsight, she wondered if this was akin to the world her mother had envisioned when she tried to send her off to Fisk to find a Meharry doctor for a husband. She thought not. She knew her mother was merely trying to ensure she had the best future possible and that was the same goal she sought for her daughter. So, when she lived in the primarily white world of upper-middle-class northern Virginia, she felt Jack and Jill would be the way to provide balance in Desi's life. She wanted to expose her daughter to the black community she felt was missing from her everyday world. Veronica liked the northern Virginia chapter of Jack and Jill.

"All of the women were welcoming and warm, nothing like the bourgeois community I had stereotyped in my mind."

Veronica found this to be such a dominant force in her life that Jack and Jill became the Valianette equivalent of her early adult years. This wasn't merely an influential social channel for her daughter. It was a powerful outlet for her. Joining in 1988 when Desi was seven, by the time Tony and Veronica's second child, a son, Vachon, joined the family, Veronica was the chapter president.

It was the Jack and Jill mothers and some close professional colleagues who had supported Veronica as she and Tony tried to become pregnant the old-fashioned way. When that didn't materialize, unbeknownst to me, they choose the adoption route as I did. What incredible support we could have been to each other, but by then our Valianette connection didn't exist. It seemed dead, but it wasn't. It was dormant. Life was providing the time and space for families to grow, for careers to flourish and for us to be ready to appreciate the importance of this powerful friendship as we entered the middle-age phase of life.

Veronica is the married mom of two adult children and a retired school administrator, having worked in the public school systems in D.C., and both Fairfax and Prince William counties in Virginia. She lives in northern Virginia.

AND THEN THERE'S ME:

While Debby was the first to marry, hers was not the first marriage to end in divorce. Mine was. I had married that high school football player you read about earlier. It didn't happen in a fancy ceremony in a church. I married him at city hall with no friends or family in attendance. My parents didn't approve of him. And they had been right. He was not the right man for me, and we divorced three years after marrying.

But, Renée's was not the last wedding for one of the Valianettes. On July 23, 1988, I married for the second time. No lonely justice-of-the-peace gathering; the second wedding was a huge, romantic affair on a summer evening at a beautiful botanical garden in Richmond. One of the Valianettes, Marsha Ford, was a bridesmaid. Everyone loved the second husband, handsome, charming and financially on the right path. Only one problem, he lived in Washington; so off to Washington I went. After my earlier divorce, I had focused on career. That was good because once I moved to Washington, I was well-positioned for several career opportunities. I had flourished after the divorce, moving up the career ladder at a state agency focused on child advocacy. I had started there as a graduate intern and stayed for almost a decade steadily climbing the ranks. During this time, I gained visibility and a solid reputation with state legislators and governor's staff as I worked to advise them on children's issues. One of the people who would be influential and important to me in Washington was then Virginia State Delegate Bobby Scott. Delegate Scott, an African-American, had been elected to the Virginia legislature in 1977. The number of African-Americans in the state legislature and in policy positions in state government was still meager. It was still unusual to walk across Capitol Square, the seat of state government, and see someone who looked like me; so, it wasn't difficult to know all of them. I did, and they knew me. As a child advocate himself, my connection to Scott was strongest.

It was a remarkably quick job search once I was in Washington. I became the Director of the Southern Regional Project on Infant Mortality, an initiative that had been formed with involvement by now-Virginia State Senator Bobby Scott. There was a higher incidence of death for black infants in the South in the first year of life than for white babies, but for all babies in the South, it was high. This became my new work continuing to fight for needed services for those who couldn't fight on their own behalf.

One day, my phone rang, and it was now newly-elected Congressman Bobby Scott inviting me to join his staff. Seeing the opportunity to be a change agent on a much more significant field—the United States Congress, I left the Project on Infant Mortality to become Scott's Legislative Director. Not too long after that, my husband and I adopted a baby. The long hours as a congressional staffer and a new baby weren't compatible; so, I left Scott's office to be a full-time mom. Marsha decided to have a baby shower for me. Who would she invite? The Valianettes, course.

It was 1994. The Valianettes had been apart for 25 years.

BACK TOGETHER
1994—2018

CHAPTER 14
NOURISHMENT OF OUR SOULS

"The Valianettes' link was re-formed around food—in my kitchen as I fed my infant son."

When one thinks back on memories, they often revolve around food. The smell and taste of the apple pie your mom used to bake. The abundance of all the food spread out on the table for Thanksgiving dinner or how captivated you were by the family stories shared while out on the river crabbing or fishing. Food doesn't only give us nutrition for our bodies, it seems to give us sustenance for our souls. It has textures and flavors, scents and even spicy sauce just as life does. Food and the act of dining are core to so much of our personal story and food was, and is, a critical ingredient of the Valianettes time together.

We don't remember our earliest connections to food, but that was the primal connection. By the time we were born in 1951, the first packaged liquid formula for infants, Similac, short for similar to lactation, was on the market. And over 50% of babies were bottle-, not breast-fed. Breastfeeding had declined in the 1920s and 1930s with the introduction of evaporated milk. Homemade recipes or formulas had become popular in the 1940s when extra ingredients like sugar and honey were added to the evaporated milk. Most of the Valianettes were in that group of babies born to women following the new, modern way. By the 1950s, breastfeeding was increasingly viewed as old school. So, even though our earliest introduction to food may not have been literally at our mother's breast, the bonding between mother and baby was still there since mothers took care of the infants as dads went off to work. Our bodies and our psyches were connecting to our mothers as a source of nourishment, and the connection with food as a central character in all of life's stories was beginning.

We remember our mother's packing our lunch in shoe boxes with a string tied around it for a handle as we got on the school bus in elementary school for a class trip to Jamestown or boarded the train at the Broad Street Station to visit Washington, D.C. We didn't know the white kids across town had lunch boxes with Roy Rogers or Dale Evans, the western cowboy stars of the time, on them. We had shoe boxes. They were easily available. Everyone had a shoe box at home, and no one was stigmatized because his or her family didn't have what we would have thought of as a fancy lunch box.

We remember our mothers frying that ever-present chicken and cutting up the potatoes for potato salad as we got ready for family vacations. Our dads would go to the store to buy ice for the cooler. Then we would stop at a roadside table on our trip to South Carolina, or Ohio or New York, take out the tablecloth and set up a feast.

We remember the food fights that happened in the cafeteria at Chandler Junior High following integrating the school. We didn't go home and tell our parents about them because even as young teenagers we could sense there was a much bigger stage as our parents watched the news coverage of college students sitting in at lunch counters protesting for blacks to have equal access to restaurants. Food had become a proxy for all constitutionally-guaranteed rights, and the denial of that food was a denial of the sustenance we needed and deserved as Americans. During this time, food had become the source of stress, not of fulfillment for African-Americans, as it became central in the fight for civil rights.

But even during the sit-ins and the food fights at school, food was also central to many good memories for the Valianettes. We remember the lunches that were the central part of our Valianettes club meetings, usually prepared by our moms and modeled after their own adult club meetings. We remember feeling like grownups as we went to the Jade Isle or other Richmond restaurants for dinner before the big high school proms. Dining has always been a natural event around which friends and family connected and memories resulted; so, it is not all surprising the Valianettes' link was re-formed around food—in my kitchen as I fed my infant son.

CHAPTER 15
TENUOUS CONNECTIONS (AT FIRST)

"'Let's do lunch'... with that backdrop, there emerged an overlay to our outings. Often some element focused on our racial identity and racial pride."

On March 12, 1994, Andrew Jordan "AJ" Copeland joined the family. He was a perfect baby boy—five weeks old with deep brown, pensive eyes that wordlessly spoke the wisdom of an 80-year-old. Then when he smiled, those eyes would sparkle with an innocent's joyfulness that would melt my heart. Remarrying later in life, pregnancy didn't come; so, adoption seemed the way to bring a child into our family.

In 1993, my husband Rick and I became a part of a unique black adoption initiative. A public agency in Virginia had recognized the travesty of children remaining in foster care for too long missing the moment of infancy or young childhood when most children are adopted. They aggressively sought adoptive parents and actively marketed this program to young pregnant women who felt they couldn't care for their babies.

AJ was born on February 4th to a 19-year-old mom and a 24-year-old dad. While a stable couple, they felt they couldn't take care of a baby. They contacted an adoption agency. The agency welcomed them. The couple was shown a literal catalog of possible parents, including photographs and autobiographical statements each potential parent had prepared as part of the adoption process. Ironically, also in the directory was Valianette Veronica Dungee and her husband Tony who had also grown their family through adoption. From this book of possible parents, AJ's biological parents chose us to parent their son. By statute, the biological parents in Virginia had one month to change their minds. So, even though the baby had been released for adoption before he was born, he remained in foster care until he came to live with us, his new parents.

No matter how old you are, a baby entering a household is an adjustment. For us, it was no different. We had created a beautiful room for the new baby. Not knowing if we would adopt a boy or a girl, we opted for a soft, gender-neutral, seafoam green for the walls with matching striped sheets and comforter for the crib. Into what we thought was a tranquil setting for the baby, came a screaming insomniac who was so ready to embrace his new world he could only sleep for two or three hours at a time before he demanded to see the next act of his life.

Marsha and I had remained in contact throughout our young adult years. When we both lived in Richmond, we would go to play bingo together with Marsha's aunt, and we took a great exercise class together which we often followed with dinner. Then once Marsha moved to Roanoke, and I moved to Washington, we still connected whenever Marsha's travels brought her to Washington. So, it was not surprising that Marsha hosted a baby shower for me, the new mom, and it fitted that Marsha adapted the name of a popular movie for the theme. She called the shower, "Sleepless in D.C."

It was a beautiful summer day when most of the Valianettes and other friends came to my home in Washington, D.C. for the shower. Everyone brought wonderful gifts. Madeline had knitted the most beautiful soft yellow sweater for the baby and had also crocheted a blanket for his bed.

Others brought adorable outfits, books, and toys to keep AJ entertained. He'd been great at the party, going gleefully from one person to another.

Friends Gathering at AJ's Shower

We'd all enjoyed a lovely lunch when he cried alerting me it was time for his lunch, too. The party had shifted from the living room to the outside patio but had now found its place, as is so often the case, in the heart of every home, the kitchen.

I cuddled AJ in my arms, opened the refrigerator and took out a bottle of baby formula. Continuing the conversation, I sat down and gave the baby the bottle.

"Aaah!" gasped the mothers in the room with an audible intake of air.

Somehow, they had all lined up on one side of the small kitchen. The non-mothers were continuing the conversation until they realized that another discussion, more passionate and energetic than had been heard during the day, had started in another part of the kitchen.

"Aren't you going to warm up AJ's bottle?" asked Debby, the mom with seniority since her children were the oldest.

"Nope," I quickly responded. "I asked the pediatrician. She said it was fine."

"Really?" said Debby not believing me.

"Really! She said if he is okay with it, it's fine," I assured her.

AJ looked fine as he happily consumed his bottle. They laughed at their jokes about how he wouldn't want hot food as an adult, and they quietly wondered if he would feel less nurtured as he drank cold milk. They cared. They cared that AJ was well taken care of and they cared that I would be a good mom.

We were back together again. We were that caring group that had protected and nurtured each other twenty-five years earlier. Maybe we hadn't articulated our caring, but we had shown it in the then-teenage way of being there for our friends. We were not mean, not jealous or malicious around each other. For teenagers, those qualities were remarkable.

AJ was now surrounded by that same love and care. Food became the core of how his mother's girlfriends would see to it he was taken care. They hadn't been there for the others in the group as they began their respective motherhood journeys. They were all having that experience at roughly the same time, and miles and circumstances had separated them. But for the last Valianette to become a mother, they would walk this path with me.

The baby shower was the first time a large number of the Valianettes had been together in twenty-five years. The last time we had gathered as a group was on the spring day when we had graduated from high school in 1969. Now the girls had grown into women who could demonstrate their friendship in supportive, understanding ways and who could and who would articulate opinions, ideas, share knowledge and mentor each other actively and lovingly. Somewhere in the midst of all the laughter about the cold milk and the catching up on what had happened over the years, the chemistry was evident. Everyone had such fun and clicked like time, and miles and circumstances hadn't separated us. When the day ended, everyone said how much fun it had been, and they wanted to do it again. It's not clear if anyone thought it would happen, but it did, we were back together.

Not only were the Valianettes getting back together; so too was the entire 1969 graduating class of John Marshall High School. There would be a 25th reunion celebration that same year, in the fall. While there may have been other gatherings, the Valianettes hadn't heard about them. This time Debbie Riddick was on the planning committee, and she was encouraging the Valianettes to attend.

"Come on, y'all," Debbie said in her soft, mellow southern tone, "It'll be fun."

And a few did. Veronica, Debbie, Jeannie, and Renée went. Others commented they hadn't been treated that well at John Marshall High School; so, didn't see any reason to go to a reunion, but that wasn't the opinion of most.

The event was held at a downtown hotel that hadn't existed when we were attending high school. It was a part of the much hoped for, but short-lived, revitalization of downtown Richmond. About 150 people attended. Considering non-Jayem spouses or guests, Debbie estimated approximately 100 students came, roughly one-fourth of our class. Jeannie wore her Miss Justice crown and someone had even thought to bring a banner for her. The Johnson sisters—Debbie and Jeannie—were voted as the attendees who looked the most like they had in 1969. The band did a good job of mixing the music of the late '60s with the music of the day. People danced and had a good time. But like most of the years at John Marshall, the whites and blacks didn't mingle. Time hadn't blended the races anymore in 1994 than in 1969. No friendships had emerged after high school between the black and white students; so, after initial pleasantries across racial lines, the black attendees gathered in one part of the ballroom while the whites collected in another.

After a long separation, this was now the second time in less than six months a group of Valianettes had come together. Even though only four attended, there had been several telephone calls and conversations to determine who was going. It felt like the old high school conversations of twenty-five plus years earlier. Then, we would discuss where a party was being held on Friday night, who was going, who would drive and who did we think would be there. 1969 or 1994, it was the same conversation, and it felt right. For those who attended the reunion and for those who didn't, there was only one question afterward, "When will we get together again?"

We all had other friends, some close, dear friends, but it wasn't the same as childhood friends. When we exchanged Christmas cards with other Valianettes that year, the number of times that special notes were included and the terms 'forever friends' or 'childhood friends' was used was revealing. Ours was a special bond that had been dormant for twenty-five years, but it had never broken. Now it was slowly coming back into its own.

We wanted to reconnect, to spend time together, to feel that bond that had been there so many years ago. I was a new mother, trying to balance motherhood and a job. Marsha was thinking about divorce. Debby had divorced and was now trying to manage her son's bipolar diagnosis as she entered graduate school. Jeannie was also in graduate school, but the two didn't discuss the difficulty of juggling family and school. They didn't talk.

We were in our forties, entering the middle years of soaring and demanding careers. Of marriages being tested by many years of familiarity, of children not in the terrible twos (except for me) but in the terrible teens and twenties. And of being sandwiched between the demands of the nuclear family and the demands of aging parents. We didn't know Renée's parents, pillars of the black community in Richmond, were divorcing after 44 years of marriage. Divorce among our parents was a rarity. Their divorce was devastating Renée as much as it would if she were a young child, but we didn't know that. We were 40 plus-year-old adults with the social, familial and work-related challenges that face most in this age group.

And then there were the physical challenges affecting us, high blood pressure, high cholesterol, arthritis; the maladies many Americans of our generation faced. We were all probably overeating rich food while not getting the exercise we needed. Some conditions were not driven by our relatively sedentary lifestyle. The most severe diagnosis facing any of the Valianettes was Marsha's breast cancer. I knew about it, but I didn't know who else knew. Not once did we come together as a group to support Marsha during her treatment. Individually, some Valianettes sent notes, made calls or sent small gifts intended to comfort her, but never did the group get together. Upon reflection, this seems strange if you think about our friendship. But it not that odd if you only focus on cancer. It hadn't been too long ago that people said the word cancer in a whisper almost as if speaking it out loud intensified its impact. The pink ribbon signifying a breast cancer survivor or a breast cancer research supporter hadn't gained popularity yet. It had been in 1991 that the Susan G. Komen Foundation had given them out to survivors who participated in their race in New York. We probably had no idea whether our friend had been given a death sentence when she was told she had cancer. We didn't know how to talk about it and didn't know how to support her as she went through the chemotherapy and radiation that would shrink the cancerous growth and make her a survivor.

Our friendship was familiar, but that bond of confidentiality, of closeness and of true friendship wasn't there yet. Subconsciously we thought these might be the friends who would always hold our confidences, who would give us thoughtful advice and who would help us through whatever challenges we faced, but we weren't sure, at least not yet. We had to test the waters. We kept our expectations low and behaved somewhat tenuously as we would have if we were making new friends, at least at first. Certainly, we could get together every now and then.

The expression "let's do lunch" emerged in the Hollywood film industry in the mid-'80s. It was a way to politely end a conversation, knowing neither party intended to ever take that next step of scheduling lunch. However, a decade later when the saying had made its way from the trendy west coast to the more traditional Washington, D.C. area on the east coast, it did mean let's get together for lunch.

And so, we did. We'd had such fun at the baby shower for AJ and at the high school reunion. We could tell there were still embers glowing from our prior friendship. They needed to be stoked to come back to life. We decided we would get together once or twice a year. It would not be anything elaborate, just lunch.

We started with folks volunteering to plan a gathering. Veronica hosted us at her home in northern Virginia a couple of times. We even went to Virginia Beach, the city that was farthest away for the core group. Marsha had moved there in 1996 and was getting used to all the city offered. She'd been reading about this great seafood restaurant called Mary's and a visit from "the girls," was the perfect opportunity to check it out.

Yes, we were 'the girls.' We didn't think of ourselves as the Valianettes anymore. That was definitely a name from the '60s, and it didn't have the right feel for who we had become. We were in our early 40s, career women, and well regarded in our respective communities. We weren't a group, so we didn't need to have a name. That felt so high school, but we had to refer to ourselves as something. So, our group of 40 somethings became the girls.

With four of the girls—Madeline, Veronica, Debby and me—living in the Washington, D.C. area, Washington became the site of many gatherings. We went to black-owned B. Smith's restaurant in Union Station and to a restaurant then called Potomack Landing, in a lovely setting right on the Potomac River, off of the George Washington Parkway. The goal was always good food, and if the ambiance was interesting, too, that was a bonus.

When it became my time to host lunch, I suggested a different spot. I had heard good things about a crab house on the outskirts of D.C. I thought I'd recommend that to the girls. Like many who lived in Maryland or Virginia near the Chesapeake Bay, I had grown up eating crabs all of my life. My earliest memory was of my mother holding one hand and one of my mother's sisters the other as we walked out on a pier in the Rappahannock River to go crabbing. To a 3 or 4-year-old, the spaces between each plank seemed wide enough to fall through. I knew my mom and my aunt would keep me safe. I remember my dad walking through water so clear you could see the crabs swimming as he scooped them up with the net. Those wonderful memories told me a crab house would be a fun locale for all of us. Crabs were typically a summer treat, but this gathering was in the winter. Would this work? The Bethesda Crab House I heard about was in an urban community, not along the water as so many crab houses were. We couldn't sit outside and feel the summer breeze, but I still thought the notion of newspaper spread out on a table with hot steaming crabs, spiced shrimp, and a cold beer would be a fun and surprising winter outing. The plan was made, but then it snowed. Were we still going? As long as the crab house was open and they had crabs, we were going. It was open. They had crabs.

"Come on over" urged the owner. "The crabs will be ready when you get here."

We piled into two cars, pulled out our Mapquest directions as we ventured beyond our typical downtown D.C. safety zone and laughed and joked all the way there, not believing we were going to a crab house in a snowstorm in January. We were becoming a group. A memory was being born.

January had become our regular time to get together. The long weekend for Martin Luther King's birthday celebration became the time for our gatherings. With that backdrop, there emerged an overlay to our outings. Often some element focused on our racial identity and racial pride.

One of our first luncheons was held at Georgia Brown's restaurant in downtown D.C. It had opened in 1993. With its focus on low country southern cooking and its signature sweet potato cheesecake, it spoke to Madeline's South Carolina roots, the state where her mother had been born. So, it was Madeline who suggested we have lunch there one Saturday. It was perfect. Collard greens, fried chicken, jambalaya and fried green tomatoes; the down-home nature of the menu combined with the possibility of seeing African-American political leaders, movie stars or athletes. This restaurant was getting a reputation among blacks who lived in Washington, D.C., but also those who came into town regularly as a place to get great food and to see and be seen. We joked about being only steps away from the White House and wondering if the first 'black' president ever dropped by.

Bill Clinton had been elected president in 1992. Known for his love of food, appreciation of jazz music and natural affinity for black people, a few years later he would jokingly be referred to as the first black president. Some say it was black comedian Chris Rock who first used the term. Others say it was black author Toni Morrison. Regardless, it was a testament to his natural fit in the black community and probably to a belief Clinton might be the closest we would get to a black president for years to come.

At Georgia Brown's restaurant and on our many other outings, we were developing more and more memories. We laughed together as the group chided me for not knowing I had to push the 'send' button to receive messages on my bulky, box new cell phone and we lovingly berated Veronica for holding our newsletter hostage in her northern Virginia home.

Yes, the girls had a newsletter. During these early gatherings, I had decided we needed a newsletter. With my master's degree focused on community organizing and social (policy) planning, it seemed I was ready to dust off those organizing skills with the girls. One day it suddenly occurred that we needed glue to hold us together between our luncheon outings; so, I suggested a newsletter. Remember this was still the mid-'90s. America Online, the connector for the internet, had gone global in 1993. Electronic or email hadn't become the ubiquitous communications tool it is today, or it would become in a few years. It wasn't until the late '90s that texting was even possible. We still relied on the U.S. postal service and the telephone. I thought it might be fun to share stories about our lives in between our lunch gatherings; so "the girls" newsletter was born.

There were an order and simplicity to the plan for the newsletter. Person 1 wrote two pages about all that was going on in her world and mailed it to person two. Person 2 got the full scoop on person one and then added her two-page update and sent it to Person 3 until it got back to Person 1 with everyone's story and started over again with new information. If we could keep it going, it would have been a great way to keep up-to-date on everyone, but life got in the way. The newsletter hit a big snag at Veronica's house. She read all the news about everyone before her, but she couldn't find the time to add her own and mail it on to the next person. The newsletter idea failed. For some unknown reason, folks didn't pick up the phone to call each other. It was almost as if we still didn't have enough shared experiences or current common ground to make regular communication happen. We weren't comparing outfits for a party on the coming weekend, gossiping about boys or asking about homework. We didn't have a reason for the natural, regular calls that happen between friends.

Picking up the phone to call a Valianette and talk about the day, ask for advice or get a recipe didn't occur to us yet. All of our news was shared in relatively superficial snippets when we gathered for lunch. No one talked sincerely about their lives. If we'd known, maybe we would have been more supportive of Renée when she left Virginia state government and went to work for a private corporation. We didn't know she had been called into her new boss's office after working there for a short time because she had put her hair in cornrowed braids and pulled it back into what she thought was an elegant chignon. Renée had been told, unofficially, her hairstyle might prevent her from moving up in the company. Ph.D. or not, it would be the outward appearance of hairstyle, not her intellect, that would determine her success in the company. In her mind, she recognized the texture of her hair and the fashion of the times by adopting this new hairstyle. In the minds of the company executives, this was a negative 'hood hairstyle that was being responded to somewhat similarly as the afro had been in the late '60s and early '70s. Back then, the afro was a visual symbol of militancy. Now cornrows were perceived as connecting to the black community or the 'hood as it was sometimes called, originally with a purely derogatory connotation. With both hairstyles, the wearer was underscoring the fact he or she was black, not trying to adapt their black, textured hair into a white, straight-haired style. In this part of their beings, they weren't trying to assimilate. Renée's work ethic, knowledge, and ideas were being minimized as the company's leaders focused on her hair. It was years after this happened that we learned of the incident.

If we'd talked seriously about what was going on in our lives, maybe we would have known about Renée or why Marsha left Roanoke to accept a position with Al-Anon hundreds of miles away in Virginia Beach. But we didn't talk. Perhaps some of us would have gone down to help Marsha pack and to close out that chapter of her life. Maybe we would have been far more supportive as she adjusted to this significant life change, but we didn't share, and we didn't ask. What we often shared during our lunches was the top layer of information—the facts—just what was happening. Because there were several of us at lunch, all often talking and laughing simultaneously as multiple conversations wove in and out of each other, rarely did we get to the reasons we were making specific choices or how certain events were affecting us at our core. We rarely got to the why and how we felt about events in our lives. We were having lunch, having fun, perhaps we didn't want to change the celebratory, happy feel of these gatherings. So, even though our meals weren't unveiling information about us as individuals, they still strengthened our friendship. We again built that collection of shared experiences that are the bedrock of friendship. Without ever discussing it, we had also become more intentional in adding an element of our racial identity to our lunches and learning more about our history or about the black experience. So much about us had been left out of our education and how the black experience fit into the history of our country and affected who we had become. We were filling in the gaps.

One of our most memorable gatherings was a visit to the Frederick Douglass house. We watched the movie that recounted the many accomplishments of this noted abolitionist, orator and presidential appointee before touring the house. Called Cedar Hill, the 21-room Victorian house sits on 15 acres overlooking the federal city, the central section of Washington. While in high school or college, we had all read

Narrative of the Life of Frederick Douglass, an American Slave, but coming to his house and hearing the U.S. park ranger discuss Douglass' accomplishments with an audience of blacks and whites somehow made his story even more moving. By now, we were at an age where we could appreciate the trauma of what he had experienced. We could understand the impact of his sharing his story of enslavement with white audiences. An eye-opening, first-hand recounting that probably had a similar impact on white audiences as did seeing police with vicious dogs and powerful water hoses attacking protesters in the 1960s or as viewing the cell phone videos of police violence has had today. As adults, we could understand Douglass' pride at being asked to advise President Lincoln and then later serving as the keynote speaker at the unveiling of the Emancipation Memorial in Lincoln Park near where I live today. And, we could appreciate the feelings of his friends, children, and colleagues when following the death of his first wife, Anna, who had been born a free black, he married the daughter of a white abolitionist friend. Frederick Douglass was a complex man working for opportunities for his race when few existed. As we walked through his home and listened to his story, we could only imagine that the opportunities must have seemed massive in the late 1800s to someone who had experienced both the pain of the overseer's whip and the respect of the president of the United States.

We supported African-American entrepreneur Bob Johnson by visiting his Black Entertainment Television (BET) Soundstage. Johnson, the owner of BET, had modeled his restaurant by day, club by night, after the trendy Planet Hollywood chain. With black music playing in the background, he created a setting in which you felt like you were dining in a music studio. This restaurant in Prince George's County, Maryland, where Madeline lived, was to be the flagship of his chain of restaurants. Prince George's County, a county that abuts Washington, D.C., was home to the largest number of African-American millionaires in the country. Johnson, who in a few years would become America's first black billionaire, felt that success was the only destiny for his enterprise. We weren't as hopeful. We remember we didn't find the service or the food to be up to our standard, but we still had a good time. With a black owner, soul food, and the BET imprimatur, it's not surprising this restaurant was one destination for our lunch gatherings. It was disappointing it didn't achieve the success Johnson had envisioned.

The Corcoran Art Gallery, only blocks away from the White House, became the venue for another memorable gathering. We followed the advice of Debby Anderson's sister, Anna, a docent at the Corcoran when she suggested the 'girls' might enjoy the Gordon Parks exhibit. We had all heard of Gordon Parks and were familiar with his iconic photograph of a Washington D.C. cleaning crew worker holding a broom and a mop posed similarly to the famous Grant Wood painting *American Gothic*.

We had heard of him, but we didn't know a lot about the man. We learned Parks had been born less than 20 years after the death of Frederick Douglass. He had worked as a busboy, a piano player, a dining car waiter and a basketball player before finding his passion, photography, and his mission of using photography to capture images of social injustice. We were quiet as we walked through the Corcoran's galleries that Sunday admiring Parks' ability to capture hope and degradation in his photographs. He was a social commentator reflecting the 1940s world of our parents and the civil rights world of our youth. We hadn't known a lot about Parks as an artist, a filmmaker, directing the 1971 iconic black film *Shaft* and a poet. We didn't know. This was one more outing that helped to fill in the holes of our education about those in our race who had both contributed to the culture of the country and those who had captured its essence. This was definitely food for our souls, but as we left the gallery, we noticed they were hosting a brunch. As always, we were also interested in great food for our tummies. We hadn't made reservations. The Corcoran's gospel brunch would be our destination on another day. No food this time.

My organizing resurfaced during this time as I encouraged two other friends to form the Metropolitan Area Strategic Investment Group, MASIG as it would be called. I wanted to maximize my resources by joining with a few others to make what might seem to be slightly risky investments. I believed if the individual financial commitment were relatively low, the loss would be small, but the gain might be high if it worked. Each of the MASIG founders invited three people to the group to form a core of twelve, African-American women. When I thought of which of my friends in the

Washington, D.C. area might be interested in this opportunity, I immediately thought of Madeline. Actually, I thought of all three of the other local Valianettes but knew Debby had too much on her plate with school, her sons, and her jobs and Veronica always seemed immersed in Jack and Jill activities. They couldn't do this, but Madeline was interested. Through the monthly MASIG meetings, Madeline and I connected differently. It wasn't long before racial identity, and ethnic pride became an undercurrent of this group, too. Maybe that is merely a reality whenever a group of African-Americans comes together. We don't know, but it always seemed to be right below the surface for us.

Somehow, I had learned about the October Gallery, a Philadelphia art gallery owned by an African-American couple, Mercer and Evelyn Redcross. The gallery featured African-American artists. In the early 1990s, my husband and I had started attending the gallery's annual art showing and had begun collecting the works of an artist we liked named Andrew Turner. Turner captured everyday images of African-American life, women in the pews at church, older men playing chess in the park, jazz musicians hitting the perfect note or a youngster playing the piano. To me, Turner's use of color and the composition of his paintings made his works reminiscent of Henri Matisse, but never would he gain that level of fame. Building on my love of art, I suggested MASIG could grow the funds in the investment pool by hosting a fundraiser, somewhat like the pay parties the Valianettes used to host in each other's backyards decades ago to support the other things we wanted to do. I knew Mercer would give the group a percentage of the sales if we hosted a show. I also thought it would be a great way to introduce our friends to the works of both up-and-coming artists, like Andrew Turner, and to well-known African-American artists, like Annie Lee, Ernie Barnes and Charles Bibbs, while also supporting a black-owned business. While many knew white artists, the broad repertoire of black artists was still little-known. This would be a win-win-win-win, a win for the gallery, a win for the artists, a win for our friends and a win for MASIG. So, began an annual MASIG tradition. With almost one-half of the MASIG group having roots in Richmond, one year we hosted our yearly art show there, inviting all of our Richmond friends, including the Valianettes.

Throughout the mid to late '90s whenever we got together, we learned something about our heritage or patronized a black-owned business or restaurant. We didn't discuss doing this. It happened naturally. And on the rare occasions, when we didn't go to an art gallery with a black-focused show or dine in a black restaurant, race would still often surface in conversations as we discussed current events. It was a part of the lens through which we saw the world, but our lens was also factored by our gender, our education, our professions, our home state, our life's experiences and many, many other ingredients that made us who we are.

We knew what was going on in the world that affected African-Americans, and we talked about it. By now, we fully understood the impact of these occurrences and wanted to hear the views and perspectives of the others in our group. When Nelson Mandela was elected the President of South Africa, we gloried that his struggle and that of his people for equality had ended. We saw South Africa as having arrived at the point of racial equality we felt existed in our country. We were elated when then-President-elect Bill Clinton asked African-American poet Maya Angelou to recite an original poem for his inauguration and then named African-American Ron Brown as Secretary of Commerce, a first for our race, and African-American physician Joycelyn Elders as United States Surgeon General, another first. The president of the United States was acknowledging the artistry of someone in our race along with the leadership and intellect of others. We felt these were all indicators we had arrived as a race as our parents had felt when they could have lunch in the Tea Room in a once-segregated restaurant in a Richmond, Virginia department store. Against the frame of reference of the times, in the '60s and in the '90s, in both instances, we had arrived, but only to the next plateau.

Like a lot of other people, we wondered what would happen when Minister Louis Farrakhan and the Nation of Islam announced a desire to attract one million, black men to the nation's capital to focus on self-help and economic power. We didn't know what to expect. Most of us had insufficient knowledge of the Nation of Islam. The little we knew of it was because of Muhammad Ali's conversion or what we had learned from watching the movie or reading the book, *Malcolm X*. There was a mystery about the faith and an undertone of militancy. The Million Man March was held on October 16, 1995. Washington, D.C. was ready for rioting as it had been following the 1968 assassination of Martin Luther King, or five years earlier when Dr. King organized the March on Washington. Instead, what the country saw were dignified, respectful and determined African-American men—one million of them—committing to raising their children, pledging to be a part of their communities and committed to helping lift this country. We were so pleased. Our country was seeing what we knew. Although the media often focused on the negatives of black men committing crimes or being incarcerated, we had the examples of our fathers, our uncles, and our brothers. The men who we knew had always cared for their families, had been focused on success and had always set a positive example. For one amazing day, Farrakhan had taken the country's eyes off the negative and shone a light on all the positives of black men. We were proud.

But the year of the Million Man March was also the year that noted African-American athlete, O.J. Simpson, was exonerated from a charge of murdering his wife and her friend both of whom were Caucasian. Reaction to the verdict divided almost fully along racial lines. Many blacks were convinced of Simpson's innocence. Some just believed he could not get a fair trial. The decades-old fear of black boys and men being lynched for whistling at a white woman had been escalated a hundred-fold in the Simpson case. The sexual undercurrent of black men attacking white women, endemic to race relations in this country, streamed through this trial. Even the media played a role when both *Time Magazine* and *Newsweek* featured Simpson's arrest photo on the cover. *Newsweek* merely put the mug shot on the cover. *Time*, however, darkened the image thereby, some said stereotypically, making Simpson appear more sinister. The public was so caught up in this trial that it was broadcast on television daily and became a tragic, real-life soap opera and a racial morality play followed by thousands. The verdict was read live on television even though it happened in the middle of a workday. This was the magnitude of interest in this trial by 1990s Americans. Everyone wanted to know immediately what the outcome would be. The United States was still a racially-charged, not racially-neutral, country. No matter how much we wanted to think the country had moved past the divisiveness of race, we knew it hadn't when the national news cameras panned the hundreds of people outside of the

California courthouse. What you saw were black people cheering and white people looking stunned. What you heard in offices across America was silence. In the middle-class workplace, no one—black or white—knew what to say. Many blacks were thinking, "Had a black man finally gotten a fair trial in America? Or had green, not black or white, been the color of importance at this trial since Simpson's wealth enabled him to hire a dream team of attorneys and legal assistants." At the same time, some whites thought, "Is our country trying so hard to compensate for what it has done to black people that the system just let this man get away with murder?" Regardless of what you believe, this trial proved race was still a huge factor in America.

The skewed perspective of some white's concern about the politics of 'correctness' was also an ongoing issue in Richmond, Virginia. Soon after the death of hometown hero, Arthur Ashe, conversations started about how Richmond might honor his legacy. He hadn't only been the first African-American to win the coveted Wimbledon title, he had spoken out again apartheid in South Africa and against racism at home. The Richmond Planning Commission approved the placement of a memorial honoring him on Monument Avenue, the revered Richmond boulevard. Until then, only Confederate soldiers had been honored with larger-than-life statues on this street. The Richmond city council recognized this decision had created a huge issue. They met with citizens who visually expressed their views even before speaking by wearing African-inspired clothing or Confederate soldier uniforms. Should a renowned Richmond son be remembered on this grand thoroughfare? Monument Avenue definitely had the stature and primacy in Richmond as *the* venue for recognizing sons of the South; however, with its very visible salute to the Confederacy was this an inappropriate place for a tribute to an African-American? The community was mixed. The family of the late Arthur Ashe did not want his statue placed there, but ultimately it was. The proponents felt this placement would be a powerful testament to the ability of the Old South to recognize the contributions of all of its sons. Over twenty years later, this decision still elicits racially-charged comments.

Sometimes race wasn't an undercurrent as it was with the Ashe statue, sometimes it was all that an event was about. The specter of pure racial hatred was apparent in a way unheard of for decades when James Byrd, a black man in Jasper, Texas, had a noose placed around his neck, was tied to the undercarriage of a pickup truck and dragged to his death by three white men before his body was left in front of a black cemetery. This was 1998 America. This was the America that surrounded us as we had lunch and visited museums. Our worlds were relatively calm and not overtly racially-charged, but the impact of decisions and actions driven by race was still all around us.

Unlike our ancestors, our lives were not guided by constant fear of white people, always afraid of doing or saying the wrong thing or being black in the wrong place. We knew what happened to James Byrd was an anomaly, but so too was what happened to Ron Brown. We knew that Byrd's death was because he was black. We hoped Brown's appointment to President Clinton's cabinet was because of the content of his character, as Dr. King would have said, not the color of his skin, but we knew skin color played a role in that, too. President Clinton had hundreds of candidates for every cabinet-level position. What were the factors that led him to choose Brown over all the other qualified possibilities? Certainly, his race was one of those elements. We understood that, too. Just as we were sought, to a certain degree, for management and leadership positions in the '70s and '80s, blacks were now pursued in the same way, but on a much higher stage.

Every time an African-American rose to a position that had never been held by another, we knew another door had opened, and every time a tragedy occurred, we knew there were still so many hatreds and stereotypes—along with hidden structural racism—that kept race as an ongoing source of division in our country.

Race percolated all around us, affecting almost everything we did. It almost always came up in conversation when we got together. We would talk about it when something monumental happened like O.J. Simpson and James Byrd or the release of Nelson Mandela, or we'd remember an incident from high school.

While the reality of race was ever-present, it's also true it wasn't on our minds. Being black and living in a world in which race remained a key factor wasn't always foremost for us. It just was. Like everyone else, we talked about the issues of the day large and small. Sometimes our conversations were in the context of race, but not always. We were not activists, like Jesse Jackson, Sr., fighting for racial parity or academics, like Cornel West, focused on examining the impact of race on society. We were merely a group of black women, friends getting together. We were rebuilding our connection. Mostly, we were having fun.

Our gatherings were episodic, and most of our conversation was still somewhat superficial. We'd spent twenty-five years apart. During that time, we'd suffered tragedies—the loss of a parent, the end of a marriage or long-term relationship, the loss of a job—and other setbacks, difficulties and disappointments. We'd also had significant accomplishments. Madeline's gospel choir, the Sargent Gospel-Aires, had won a prestigious singing contest and had recorded a CD called "God Did It." I had been named the president of a national child advocacy organization, Voices for America's Children. Renée was on the road to becoming vice president for human resources for Service Master, a Fortune 1000 company and Veronica had achieved her goal of becoming an assistant principal. As these things happened, we had probably shared the event itself with the rest of the group, but we didn't share the backstory. None of the Valianettes knew that to reach her goal, Veronica had to volunteer for two summers to work with an assistant principal. Volunteer. Her degree in home economics placed her behind candidates with degrees in math, science, English or history, so she had to work doubly hard to demonstrate her abilities, and she did. We had always been programmed we had to work harder. Veronica was doing what she'd known she'd have to do all of her life. Work harder.

When bad things happened, it wasn't to a Valianette we turned. It was someone we'd met on the job, at church, or at our child's school 10, 15, 20 years ago. It was husbands or siblings or cousins who had held our hand in the past or who had guided us through an earlier tough passage in life. And these were also the people who we turned to when we wanted to celebrate. We had vacationed with them, had hundreds of meals together and had shopped and gone to the movies together. Our lives were intertwined with theirs. We had built a stash of memories, both joyful and sad. These were the people who had shared our experiences as we were becoming women.

We knew we could trust them with our innermost fears and desires. These were the friends and family, not the Valianettes, who had earned that trust. We—in our mind's eye—saw the Valianettes as teenagers really. We were getting to know who they had become as adult women, but we still weren't there.

Once I was told that a true friend was someone who you would call, without hesitating, at 3 o'clock a.m. if you needed them. If you believe that definition, most of us have only a handful of true friends. And, maybe the notion of a group being friends is a fallacy. While the Valianettes as a group existed, perhaps it was the dyads and triads that were the friends. And with the passage of so much time, could those dyads and triads ever come back together as they had been when we were teenagers?

By the end of the 1990s, the girls had gotten into a rhythm of gathering at least once and sometimes twice a year, but the old friendship of high school hadn't re-emerged yet. No one commented on that, and it is only in hindsight that that reality is apparent. Was that kind of connection needed or even possible as we approached our 50th birthdays? Maybe friendships that develop in your 40s and 50s are different. Maybe they aren't the joined-at-the-hip friendships of eleven-year-olds. Maybe they are loose connections that weave in and out, no longer the best friend you share everything with like you did when you were fifteen. Our friendship, like most friendships, had been born from shared experiences. Maybe in the rekindling of that bond, the experiences would now be more solely fun and pleasure, not interspersed with the angst and drama of earlier times. Not that our lives were now drama free. But did we have the trust to share those parts of our lives? So much had shaped who we had become and so much was determining how our friendship would develop. Maybe there was a different kind of connection that would characterize our friendship group now. We'd see.

CHAPTER 16
BECOMING DIVAS

"Some might think to be black girls raised in the South in the '50s and '60s, we had been taught to be cautious, demure and mindful of the world order. We were not. We were taught to examine circumstances, to assess the pros and cons of acting in specific ways and then to stand up for what was right, to voice our opinions, and to be a part of the change we wanted."

It was Y2K, the start of the new millennium. Soon we would be 50 years old. We couldn't believe it. Like our parents—old people—we now said, "Where has the time gone?" People saying to us, "You look really good for your age." These were words we both wanted to hear and didn't want people to say. Looking good for your age meant you were old. Otherwise, no one commented. The prospect of 50 was sobering. We knew there was no question we had more days behind us than ahead. Enjoying life gained an urgency it had never had before.

Madeline suggested we start off the new century by pampering ourselves. Jeannie, the Valianette who lived in Birmingham, Alabama, would be in Washington for the Martin Luther King, Jr. weekend. Our MLK weekend gathering wasn't going to be a culturally enriched this time. We would start 2000 utterly focused on us. We would take care of our bodies with massages and facials, manicures and pedicures.

While the medicinal benefits of warm and hot natural springs had been known since ancient times, the concept of the day spa had a relatively short history. Elizabeth Arden had opened the Red Door in New York City in 1910. It wasn't until the late '50s that Deborah Szekely opened the first destination spa, Rancho La Puerta in Baja, California. Although we'd known about spas for a while, it was only recently it had moved from being

176

a destination for wealthy, white women who wanted to be pampered to being a source of relaxation and aesthetic services for the average woman.

Madeline had frequented a black-owned salon near her home in Mitchellville, Maryland, right outside of D.C. She thought a spa day would be what we needed. We were nearing the big 5-0 birthday. It was definitely time to take care of the tight muscles, to ease the stress we held in our bodies while also getting the latest shade of nail polish; so, Madeline arranged for the Valianettes to have spa services and then a lovely lunch. What a day this was as we moved from one glorious treatment to another. During the day, Jeannie mentioned how much she wanted to be a part of the girls' outings but living in Birmingham made this rarely possible. Jokingly, she said, "Why don't y'all come down to the 'ham for the next girls outing?" And, with that comment, we planned for a real adventure. For our 50th year, there would be a trip. The Valianettes were going to Birmingham, Alabama.

Birmingham had been founded in 1871 soon after the end of the Civil War. It was to be an industrial hub for the South, named intentionally after Birmingham, England, another industrial city. Knowing the recently freed blacks needed jobs, the city founders saw them as cheap labor. So, they planned to use them to grow Birmingham, Alabama into the steel and railroad center of the South, and they did. Right through World War II, Birmingham was known as an industrial center.

That changed in the '50s and '60s when Birmingham moved from being the center of industrial growth to being the center of the civil rights movement. Reverend Martin Luther King, Jr. had come to the city to work with local leader Reverend Fred Shuttlesworth. Unlike our experience in the Richmond, Virginia schools, Shuttlesworth had been beaten with chains, and his wife stabbed as the couple tried to enroll their children in school. This happened while city police watched. In 1956, two years after the Brown v. Board of Education school desegregation decision, the state forbade the NAACP from having a chapter in Alabama. Dozens of parks, playgrounds, swimming pools and golf courses had been closed instead of complying with federal desegregation statues. Newly-elected governor,

George Wallace, was determined to maintain the racial inequity that had been the hallmark of this city since it was founded.

The Valianettes were twelve years old and in the 7th grade when Shuttlesworth and King and other civil rights leaders meticulously planned Project C in 1963. The 'C' was for confrontation, but not violence. They wanted to create Mahatma Gandhi-like nonviolent situations, face-to-face encounters, that would draw national media attention to the Jim Crow laws and plantation mentality that still ruled much of the South. Birmingham would be the epicenter of their work.

So, it was not a surprise that Jeannie had planned the visit around the civil rights history of the city. In 1992, Birmingham had established a six-block Civil Rights District. This area was acknowledged as a federal historic area, a place of significance for all in the history of our country. Only Veronica, Madeline and Renée traveled to meet Jeannie in Birmingham. Each remembered the excitement of this first Valianette trip and disappointment that the others weren't able to come. But what they recall foremost, is the poignancy and pain they experienced during one of the first stops on their tour of the city—the Birmingham Civil Rights Institute.

The Institute had been the vision of David Vann, a former mayor of the city. Vann had been a law clerk at the U.S. Supreme Court when the court decided Brown v. Board of Education. As a white Southerner, he knew how race had divided, but he also felt a memorial to the struggles could bring the races together. And, to some degree, it did. Not everyone in Birmingham saw his vision. Some felt monies could be better spent on addressing poverty. Jeannie, however, was a proponent of the Institute. She thought the establishment of the Civil Rights District and the memorials healed some of the pain both races felt due to a horrible time in the city's racial history and that of the country. She wanted her friends to see it.

Jeannie took them to the Institute where they walked by re-creations of scenes from our past that the Valianettes had only read about. She took them to Kelly Ingram Park where police dogs had attacked, and fire hoses were forcefully opened on those demonstrating as a part of King's and Shuttleworth's Project C. Ironically, the park was named after a local firefighter killed in World War I. Kelly Ingram had probably never thought of water as a weapon, but Public Safety Commissioner Bull Connor had. Madeline remembers her heart pounding as she walked by the sculptures of the dogs. The depiction was so life-like and the knowledge of what happened there so raw and powerful. Even decades later, with no threat of harm, it had a visceral impact on her.

Jeannie then took the girls to the park near the 16th Street Baptist Church, the center of civil rights' organizing in the city and the site of the 1963 bombing that killed four young black girls on Sunday, September 15th, 1963. While this tragedy received national media attention, it was only one of many attacks in Birmingham. One local neighborhood was even known as Dynamite Hill because of the violence that had occurred there. Birmingham was known as Bombingham, a tragic, but accurate, sobriquet for the city.

While it was important to visit the civil rights historical sites, Jeannie didn't want the visit to solely be about sadness. She capped the outing with a visit to Eddie Kendrick Memorial Park. Eddie Kendrick was a native son who had been born in Union Springs, Alabama but who grew up in Birmingham. With friends, he formed a singing group in the 1950s called the Cavaliers. They became well-known in local clubs. Even though they were gaining a following and a name for themselves in the area, they wanted more. Like thousands before them, they left Alabama and become part of the great migration that moved north for more opportunities. They ended up in Detroit, changed the group's name to the Primes and sang in shows with a local girl group called the Primettes. The Primettes became the Supremes, and the Primes changed their name to the Temptations when they signed on with Barry Gordy at Motown. The park honoring Kendrick (the "s" was added to form Kendricks as a stage name) had just opened in 1999, a few years after his death and the year before this visit. As Jeannie, Veronica, Madeline, and Renée came into the park, walking changed to dancing as they moved smoothly to the park's piped in music. The songs of the Temptations, the music of our youth, became the nourishment their souls so badly needed on this special day.

EDDIE KENDRICK PARK

2001 was our year. We were turning 50. Debbie Johnson had celebrated this milestone the previous October and had assured us all it was relatively painless. We were all marking our special day in our own way with friends and family, but one commemoration stood out. With a huge smile, Marsha said to me, "You bought us a clubhouse!"

I had decided to buy a house at the beach. I had always wanted one. Maybe my love of the water had started very early in life on those trips to the river to crab or the time spent playing in my aunt's pool. When I became an adult, an apartment overlooking the James River in Richmond was one of my early homes, and when I finally bought a house, a swimming pool was quickly added to the backyard. The swimming pool made it very hard to leave that house when I moved to Washington, D.C., but a year hadn't passed before a pond with a fountain was installed in my new back courtyard. A water element was always imperative wherever I was. The movement of the water and the sound of running water were comforting. The backdrop for idly reminiscing about the past, considering situations in the present or planning for the future; so, when I thought about what I would do to celebrate this half-century mark, I knew it was time to buy a house on the water.

I can remember a conversation with my mother when she asked me what I wanted out of life. I can still see her slightly disappointed look when the answer wasn't about attaining something lofty and noble, something with real import, but instead, my response was, "a house on the water." I can also remember being delighted when an old boyfriend gave me a pencil sketch he had done of my dream house. It was a modern looking house on a cliff overlooking the ocean. Now, I could fulfill that dream.

I had been planning for this for a while. I knew where I wanted the house to be located—in a little community called St. Leonard, Maryland—only about 50 miles away, an easy drive from my Capitol Hill home in Washington, D.C. A friend and former colleague had a second home there. I had been visiting this area since the early '90s. It was perfect. It was wholly residential, but all the necessities of restaurants, grocery stores, pharmacies, movie theaters, et cetera were within about a 10 to 15-minute drive. It felt right. I looked at houses. The first offer fell through, but my friend, John, who had a house in the area, assured me that that was okay. He knew the house I should have. It was the little one at the top of the hill, and it was coming on the real estate market soon. John was right. This, two-bedroom, white, frame cottage with a bright blue door was perfect. The eight sashed windows on the front provided an unobstructed view of the waters of the Chesapeake Bay. The house had been built in 1951, the same year I was born. This was the perfect birthday present. It was meant to be.

I was reminded of what 1951 was like for black Americans when I saw the purchase contract for the house. There it was in the deed, a notation the property could not be sold to Negroes. I knew I was buying a house in southern Maryland, a region that had a reputation for being more aligned with what was thought of as traditional southern sentiments about race. In fact, I'd discussed this with John, who is white and confident there would be no issues. And there never were.

The 'No Negroes allowed' language in the contract had been redacted due to the passage of the federal Fair Housing Act of 1968 that made such housing discrimination unlawful. It was still in the contract that was used, a clear reminder of the restrictive covenants that had defined who could live in this small community beside the Chesapeake Bay—whites only. I saw the language, thought momentarily about what used to be, and then focused on what was. It was 2001. The world had changed where many blacks could now afford second homes. That was positive. It was not a time to focus on the past. I signed the papers and invited the Valianettes down for a girls' weekend at the beach.

Everyone, but Jeannie and Renée could come. Debby, Debbie, Marsha, Veronica, Madeline, and I along with my son AJ, now 7 years old, packed that little house. No one minded being a little crowded. Somehow the three beds, a sleep sofa, a couple of sleeping bags and an air mattress along with the one bathroom worked. We were family. It was cozy. No fancy restaurants this time. We grilled hot dogs and hamburgers. When the sun set over the bay, we were sitting in the white Adirondack chairs out on the stone terrace with glasses of wine in hand. We all smiled and toasted the Valianettes and our new clubhouse. This was to be the first of many, many weekends together at my little house on the bay.

It was only a few weeks later that the world changed for all of us. September 11, 2001. Living through this day and the immediate aftermath must have been like living through the attack on Pearl Harbor on December 7, 1941, for our parents. Our parents knew immediately that none of their loved ones were at Pearl Harbor. We didn't have the same assurance. For our group, several lived in the D.C. area, and a trip to New York City was a fairly regular occurrence. Marsha worked for an international organization. I worked for a national one. Travel was an everyday part of our worlds, but fortunately, neither of us had a trip planned on that particular Tuesday. The Valianettes that came closest to being affected were Madeline and Renée. As a US Army civilian employee, Madeline had regular meetings at the Pentagon just not that day. Renée had only recently been laid off from ServiceMaster as the company downsized. Little did Renée know what seemed like misfortune would be one of her many life's blessings. She was responsible for a 15-state region on the east coast and Canada. Not wanting to fly into or out of the New York City airports due to the congestion, Logan Airport in Boston and Newark International were her airports of choice for negotiating through her territory. She could have easily been on one of the planes used by the terrorists on that day. As it happened, she was on the west coast visiting her stepdaughter. She and her husband were on one of the first planes allowed to fly after 9/11. The Valianettes would learn of this much later. Once again, when tragedy struck, it wasn't to any of the Valianettes that most of us turned. It was only after we had reached everyone in our immediate families, parents, and siblings that we turned to friends. Even then, it was just our '3 a.m. in the morning' friends we called, our closest. The only Valianettes that fell into this category were Renée and Madeline. They had always been a very close Valianette duo and their constant back-and-forth conversations on this day and in the immediate aftermath showed this was still true. They needed the comfort of each other to get through this event, particularly one that had come so close to affecting each of them.

We continued our regular gatherings. We'd grown from one gathering a year to one a quarter. We enjoyed getting together. There was almost always the January gathering on or around MLK weekend, a spring outing usually at cherry blossom time in Washington, a beach gathering typically in the summer and a Christmas luncheon.

Madeline had arranged for another spa day. This time it was at the home of an African-American woman who had transformed the basement of her upscale suburban home into a private day spa. As usual, supporting a black business or learning more about black history was an undercurrent; so, it's surprising that as we were choosing nail colors and talking about what was going on in our lives, no one remembers talking about the new museum. At the end of 2003, President George W. Bush had signed legislation to support the establishment of the National Museum of African-American History and Culture. Perhaps we didn't know about it. This is likely to have been a small item in the newspaper or on the evening news, but an accomplishment that had taken almost a century to achieve.

It was 1915 when discussions began regarding a memorial. The African-American soldiers who had fought in the Union Army led the conversations, but nothing happened even though President Hoover appointed a body to explore the possibility. It wasn't until there was a critical mass of African-Americans in Congress that this idea gained some momentum. African-American Congressman Mickey Leland became a supporter in the mid-'80s as did former civil rights activist, Congressman John Lewis. Some quietly suggested that the Anacostia Museum, a black-focused museum near Frederick Douglass' home in a predominantly black section of Washington, D.C., was adequate. It had become a part of the

Smithsonian complex in the late '60s. Others wanted a premiere museum in a prime location on the National Mall. They felt only that level of visibility would be appropriate. In 1990, seventy-five years after the first one, another exploratory group was formed. In 2001, black Republican Congressman J.C. Watt and black Democratic Congressman John Lewis (Leland had died by this time) reintroduced the legislation. Finally, in 2003, it passed Congress and was signed by the president. This museum would be a part of the Smithsonian and definitely a future venue for one of our gatherings.

We made it to that gospel brunch at the Corcoran—again good food and good music. We enjoyed the uplifting black spirituals in the lovely setting of the Corcoran Art Gallery, steps away from the White House. We went to the National Gallery of Art's exhibit of African-American collage artist Romare Bearden. Bearden could capture the human condition he saw as a social worker in and through his powerful art. He showed us the world of field hands in the South and of jazz musicians in Harlem as well as average black Americans living life. As we walked through this Smithsonian museum, we commented on the vibrancy and the poignancy of his art and on his medium. We thought back to the blunt scissors we had used in elementary school at Norrell to cut out photos from the *Ebony* or *Life Magazine* our parents read. What amazing images Bearden could produce with the same cut out pictures from those glossy magazines.

Now, we also had our beach gathering. We rarely ended up on the beach. We'd walk by it and look out on it, but our focus was always on our outing. Occasionally, we would go antiquing at a favorite local store, get a half bushel of hard-shell crabs and spread out newspaper on my dining room table, drive into Solomon's Island to explore the little shops and the local art gallery or sit out on the terrace, tell stories, laugh and relax. One particularly memorable weekend combined seeing *Dreamgirls*, a movie that told the story of a girl singing group reminiscent of the Supremes, at the local theater followed by mouth-watering ribs at a new southern barbecue restaurant in the area. Once again there was a black cultural component to our gathering as we relived our youthful fondness for the Supremes. Then there was also the constant of food, not the necessary act of having breakfast, lunch, and dinner, but an authentic food experience was definitely desired. Red, Hot & Blue, the local barbecue spot, was the closest we had to all of that. It had recently opened in Calvert County, in a shopping area about 15 minutes from the beach house. The chain had started right outside of Washington, D.C. by a former governor of Tennessee and the then-head of the Republican National Committee. They wanted good food and the blues. So did we. Blues music played in the background and photos of blues musicians looked down on us as we dined on Memphis, Tennessee inspired barbecue ribs. Life was good.

By now, there was also the annual Christmas luncheon. We'd all been raised as Christians; so, Christmas was still a primarily religious and cultural holiday, but for a couple of folks in the group, Kwanzaa was also a part of the December celebrations. Kwanzaa, the festival created by Maulana Karenga in 1966 to celebrate black family, community, and culture, was growing in popularity. It was now regularly recognized as part of the December celebrations, even by the White House, along with the Jewish Hanukkah. One Christmas, our holiday luncheon was at Maggiano's Italian Restaurant in Richmond. This family-style restaurant was the perfect venue for our family-like group. It was the mid-2000s. We were continuing to strengthen our connection.

Somewhere along the way, Renée decided the group needed a real name. 'The girls' no longer worked for her. She dubbed us 'divas.' I had always thought of a diva as a temperamental, female singer. Nothing about the name felt right, but for Renée, the term meant a woman who was successful in her career, a consummate professional, stylish and intelligent. She would quickly prove we could be defined by both definitions. We all viewed ourselves by the positives Renée attributed to the name. Certainly, Renée was stylish, smart and professionally accomplished and we liked to think we all had those characteristics, but maybe there was a bit of the traditional diva in all of us as well.

A couple of stories make that possibility clear. We were at the beach and decided to try out a new restaurant. I had let everyone know I'd only been there for brunch once. I'd enjoyed the food that time but knew nothing about the dinner service. Everyone agreed we never would know without trying it out. An adventure it would be. We climbed into two cars, drove the

15 miles to the restaurant in Solomon's Island right on the bay and got there in time for our 7:00 p.m. reservation. It was a small place about half full, a respectable crowd for this community. We were at the beach, so several folks thought about crabs. No hard-shell crabs this time, but crab cakes were on the menu. When the waiter came, Renée was clear. She wanted the crab cake, but only if would not be full of bread filler. Assured it was the best the waiter had ever had, Renée ordered it. The time passed as we laughed and talked about whatever had happened during the day, but eventually, we were starving. Called over to the table, the waiter let us know several of the staff hadn't shown up for work that evening. The kitchen was behind, but our food would be out soon. It might have been a better situation if it had never arrived. It was awful. In no uncertain terms, Renée told the waiter she had eaten crab cakes all over the country and had never had a worse one. It was full of filler and not edible. Politely, but thoroughly, she admonished him for even bringing it to the table. While she was the most vocal, she spoke for the group. The food was awful. We paid the bill—at least some of it. Renée's crab cake had been removed, and we left that restaurant never to return. Not that long ago, other African-Americans would have been pleased to have been allowed to eat there. Never would they have questioned the service or the quality of the food. A lot had changed as Renée had demonstrated that evening. Maybe there was the spark of a diva—the good, the bad and a little bit of the ugly—in all of the girls.

We were well-educated, well-read, and well-traveled. Marsha's position with Al-Anon had her working with an Al-Anon chapter in Italy one week and then the next week heading off to South Africa to meet with individuals interested in starting a group. Madeline had begun traveling right out of high school when her mother took her on a European vacation as a high school graduation present. Spending her 18th birthday in Rome and visiting the other major cities of Europe, the travel bug was nurtured in Madeline as she accompanied her mother to many countries. Not only was her mother vacationing, but she was also studying the early African diaspora. Ruth Rice Swann, Madeline's mother, was researching her book, *A History of Black Africans: To A.D. 1400*. Madeline always enjoyed these trips and learned a lot, but she never felt the strong connection some African-Americans had experienced in different places until years later when she and Renée went to Ghana. There a local man turned to her and said, "Welcome home sister." It was only then she felt like she had come home. I, too, had traveled the United States and other parts of the world somewhat extensively. While I, also, enjoyed visiting many places, I never felt a strong connection until visiting Egypt and felt that same sense of homecoming. It was a strange and genuinely unexpected feeling. Jeannie remembers feeling that her travel in the Caribbean had sensitized her even more to the abundance in this country and the poverty in which so many lived. Most of us in the group had been to a lot of places and had many experiences.

When Renée told the waiter at that Chesapeake Bay-side restaurant she had ordered crab cakes at restaurants in most of the major American cities, she had. She knew what excellent crab cakes tasted like. The reality is both she and the waiter were speaking their own truth. The crab cakes at that restaurant may have been the best he had ever had, but that was not the standard for Renée or for the others at the table. We were foodies. We had dined in fine restaurants all over the country and in many places around the globe for most of our adult lives. Did the love of excellent food also stand as one characteristic of a diva? For us, it definitely did.

In hindsight, maybe that 'diva-ness' even came out when it was only us. I had driven over to Veronica's for a Diva gathering one winter Saturday. I'd brought AJ. He was only a year younger than Veronica's son Vachon. The two boys got along very well. When I got there, I could almost pull my car entirely into Veronica's driveway, but I needed a little more space. I could tell that if the drivers of the other two vehicles pulled theirs up a bit, there would be adequate room. I sent AJ into the house to ask them to move their cars. I waited and waited. No one came out; so, I bundled myself up and went into the house to see what the problem was. I don't remember it this way, but the others say I strutted into the house with my handbag held tightly on my shoulder and a look of determination in my eyes as I pointedly asked what the problem was. Why hadn't they come out to move their cars? The two drivers got up and moved their vehicles right away. They could tell a little bit of the diva was coming out, and they didn't want to deal with it. Moving the cars was easier.

Some might think to be black girls raised in the South in the '50s and '60s, we had been taught to be cautious, demure and mindful of the world order. We might have been trained to stand back, to be tentative in the way we approached situations. We were not. We were taught to examine circumstances, to assess the pros and cons of acting in specific ways and then to stand up for what was right, to voice our opinions, and to be a part of the change we wanted. Renée remembers her father telling her how important it was to have her own ideas, to understand what led to those views and to speak her truth. Her father was afraid Renée was so concerned with everyone liking her she wasn't developing the backbone necessary for her to rise in her field and succeed. He wanted her to stand up for herself and for her views. He didn't have to worry. She developed that strength as we all did. We stood up for what we believed in conversations among ourselves and in more public situations.

It wasn't only our parents who sought these qualities in us, these were the core qualities that had been wanted by our race for all children ever since black people had witnessed the power of visible leaders like Frederick Douglass or Marcus Garvey, Martin Luther King or Malcolm X. The messages of these leaders weren't uniformly supported by all in our race. The power of the words, the ability of these leaders to stand in front of audiences and say what others were thinking and to lead people to act was what our parents, our grandparents and our great-grandparents saw as vital to improve the conditions of our race.

We spoke our minds and shared our opinions with clarity and poise. Whether I was standing before a state senator or a governor. Or an audience of hundreds of people. Renée before a major corporate executive or Madeline before another scientist or a general in the United States Army. We, like the others, knew how to craft our positions, share them cogently and in an engaging manner and base them on the research and other available evidence. Even if we didn't feel it, we walked into any room overtly with confidence, able to negotiate whatever cultural behaviors were needed. We were, and are, adept at code-switching, as it is called, knowing how to talk and act with anyone in our race or in other races regardless of their station in life. Having been around whites since our early years, we also felt comfortable the many times we were the only or one of few blacks in the room. That still happens often in our professional lives even now.

And as our parents had wanted: we stand up for what is right whether that means Veronica advocating for one of her students or Debby speaking out before members of Congress about services for the homeless. Or me being arrested on Constitution Avenue beside the U.S. Capitol as I protested for congressional representation for the citizens of the District of Columbia. We are articulate, self-assured and assertive. We may have had to overcome internal nervousness or feelings of inadequacy, but we do not present that to the outside world. We have become the adults our parents and others in our race had groomed us to be. The stage for our message might be relatively small, our school or our community or maybe an occasional national platform within our professional world, but we learned that the size of the stage does not matter. We were taught that from the time we put on our Sunday best clothes to board that segregated train at Broad Street Station on our elementary school trip to Washington, D.C. We were told you only had one opportunity to make a good impression. We knew, as all blacks do that we weren't just making that impression for ourselves or for our families, we were representing an entire race. We understood how important that one opportunity was.

Our position in the world might have been different, but our understanding of the impact of our actions and of our words was no different for us than for Barack Obama, Rosa Parks or Condoleezza Rice, three African-Americans that had a tremendous impact on us and on the country in the mid-2000s.

No one had ever stood as tall as Barack Obama did on the stage of the 2004 Democratic National Convention. Most of us had never heard of this then-state senator from Illinois who had been given the coveted keynote address at the convention. There had been keynote addresses by other notable African-Americans, Barbara Jordan in 1976 and Jesse Jackson, Sr. in 1988 were both memorable but never had there been a speech as rousing and impassioned as that delivered by Obama. When he said, "There's not a Black America and a White America and Latino America and Asian America; there's the United States of America," it felt as if the entire country was cheering. He was speaking to us all. Obama's message was clear. For far too long, the country had been separated into racial camps. Stereotypes and prejudice had fueled efforts to divide the country. Even the famed Kerner Commission, formed by President Lyndon Johnson after the deadly 1987 Detroit race riots, had proclaimed, "Our nation is moving toward two societies, one black, one white—separate and unequal." As someone born of a black Kenyan father and a white Kansan mother and who had been raised in the Philippines, Obama personified the melting pot that is America. His message was about a healthy country bound together as states united, people united, not as a country divided by race. His message of the blending of perspectives and races and values buried the Kerner Commission's famous critical sentence, at least for a moment in time. Was he articulate? Was he impassioned? Articulate and passionate are far too inadequate words to define Barack Obama's speech that July night in 2004. He was transcendent, inspiring us to believe, as he did, in the audacity of hope. America could be an America for all.

The next year, an African-American icon passed away. It must have been that same audacity of hope that led Rosa Parks fifty years before her death to quietly and courageously remain in her seat on a bus on that December day in 1955 Montgomery, Alabama. She was already in the colored section of the bus, and now she was being told to give up her seat so a white man could sit down. She wouldn't do it. Regardless of the training Rosa Parks received on civil disobedience and social justice at the Highlander Folk School and irrespective of the support she was receiving from her employer, the Montgomery, Alabama chapter of the NAACP, Rosa Parks was still alone on that bus. She knew she was breaking the segregationist laws of her state and she was likely to be arrested.

While a legal team was ready to get her out of jail immediately, it was still the South, and she knew all of the horrible things that could happen to her. It had only been four months earlier that Emmitt Till was murdered while visiting his family in Mississippi. This black 14-year old was supposed to have crossed the most sacrosanct of southern boundaries. It was said he had whistled at a white woman. He had been told by his mother before coming to the South he must mind his ways in the South, but this Chicago teenager probably didn't even know what those words truly meant.

190

Following the recovery of his brutalized body from the Tallahatchie River, his mother insisted on an open casket funeral so the world could see what had happened to her son. Rosa Parks knew all of this. In fact, the vision of Emmitt Till may have been the catalyst that told her now was the time. Someone, something, had to ensure there would be no more Emmitt Tills. Not many of us would have had the strength of character, the actual self-assurance, to do what Rosa Parks had done. Not many.

I wonder if any of us would have had the strength of character to accept the call as Condoleezza Rice did. Republican President George Bush named Condoleezza Rice Secretary of State in 2005, the same year her fellow Alabamian Rosa Parks had died. The position of Secretary of State would be a logical career goal for her academic and professional background. Only sixty-five others had ever served in that role in the history of the country. While seen as the pinnacle of a political scientist's career, Rice probably did not see that post as necessarily attainable. She had been an assistant professor of political science at Stanford University when she came to the attention of the Republican power brokers. In his first term, President Bush appointed her national security advisor. While prominent, it was a backroom position. Most people didn't know her or her work. Her time in the public's eye emerged when she was named the second African-American Secretary of State following General Colin Powell.

Historically, the black community has cheered as other blacks rose to positions of prominence; however, this was not always the case with Secretary Rice. People wanted to support her, but she was working for a Republican, not just a Republican, THE Republican, the president of the United States. At one point a black *Washington Post* columnist asked, "How did [Rice] come to a worldview so different from most black Americans?" While Republican President Abraham Lincoln freed the slaves, most African-Americans have been supporters of Democratic candidates for decades. Most African-Americans have perceived the Democratic Party as the party of the people and see the Republican Party as the party of business and the rich, the party that always leaves our race behind. Rice had aligned herself with the Republican Party. Perhaps that position may have been tolerated if it hadn't been for Hurricane Katrina.

When Hurricane Katrina struck Louisiana and the levees holding back Lake Pontchartrain broke, the residents of the ninth ward in New Orleans were the most affected. They were 90% black, and a third of them were poor. Many didn't have cars or money to leave the city when the evacuation order was made, and if the ninth ward mirrors the national statistics for African-Americans, 70% of them couldn't swim to safety because they didn't know how to swim. When the cameras panned the people on rooftops waiting to be rescued as the water closed in on the second stories of their homes or the thousands that wrapped around the Superdome seeking shelter after the storm, viewers saw predominantly black faces. When reporters talked about the thousands who had been displaced, they often referred to them as refugees. Was the ninth ward a part of their country? Now that they had left that part of the city to come into mainstream New Orleans were they in another country? Even the terminology suggested a worldview that relegated these victims of this natural disaster to a very unique and inappropriate status in the history of our nation. This perception was compounded and reinforced when President Bush did not immediately respond in a visible way that suggested concern and caring. Instead, he continued his Texas vacation. When he left Texas for Washington, he only flew over New Orleans as opposed to stopping in the city and being, on the ground, with the citizens of this country who had experienced such a tragedy. Many African-Americans, including the Divas, immediately thought his response would have been different if those affected had primarily been white. The victims were poor and black, a combination that rarely demanded the attention of people in power.

Condoleezza Rice's realm was international. She had no role in the domestic situation that was Hurricane Katrina. Many wondered how she could remain in an administration that had demonstrated such a lack of sensitivity to the needs of people, people of her race in particular. When criticized for how she responded to some situations differently from many black people, she commented "The fact of the matter is I've been black all of my life. No one has to tell me how to be black." I wonder how many of us would have had the strength of character, the assertiveness, to voice this strong a position in the face of so much backlash from members of our own race. Not many. Most African-Americans could not see themselves working for President George Bush. Rice was true to herself, true to her beliefs, able to stand tall before those in her race and those outside of it for what she believed in. Self-confident.

Over our lives, life has given us many indicators of what it means to be black in America. Burning crosses and BET, Rodney King asking "can't we just get along," and Oprah Winfrey introducing us to her favorite things, the words of playwright August Wilson and the actions of Cassius Clay (Muhammed Ali). The jails overcrowded with black men and Morehouse men graduating from college. Sometimes race was merely an always-there overlay, like wallpaper. It was there, but you didn't pay much attention to it. Other times, circumstances made it starkly central to how we thought about ourselves. That was the case in the late summer and fall of 2008.

CHAPTER 17
THE OBAMA EFFECT

*"The connection to racial pride and the century-plus
fight for civil rights has probably never been felt as
uniformly by millions as it was on that election day."*

After a whirlwind, miraculous campaign, on August 28, 2008, African-American U.S. Senator Barack Obama claimed the nomination for president of the United States as the Democratic Party candidate. President. We had gotten goosebumps when he spoke in 2004 at the Democratic convention. We knew his political star was rising, we didn't think it would climb so far so soon, and we didn't know if a black candidate's time was now. Many had been concerned when in February 2007 he announced his candidacy for the office. Former First Lady Hillary Clinton had announced her candidacy the previous month, and many felt she was a shoe-in. She had been in the U.S. Senate since 2001 and already had eight years in the White House as First Lady. Many supported her because they had helped her husband. With Obama's entry in the field of candidates, the question of who would be the nominee was now very uncertain. A woman, an African-American or the traditional white male?

There had been other African-Americans who had been nominated. Frederick Douglass had received one vote at the 1888 Republican Party convention. The little-known name, George Edwin Taylor, had run in 1904 as the candidate of the National Negro Liberty Party. More recently Congresswoman Shirley Chisholm ran in 1972 and Jesse Jackson, Sr. in 1984 and 1988, but never had an African-American been THE presidential candidate of one of the two major United States political parties.

Eighteen months after his announcement, Barack Obama accepted his party's nomination for president. For this historic moment, the Denver convention center, site of the convention itself, wasn't large enough.

84,000 people watched as he walked out on a newly-created stage at Invesco Field in Denver, Colorado as millions of us sat glued in front our televisions. We were mesmerized. Again, he reminded the crowd of his African and of his American roots and the improbability of his candidacy. The crowd cheered this African-American son and became electrified at the end of his speech when he reminded us it had been 45 years ago to the day since a Baptist minister had spoken before a crowd of thousands on the Mall in Washington D.C. The March on Washington and now the nomination of the first African-American to be president of the United States—this was a monumental confluence on the same day in history. We knew our country had taken another step toward achieving Dr. King's dream. Barack Obama had been judged, we thought, by the content of his character, not by the color of his skin.

Regardless of the clarity of his vision and eloquence of his message. Regardless of the millions in campaign contributions received in five and ten-dollar denominations or the power of his intellect and regardless of the polling numbers, we still knew this was America. Racial hatreds, misconceptions, and fears were rife. As over age 50, African-American women, we were enormously proud of his candidacy but did not believe he could be elected. We thought we lived in a country that continued to be driven by race. We knew barrier after barrier had been removed. But we also knew millions lived in environments in which black people were not a part of their worlds. And much of what they knew of black people, they learned from the negative images on the evening news or what some viewed as the denigrating rap music occasionally heard as they turned the radio dial. They had a warped view of who black people were. We felt even those whose views were informed and accurate might say they would vote for Obama but would not when they got into the polling booth. This behavior has a name. In 1982, when Los Angeles' black mayor Tom Bradley ran for governor of California. The polls showed he would win, but post-election research showed that fewer people voted for him than said they would. That action (or inaction) became known as the Bradley Effect. Before the election, some whites make the politically correct pronouncement that they would vote for a black candidate, often noting that person's credentials and appropriateness for the position, but once in the voting booth, other factors drive their decision. We expected the Bradley Effect on November 4, 2008.

Millions stood in lines for three and four hours to ensure their vote counted. Some as long as ten hours. It didn't matter. Many of us felt we weren't only voting for ourselves, but we were voting for our parents and our grandparents. The connection to racial pride and the century-plus fight for civil rights has probably never been felt as uniformly by millions as it was on that election day. Age, illness, weather, the length of the voting line—nothing would have kept most African-Americans from voting.

Surprised? We were in shock. No one was as surprised by Obama's election as black Americans over age 45 or 50. All Democrats under that age heartedly believed in his slogan, "Yes we can." We said the words, and we hoped, but deep in our souls, we didn't think the country would elect a black man. Not yet. We thought the Bradley Effect would prevail once again. And, we thought we might see a protracted process as we had with the counting of votes in the Gore-Bush election eight years earlier. We expected the worse because that is what our life's circumstances and experiences told us was likely to happen.

No African-American can remember in his or her lifetime a moment of greater pride than when President-elect Obama walked out on the stage of Grant Park in Chicago on election night. Tears streamed down the faces of those in the audience and those of us at home. Cameras panned election night vigils in countries around the world as we had watched the New Year's Eve celebrations in previous years. Never had the world watched an election in the United States as they watched this one. Citizens of the world thought it signaled a new era of diplomacy and engagement on the world stage. This was definitely a new day for America. Maybe we could be a country united. Maybe we could stop being a Black America and a White America, red states signifying Republicans and blue states signifying Democrats just as Obama said. President Obama would be our hope. Maybe we, as older African-Americans, could stop anticipating the worse and join the President-elect in audaciously believing Dr. King's dream had been achieved.

CHAPTER 18
A Time for Togetherness

"At our 40th high school reunion, we were surprised to see Carolyn Mosby, the first African-American teacher at John Marshall. We remembered her, but we were surprised first that she remembered us and then by her comment. 'I knew you would all be together,' she said. 'You were always together.'"

While we were putting our faith in President Obama to correct the societal and economic ills that faced our country and our people, the Divas were also being driven in a small, almost subliminal way, by messages from the First Lady. Michelle Obama had taken two issues as her personal platform—the needs of military families and obesity. None of us fell into the first category, but far too many of us were getting perilously close to that second type. Perhaps, we were not obese, but we definitely had a few too many extra pounds.

By the late 2000s, what defined us most was nothing as philosophical as what it meant to be black. It was that expected bug-a-boo, middle-age spread. That was a big part of our conversations now. We talked about it as I made guacamole and margaritas at the beach.

"Girl, I just joined Weight Watchers. I've got to get rid of these pounds."

"I've started walking every day. It's making a difference. I've lost an inch or two."

"I looked at a picture of myself. I can't believe how much weight I've gained."

"I've got diabetes. I have to eat differently."

"My cholesterol is high. I have to eat differently."

"My blood pressure is up. No more bacon for me."

We talked about our expanding waists and hips when we returned to Maggiano's for our Christmas luncheon. We talked about it when we went back to the Bethesda Crab House and when Veronica made us the most delicious pancakes for Sunday morning breakfast. We talked about it and talked about it, but we weren't ready to do anything yet.

AT BEN'S CHILI BOWL - U STREET

We continued that conversation when we went to that iconic D.C. restaurant, Ben's Chili Bowl on renowned U Street. We noticed that U Street which had been the center of the black entertainment district in the '30s and '40s like 2nd Street in Richmond had now become a bustling yuppie community of condos costing hundreds of thousands of dollars purchased by far more white residents than black. But what we noticed most was the hot dogs, and half smokes covered in chili and served with fries and tall cups of sodas that were the mainstay at Ben's. They covered our table as they did every table at Ben's. We dined on this quintessential Washington, D.C. food as we listened to songs on the jukebox by D.C. native son Marvin Gaye and native daughter Roberta Flack. Today wasn't the day to start our diet. Today was the day to memorialize our visit. We couldn't help but notice the pictures on the wall of local and national leaders, black and white, dining at Ben's. We decided to recreate one of those pictures as we posed with Mrs. Ali, the owner, outside the restaurant. We'd start dieting on the next gathering.

We went together to see the posthumous Michael Jackson documentary/concert, *This Is It*. We hadn't focused on Michael Jackson in an awfully long time. He had become almost cartoon-like in his behaviors in recent years, derided by many, overlooked by others. This film brought us back to the music of our youth and to his fantastic talent, so sad to be reminded in such a way. We ate lots of buttered, artery clogging, popcorn as we watched a driven, creative Michael who seemed so alive and ready for the upcoming London concert that would never happen.

We went to the Tobacco Company restaurant, in the Shockhoe Slip/warehouse section of Richmond, still trendy several decades after it was opened, for the next holiday gathering. This had been a major, after work, hangout spot when we were in our twenties, a place to be seen and to see others. That day, we didn't look around to see who was there as we used to. We ordered lunch with a couple of glasses of champagne for our holiday toast and again bemoaned the fact our clothes were shrinking.

My house had become the central gathering place. I loved to cook; so, when the girls arrived on Friday night for the weekend, I would have prepared pot roast or chicken in a creamy sauce with rice, seafood pasta or lasagna roll-ups. Dinner was always ready, but first, we needed a wee snack to whet our appetites. Guacamole with chips was one of the favorites I'd sometimes have ready when everyone arrived. Other times, there would be trays of hors-d'oeuvres of cheeses and smoked salmon, peppered sausage and crackers to go with my favorite red wine or whatever beverage others had brought. Food was still at the core of our gatherings— plentiful food, delicious food, fattening food.

Finally, we decided that at our next meeting, walking would be an essential part of the outing. It was spring, time for the Cherry Blossom

Festival in Washington, D.C. I reminded everyone to bring their walking shoes. We would walk to the Tidal Basin from my house on Capitol Hill. The distance was 3.1 miles. This seemed like a perfect distance. Seeing the beautiful cherry blossoms would be our reward.

We still had to have something to eat before we started. To build our stamina for this walk, we jokingly decided we'd have to start with lunch. It was a straight line from my house to the cherry trees. We'd walk down Pennsylvania Avenue heading south-west, passing restaurants as diverse as French bistros, sub shops, Indian cuisine, Thai, or sandwiches, whatever you wanted could be found in this section of Capitol Hill. The group decided on Mexican. About a third of the way into our outing, we stopped for lunch. Burritos, enchiladas, and tacos would sustain us for the rest of the walk, and since we were walking, we'd walk off whatever calories we were consuming for lunch. We laughed. It was okay to eat.

It was a beautiful day, a little chill in the air that disappeared as you got into the walk. We walked down the hill pass the U.S. House of Representatives office buildings where I had worked for Virginia Congressman Bobby Scott. Scott was a member of the Congressional Black Caucus, representing the Northside section of Richmond where most of us had lived. Being next to the capitol, conversations quickly went to the election. We were still amazed an African-American man had been elected president of the United States. We walked past the U.S. Botanical Garden and the Museum of the American Indian that had opened in 2004.

We were laughing and joking and in fine spirit as our walk continued past the Smithsonian Institution's Air and Space Museum, the Freer Gallery of Art and the National Museum of African Art. The crowds got a little bigger as we crossed 14th Street and passed the back of the Holocaust Museum and came directly to our destination. We'd made it. We'd taken our first official urban hike, a little over three miles to see the cherry blossoms. They were magnificent that year, so ethereal looking. As you glanced around the Tidal Basin, you felt as if you were looking at a creamy, light pink cloud. It was a wonderful moment, another to be memorialized by a photo taken together.

CHERRY BLOSSOMS

Okay, we'd seen the cherry blossoms. What was next on our Saturday? Food! I remembered how much the group enjoyed my guacamole, so I suggested a mid-afternoon snack of made-at-the-table-side, fresh guacamole and the most amazing pomegranate margaritas from a restaurant near Chinatown in the now trendy Penn Quarter section of Washington. It was a few blocks away; up 14th Street the group went, over to F Street and finally, we arrived at 7th Street where the restaurant was located. Maybe it was a little more than a few blocks. The urban hike had continued, but everyone was still happy, and there was a reward when we got there. A bit pooped when the sign for the Rosa Mexicana restaurant appeared, everyone happily entered the restaurant and ordered drinks and guacamole. We may have been a little tired, but now—inside the restaurant—we'd gotten our second wind.

The group was psyched. We had walked four miles or maybe a little more. The day was still beautiful. Could we walk back home became the question? The group didn't know it, but it was another 2 ½ miles back to my house. Tennis shoes still feeling good, off we went, walking toward Union Station. The train station was roughly the mid-point between the restaurant and my house. Washington is such a lovely city. The scenery was beautiful as was the weather that day. There was the beginning of that feeling of spring fever. Everyone was still feeling good, laughing and talking as we walked. We'd lost Debbie Johnson who had to go to meet her daughter, Jen and her Aunt Martha, but the rest of the group was intact.

Renée had regularly been walking for some time now. Her stride was long, and her endurance was good. I had a personal trainer, so I was in good shape, stamina-wise too. The two of us had been out in front for much of the walk. The group made it to Union Station. You could see the energy level dropped as several asked how much farther to the house. About one mile, they were told. They kept walking, but the pace had slowed significantly, the laughter lessened, and grumpiness came out. Abruptly, the group stopped less than half-a-mile from the house, right at Lincoln Park. They were not walking any farther.

There we stood, within view of the Emancipation Memorial, a statue of Abraham Lincoln and a freed slave built with funds collected from the post-Civil War black community where Frederick Douglass made the dedication speech. Any other time, they would have walked into the park. This afternoon, no one was moving the fifty steps to get close enough to read the plaque on the statue. If they had, they would have learned that fellow Virginian Charlotte Scott made the first contribution for the memorial. She used her first pay after being freed from slavery to start the fund. The group didn't care. They weren't in a learning mindset. They were tired. No one was paying much attention to this statue or to the one of noted African-American educator Mary McLeod Bethune at the other end of the park. They had run out of energy, completely. They announced they could not walk one more block. Renée and I would have to get a car and pick them up. The urban hike was over. The Divas had spoken.

My home was only about five or six blocks away. Renée and I went to get the car. Renée decided she would stay at the house. Without much thought, I got in my car and drove to pick up the group. When I came around the side of the park and pulled up to pick up the girls, I noticed they were looking at me with these, "I can't believe this" expressions.

Someone said, "How are we all going to get in there?"

Instead of driving Renée's spacious Lexus back to pick up the group, I had automatically driven my tiny, Easter-egg blue, Volkswagen Beetle. Fortunately, Renée hadn't come, and Debbie had split off to catch the metro right after guacamole and margaritas. There were still four adult women left to climb into the car. These four curvy, self-described as needing to lose a few pounds, women had to get into my tiny, compact car. The tallest, Madeline, knew her long legs would place her in the front seat with me, leaving Debby, Marsha, and Veronica to contort their bodies to get into the back seat of this little car. Hips here, elbows there.

"You move up, no you go in sideways. This won't work."

Getting into the back seat proved a challenge. Before I could drive off, I had to take a photo to remember this occasion.

"What are you doing?" they screamed at me as I took the picture. "Drive, I'm getting a cramp."

Fifty plus years old and giggling like teenagers. There was so much laughter, tears-streaming-down-your-face laughter. Another memory was born.

BACK SEAT OF THE VOLKSWAGEN

It seemed as if we hadn't blinked and it was time for another high school class reunion, our 40th. We can remember going to the iconic Armstrong-Walker high school football classic when we were teenagers and chuckling about the old alumni. The class celebrating their 20th anniversary would be announced and stand or the homecoming queen from 40 years earlier would be escorted out onto the field. We would giggle and comment about how surprised we were those people could walk without assistance. Now here we were celebrating our 40th high school reunion. Well, we could still walk, so we all decided to go to the event. It was held at a country club near our old high school, a place neither our parents nor we would have been allowed in when we were attending John Marshall High School. Just like the reunion fifteen years earlier, the atmosphere was cordial, but there was no connection between the black students and the white ones. After initial pleasantries and the requisite catching up about family and professions, there was nothing else to be said. We stayed with our little group welcoming a few who we hadn't seen in years, but not venturing far from our table. We were surprised to see one attendee, Carolyn Mosby. Mrs. Mosby, who taught math, had been the first African-American teacher at John Marshall. I hadn't had her class, but several others had. We remembered her, but we were surprised first that she remembered us and then by her comment.

"I knew you would all be together," she said. "You were always together."

We didn't know our togetherness had stood out that much, but apparently, it had. She talked about her early experiences at Jayem. Even though she had an advanced degree in mathematics, the school administration had only wanted her to teach 9th and 10th graders. She fought back and with her credentials she was allowed to teach all grades. We had never known that. We were surprised by that information, but what shocked us was learning the FBI watched over her car for a period of time fearing a bomb might be planted. This is what the late '60s was like for an adult. We had no idea. We had been sheltered from these ugly realities. We left the reunion somber due to this story of racial tension but smiling from Mrs. Mosby's memory of the closeness of the Valianettes.

The next day, there was a picnic. We had planned to go. We gathered at Renée's house. Not a cook, Renée was nonetheless the perfect host. She had gotten platters of food to make sure those staying with her or those meeting there would have lots to eat. She knew how important food was to her friends. We sat around her dining room table, nibbling and talking. Soon it became apparent we weren't going to the picnic. We were too comfortable where we were, enjoying the food and the company. Everyone who we wanted to see at the reunion was right here.

We were friends who were getting closer. Not only were we getting closer, literally, in the backseat of the Volkswagen and in the relatively small quarters of my beach house, but we also continued to become emotionally closer as friends. We were approaching 60 years old. Did we want to do something as a group to commemorate this shared occasion? One day at the beach, as we talked about turning 60, we decided this milestone had to be marked by something special. We had never taken a trip together—all of us. We'd come closest in Birmingham, but only four could go. We were going on a trip—all of us. That's what we would do to commemorate our collective 60th birthdays.

With no real discussion, we decided Las Vegas would be our destination, and we'd go in March. We were in sync. With little fanfare, we had chosen a date for our outing and a location. Las Vegas had it all—some glamour, interesting places to visit, good food, excellent shopping opportunities and over-the-top entertainment. It was a Diva-kind of city for our 60th birthday celebration. Everyone could go except Debby. We were sad we'd be celebrating without her, but seven out of the eight of us was good.

Again, with minimal conversation, we had a hotel, the Luxor, roommates were chosen, and we had divided up the responsibilities for coordinating the trip. We knew we didn't want to spend every minute together as a group but wanted one group activity every day. We decided on specific restaurants we wanted to visit, what we wanted to see in and near the city and what shows to see. One show's title caught our eye, 'Hitzville: the Motown Revue.' No matter what we did, we were never too far from our roots. A Motown revue would definitely be entertainment that would bring back memories of our heyday, our time as Valianettes. We went to see "Hitzville" and what fun it was. We sang and danced in our seats along with the rest of the crowd knowing every word to every song that was performed.

We rented a limo, bought champagne, got dressed up, and cruised the Vegas strip at night. We stopped to line up beside the limousine and take the obligatory picture beside the Las Vegas sign. We sang along to Frank Sinatra singing 'Luck Be a Lady' while the fountains danced in front of the Bellagio Hotel. Every now and then, a quarter was put in a slot machine as we moved from the Bellagio to the Venetian, Paris to New York, New York, one magical hotel after another. No one won. No one cared. Gambling a little was a part of the Vegas experience.

THE DIVAS - LAS VEGAS

The highlight of the trip didn't come in a casino, at a restaurant or from watching a show, it happened while Debbie, Jeannie and I were out walking and casually shopping. The rest of the group had taken an all-day bus tour of the Grand Canyon. Strolling down the strip, it seemed like we all saw it at the same time. A t-shirt had caught our eye. It was red and emblazoned with sequins that read "Diva Las Vegas." Nothing could be more appropriate. We bought shirts for everyone. Some were red (the Delta Sigma Theta sorors in the group liked that color choice). Other shirts were black. The color didn't matter. The bling and the message did. Everyone donned their shirt and posed in front of the Luxor Hotel for our now-required group photo. Silly grins were everywhere as another tourist captured our moment. This was what sixty would be like for the Divas. We were having a great time. We were friends. We were sisters. Nothing could have made this moment better.

While Las Vegas had been a wonderful vacation, every gathering couldn't be a Diva Las Vegas moment. The clubhouse, as Marsha had dubbed my beach cottage, continued to be our go-to spot for weekend gatherings. It still had the cottage-feel, but I had added a second floor for another bedroom and a second bath. We were getting too old to double up in tiny spaces. Perhaps too old for some things, but in other ways regardless of the date on our drivers' licenses, we were still stylish divas. The pinks, reds, and oranges of nail colors had been replaced by greens and blues and even purples. It took us a minute to embrace this new color palette, but when we did, we were fully in.

To celebrate our evolving color sense, we shared a photo of our beach toes on Facebook. When we looked down not only at the different colors of our polish, we also saw the different shades of our skin. As a group, we covered a broad spectrum of the black skin color wheel. But somehow, skin color had never been an issue with us as it was with some in the black community. In hindsight, I wonder why. Even with a great deal of reflection, I can only attribute it to how we were raised. In a time when black people were trying to get ahead however they could. Our parents instilled in us the value of the group. We never tried to get ahead at the expense of someone else. We never thought we were better than anyone else and skin color was a non-issue for all of us.

CHAPTER 19
A LONG JOURNEY

"By no means did the election of Barack Obama turn this into a race-neutral country. Nor did his re-election."

When our story started Brown v. Topeka, Kansas Board of Education had only recently become the law of the land enabling our future access to integrated schools. Our parents had integrated an all-white neighborhood, but downtown Richmond restaurants still denied service to those who looked like us. It was then-President Eisenhower who was able to integrate the military even though his predecessor had signed the Executive Order making it possible. Separate and unequal was the reality in the mid-'50s in Richmond, Virginia. This was the world in which we started our lives.

Now in our 60s, we have lived to see not only the election but the re-election, of Barack Obama. Amazing. Some suggest that an African-American family as the first family of the nation is the only gauge needed to show what has been achieved for black Americans. No one can minimize that Obama had, to some degree, foretold in his 2004 speech to the Democratic National Convention, Black America, White America, Hispanic America and Asian America coming together as the truly united United States of America to support what they believed in. In 2008, that shared belief was in the rightness of his candidacy for president. In our lifetime, a black man had become president of the United States. Phenomenal.

But, in the first year of that president's term, a United States Congressman, Joe Wilson from South Carolina, interrupted the president with the vitriolic comment, "You lie" as the president spoke before a joint session of Congress. While such horrible behavior may have happened in the country's history, never had such disrespect of the office and of the office holder been captured on live television and witnessed by millions. Similarly, there have been no other instances that can be recalled when any sitting president has been asked to produce his birth certificate to prove he is a United States citizen. And the sight of a governor, welcoming the president to her state by shaking a finger in his face as she publicly admonished him for his policies on immigration is another level of disrespect that would not have happened had the president been white.

When we get together, we share our belief that President Obama has been the most disrespected president in our lifetime and in all of reported modern history. We believe that reality is solely a function of race, exclusively. What other reason would lead the Senate Minority Leader to state his number one political priority was to see to that this president did not have a second term? He was not focused on the addressing the jobs situation in the country, the housing situation or even a war that has cost so many American lives. His number one stated political priority was to defeat President Obama. White Americans or Hispanics or Asians might attribute other explanations for the behavior of Congressman Joe Wilson, then-businessman Donald Trump, Governor Jan Brewer or Senator Mitch McConnell. Some might say these individuals were passionate about their beliefs, got caught up in a moment or accidentally misspoke. Most black Americans will tell you these were racist actions of people who wanted to demonstrate their superiority while bringing down a black man regardless of, or perhaps because of, the position he held. By no means did the election of Barack Obama turn this into a race-neutral country.

Nor did his re-election in 2012. Once again, we thought Obama would not be victorious. We still thought it was almost a fluke that he was elected in 2008. I'm not saying that he wasn't eminently qualified, hadn't demonstrated an unwavering desire to work across political parties, and represented the country with dignity and intelligence on the world stage. No, that is all true, but he was still a black man in America. We thought the racist elements in the country had not been fully organized the first time, thinking that his election could never happen. We thought that backroom organizing would happen. There was no way that he would have a second term. Then he did.

Not only was Barack Obama the first African-American president, but he was also a two-term president. We wouldn't miss sharing this moment together. We didn't have tickets for the inauguration, but we still walked from my house to the capitol area to feel the energy in the crowd. Then we walked back, ladled out warm bowls of chili, turned on the big-screen TV in my family room and stood in true silly-Diva fashion as the oath of office was administered.

PRESIDENT OBAMA'S SECOND INAUGURATION

This second term must portend great things for our country, a growing racial sensitivity, a true recognition that all men are created equal.

But it did not.

Soon after the second inauguration of President Obama, George Zimmerman, born in Manassas, Virginia, only about 60 miles from Richmond, our hometown, was acquitted of the second-degree murder charge of Trayvon Martin. The killing of this unarmed 17-year old sparked a racial awakening. The Black Lives Matter movement was born, and a veil was removed from many who had believed the racial playing field had been leveled. It had not.

Even in 2012, with a two-term black president, we could still feel the overlay of race when we noticed the white person who had walked into the store after us, was asked if she needed any help. No one asked us. We could still feel the overlay when the white family at the next table in the restaurant was asked for their order for lunch before we were, even though we were seated first. Were we actually slighted? Did the wait staff think someone else had already helped us? Did circumstance other than race make them go to the table next to ours before coming us? Sometimes you don't know, but if you're African-American, race is the factor that always comes to mind.

It comes to mind also when we see others in our race not presenting their best self. When African-American teenagers wear pants that show their boxers or briefs, we wonder why that baggy pants, I-don't-have-a-belt, jailhouse image is the look some want to emulate. When cursing or the vile 'N' word is part of the everyday language we overhear on the metro or walking down the street, we're embarrassed. We don't want other African-Americans to speak what was briefly called Ebonics. We know it to be the use of double negatives or odd sentence structure, but we don't want other races to think that's how we talk. We want no one to think this is an accepted, to-be-studied racial dialect. We understand that every generation must define its fashion style and we've heard the argument that blacks should claim the 'N' word to diffuse its negative power. We know these things. Throughout history, use of the 'N' word has served to dismiss us as a people. We, perhaps because we are sixty-somethings, cannot celebrate its use. Still, we continue to believe every black person represents our race every time he or she walks down the street or opens his or her mouth. Every time. It is always our responsibility to present well. There are still so many stereotypes and misrepresentations to be overcome.

We remember and respect the 1950s and 1960s training of our parents and our grandparents. It was those generations that told us we always represented an entire race. That's what their parents told them and what we tell our children. We must still be at 110% or even 150%. We must still be dressed appropriately for whatever the occasion is. We must work harder at our professions because we have to shine brighter to be acknowledged. Those messages are still foremost in our minds. The playing field is far from level, not just for poor African-Americans. It's not level for the middle-class and even upper-income blacks. A black face still elicits stereotyped responses from many in other races far more frequently than liberal, well-informed, white people may think to be the case. They think they've been sensitized and that they understand. Perhaps they do, but only to the degree, you can try to put yourself in someone else's shoes. We never know what it's like to be of another race. It's impossible.

When unarmed Trayvon Martin was shot and killed by a white man who felt he was protecting his neighborhood and himself, a white man who for weeks was not charged with the crime, we were not surprised. Remembrances of times past when killing a black person was not a crime quickly came to mind. We know that walking-while-black, driving-while-black, and shopping-while-black are still situations that demand specific protocols even in 21st century America. Be mindful if you're walking in a predominately white neighborhood. Some people will think you should not be there and will be suspicious of why you're there. If you're driving an expensive car as a black man, some people will think you acquired the resources to buy that car through criminal activity and not because you worked hard and saved to be able to afford the car of your dreams or perhaps you're a young man driving his parent's car. If you're going to an upscale store, dress in an upscale way or some people will think you're shoplifting. And, in some places don't expect for a taxi to stop for you or to take you to certain neighborhoods. No matter how the taxi presents, the driver will say he is off duty. This is our reality. We are always expecting the negative reaction, the negative thoughts. Maybe it is this constant anxiety that leads to high stress with both emotional and physiological implications. We know of these realities as adults, perhaps Trayvon Martin didn't, or like our children, maybe he minimized the racial stereotypes that still exist. His murder became a teachable moment for many parents to remind their children of realities in America, the facts of 2012, not 1951.

When we were six, or even sixteen, our parents and other elders protected us from the negatives of race. Now that we are in our 60s, we don't shelter our children and grandchildren as much. We openly discuss situations and try to prepare them for the world as it is now. Far too often, they dismiss our analysis of conditions as we did when we were in our teens, 20s or even our 30s. They think they understand. They believe the world is colorblind. Just a few short years ago, they would have reminded us of the election of our African-American president. They would say that they live in integrated communities and have always been able to go to whatever restaurant, school or movie theater they want. We know that many believe they genuinely are judged by the content of their character, not by the color of their skin. They wanted us to feel, as they did, that the world had changed. "It's not like when you were a kid," is what they reminded us.

It's not like when we were kids. In some ways, the United States' racial landscape has become worse as it also, perhaps, became more honest, more overt in the manner in which racial prejudices are displayed, not only in same-race conversations or gatherings. There was an 'honesty' in the erecting of an 80-foot tall flagpole—flying a massive Confederate flag—over the much-traveled Route 95 North-South highway in Stafford County, Virginia near the hometown of George Zimmerman (the murderer of Trayvon Martin). As large as it is, I can't believe we didn't see it the many times we drove up and down that road. But we didn't until a year after it was put up when the wind caught it a certain way one day as Debby and I drove to some Diva gathering in Richmond. Seeing it in full reveal was a shock. Never, that I can recall, had we had a conversation about the Confederate flag. It was then we shared our anger that such an image would be allowed there. We later learned it was erected by the Virginia Flaggers, a group that puts up Confederate flags across the state, always on private property. We talked about what it symbolized and how the image of the flag would quickly mentally transition to images of the Ku Klux Klan. Seeing that flag flying proudly gave us shivers. It opened a floodgate of emotions: anger at what it symbolized and fear for the direction of the country. We talked about South Carolina, a topic that hadn't come up before. We got it. We understood that in America, you could do whatever you wanted—if it was within the law—regardless of how vile. As long it was done on private property. But the situation in South Carolina was different. That flag was on public property. How was that allowed?

On that day, the Confederate flag was flying proudly over the statehouse in Columbia, South Carolina, over a decade after almost 50,000 people, led by the NAACP, marched in protest. The NAACP wanted the leaders of the state to understand the offensiveness of this symbol to the black residents of the state. The head of the NAACP even called on the East Indian ancestry of the then governor, when he invoked Martin Luther King's query, "What would Gandhi do?" trying to remind her of the impact of the British colonial rule on her ancestors' country. Nikki Haley, then governor, now United States representative to the United Nations, supported the compromise that was reached on where the Confederate flag would fly, but not without significant furor among some citizens of her state.

Even today, while the flag has been relocated on the Columbia, South Carolina capitol grounds and no longer flies atop the dome, the leaders of the state tell the NAACP the flag isn't a racist symbol, but a visual acknowledgment of the heritage of many residents of the state. Their ancestors fought for the Confederacy, and they continue to be proud of that fact. That same sentiment holds true for many in our home city of Richmond, Virginia as the debate grows about the multiple statues to Confederate soldiers that line one of the main traffic corridors in the city, Monument Avenue.

But as we drove to Richmond that day, Debby and I focused on the honesty that has emerged from the focus on the Confederate flag and on the statues of Confederate soldiers. That the conversation about honor and pride masks a more profound and heartfelt recognition of a time when the white race was always top in the societal pecking order, a time when blacks were subservient, and the relationship between races was clearly understood. That societal reality was disrupted by the election of Barack Obama. For some, his election proclaimed what was now right in America. For others, it announced, loudly, what was wrong. I don't know if the whites who celebrate the flag and the statues would acknowledge that or if that feeling truly is subconscious. What I do know is that the support of the flag and the removal of icons to leaders of the Confederacy has unearthed a conversation buried for decades if not centuries. No politician captured the reality of the divergent feelings about the statues better than Mitch Landrieu, then-mayor of New Orleans, a city that at one time was home to the largest slave market in the country. We had visited this city a few years earlier on our third Diva trip. We went for gumbo and beignets, the music and the overall vibe or as they say in N'awlins, "laissez les bon temps rouler" (let the good times roll). Regardless of the good food and fun, we couldn't miss the vestiges of slavery in this beautiful city. The Mississippi River alone reminded us of the cotton trade and the slaves that made this possible. But the most gruesome story came on what we thought was to be a light-hearted evening. We took the much-lauded ghost tour. When we reached the Lalaurie House on Royal Street, the tour became more sinister than we were prepared for. Not only did Dr. and Mrs. Lalaurie abuse and whip their slaves, they tortured them. Following a fire that destroyed the house, the bodies of slaves were found in a hidden room chained to the walls, dismembered, tortured in a way that called to mind Josef Mengele's human experimentation on Jews in Nazi camps decades later. New Orleans was a city of finery and splendor, but Mitch Landrieu knew of its evil history and knew what the statues truly represented. One part of his historic speech on the removal of the Confederate statues from that city merits recalling. He said:

> "The historic record is clear, the Robert E. Lee, Jefferson Davis, and P.G.T. Beauregard statues were not erected to honor these men, but as part of the movement which became known as The Cult of the Lost Cause. This 'cult' had one goal—through monuments and through other means—to rewrite history to hide the truth, which is that the Confederacy was on the wrong side of humanity. First erected over 166 years after the founding of our city and 19 years after the end of the Civil War, the monuments that we took down were meant to rebrand the history of our city and the ideals of a defeated Confederacy. It is self-evident that these men did not fight for the United States of America, they fought against it. They may have been warriors, but they were not patriots. These statues are not just stone and metal. They are not only innocent remembrances of a benign history. These monuments purposefully celebrate a fictional, sanitized Confederacy; ignoring the death, ignoring the enslavement, and terror it actually stood for."

Well said, Mitch Landrieu. Very well said.

Many feel that the August 1955 killing of 14-year old Emmett Till along with his mother Mamie Till's strength in having an open casket funeral for her son gave Rosa Parks the push she needed a few months later in December 1955. And that her action then gave rise to what we know as the civil rights movement, an array of activities taken by many, from various vantage points, focused on improving the lives of black Americans. This was also the case with the killing of Trayvon Martin. A cascade of actions and counter-actions emerged between that 2012 event and today. Black Lives Matter stands as both the powerful organization that emerged and as the umbrella sentiment that captures the emotion felt by many in America. Black lives have been minimized for centuries. That reality was crystallized for many by the killing of Trayvon Martin and the exoneration of his killer George Zimmerman. Then it was magnified into a movement by cellphone video after cell phone video of black, unarmed men being killed by police. Michael Brown, Eric Garner, Tamir Rice, Freddie Gray and Stephon Clark are the names of a few as they were martyred and then embraced, by a community that always knew of this disparate treatment but didn't have the evidence. Now, deadly, stark images captured the callous treatment of black people in America. Image after image showed that black lives didn't matter.

The notion of honesty in the country's racial reality emerged even more with the election of Donald Trump in 2016. His campaign slogan "Make America Great Again" offered a clarity of viewpoint, not the false sense of equality that had shaped the country for decades, masking the racial reality. Black people across the country knew that the slogan meant "make America white again," return America to the 1950s, the time when we were born, the time when separate-but-equal was the law of the land, the time when there was an insufficient concern for black people or for other people of color. But instead of black people living in fear from the killing of so many unarmed black men. Or the killing of Heather Heyer in Charlottesville, Virginia by a white nationalist protesting the removal of a Confederate statue. Or even the election of a president who claimed there were good people on both sides in the Charlottesville confrontation. These actions have served to mobilize the black community and others who recognize that the notion of a post-racial America following the election of Barack Obama was a white America fantasy. Black people knew this, but white America did not. White America, liberal white America, seemed to think that we— the middle and upper class, black and white—had reached the promised land of a level playing field. Now, the honesty of feelings, deeply held beliefs of privilege combined with white fear, held by many, have been unveiled.

When renowned media mogul Oprah Winfrey is treated like a potential shoplifter in a Swiss boutique when the salesperson refused to show her the behind-glass-$38,000 handbag that she had asked to see, we know that we are still being judged by the color of our skin. When former NFL player Colin Kaepernick kneels during the playing of the National Anthem in silent protest of the violence directed against black people, our minds immediately return to how Muhammed Ali was treated when he refused to fight in Vietnam. The heavyweight boxing powers-that-be abandoned him for years as the professional football power structure has blackballed (I cannot fail to note here that the negative action isn't referred to as 'whiteballed') Kaepernick. And when the Academy of Motion Picture Arts and Sciences is called out for its lack of diversity in nominees, and even in presenters in one recent year, you don't have to look too deeply to see that racial injustice is still a significant part of America. Perhaps more so for the have-nots than for the haves. But when un-eyelashed, no entourage Oprah Winfrey goes into an upscale store, the salesperson only sees race and based on that, certain assumptions are made.

These assumptions were made when the little boy who brought the Valianettes back together at his baby shower, now in his 20s, came out of the front door of his Capitol Hill, Washington, D.C. home recently on a sunny fall afternoon. Two police officers riding down the street on bicycles shouted at him, "Hey, what are you doing?" When he responded, with confusion, "Coming out of my house." Their response was "You live there?" After showing his driver's license to confirm what he said, they rode off, and he called me. Although he said this incident didn't bother him, it did, or he wouldn't have called. He was not surreptitiously leaving a back exit, hiding items under his arms, running to get away quickly. He was only walking out of the front door, and locking it, on his way to a doctor's appointment. Why was he stopped? Because he was young, black and male, in a gentrifying neighborhood. This is what black in America looks like today.

Look at the statistics on college entrance and graduation rates, home ownership, wealth and poverty, job status and employment. What continues to define the negative disparities between blacks and whites? Why are blacks predominant in the statistics that present those who are

217

struggling to succeed? What has shaped an America in which we continue to be on the bottom? Think about it. Race is still our reality. It is always an overlay that impacts our day-to-day lives.

Wisdom gained from over sixty years of living-while-black has made us see the world through a particular lens. Perhaps we focus on race more than our children do, but it's because of situations like the explosive "You lie" bellowed in the United States House of Representatives to the first black president of the United States, Barack Obama. Or the election of Donald Trump, the person who questioned the citizenry of Barack Obama during his candidacy or the ongoing response of "All Lives Matter" to the refrain "Black Lives Matter." As we get closer to 70 than 60, it's unlikely we will ever get rid of that racial frame as we live through the events of today. It will always be there. We know that now and don't talk as much about the firsts anymore. A black woman has finally been named Best Actress by the Academy of Motion Picture Arts and Sciences, but only one in the almost ninety-year history of the Academy. Since Guion Bluford traveled in space in 1983, there have been thirteen other black astronauts who have done the same. Thirteen out of 536, There have now been eight black Miss Americas since the first participated in 1970 following the lifting of the ban on non-white contestants. We are in boardrooms, state legislatures, science laboratories, Congress and in the White House. Talent, intellect, beauty. African-Americans have become more of the mainstream of America. More, but not entirely incorporated or fully represented even now. We have been shaped by the events of history, and daily activities continue to guide who we are, how we see the world, and how the world sees us.

Every day we read the newspaper or listen to the news. We are surrounded by instant information about what is happening in our neighborhoods, our cities, our country and across the globe. We know history is being made. We know this intellectually, but we don't have a real understanding of the importance of any single one of today's actions. The actions of today have to be placed in a framework that combines all of the other conversations with foreign leaders on a particular topic and how those discussions relate to each other and to the order of the world. Then the reactions to those conversations have to be monitored. History is the study of past events. This study takes time. It takes time to understand and appreciate the impact of those events on our day-to-day lives.

As kids, we didn't understand the importance of an African-American being named vice-mayor of the city of Richmond or the hundreds, if not thousands, of individual, cumulative events it had taken for us to attend Chandler Junior High School or to compete for jobs in the workforce. Events were swirling all around us that had a unique impact on our ability to live the lives we have led. We didn't focus on them. How could we? We didn't even know some of them were happening. Others we knew were occurring, we didn't understand. They just were. It was life.

Civil rights, human rights, social justice are abstract concepts. Without even being conscious, we play a part of the mega-dynamic that is working toward these liberties and rights every day. Every time we put on a tailored suit, interact with a white person, speak up when we witness or are made aware of a racist, inhumane or unjust action, we are a part of an unfolding that will become the history of social change. We are working for civil rights, human rights, and social justice even when we don't think about it. We know it, yet we don't. We think about it, but we don't. It is part of the enigma of being a black person in America, living-while-black.

Civil rights and women's rights were the major social movements that shaped our destiny, but so too did family and friends. Those eight Negro girls who started Norrell Elementary School together became eight successful African-American women. Seventy-five percent have a graduate degree, a significantly higher percentage than the national figure of ten percent. Most of us ended up in a helping profession. Those were the professions that had opened up first for our race, the examples we saw. Although we all came from intact families, we have a higher rate of divorce than the national average (62% vs. 50%). Some suggest we were the first generation of women who had society's permission to divorce, not only because we had the financial resources to take care of ourselves, but also because the women's liberation movement had convinced us we didn't have to tolerate situations that weren't good for us. All except one of us still live within about 100 miles of Richmond, our home. We left the nest, but we didn't go far. We are parents or provide active parenting to the children in our lives. Many of us are also grandparents now, but only one is called Grandma. As baby boomers, we are all active, vital women. For us, 60 something is the new 40 something. We don't see ourselves as we saw our grandparents; the label 'grandma' or 'grandmother' doesn't fit for most of us. Age sixty doesn't mark the beginning of the last stage of our lives. It merely marks the beginning of the next phase.

Are we reflective of America? Yes and no. Perhaps we don't fit neatly into the normative range of statistics for America. We are, however, reflective of that subset of black Americans, focused on education by their parents, while also being products of the civil rights and women's liberation movements of the '60s and '70s. Our steps may not always have been traditional, but our goal was clear: to achieve and to achieve at a higher level than our parents. And, we did.

History shaped us. Our families formed us, but so too did our friendship. And unlike the subtle impact of history or even the subliminal and expected impact of family, our friendship has had extraordinary, ongoing implications. It has connected us to a past our parents and siblings were not privy to. It has given us a true peer group that will always be there for us. Friends who can finish the stories you start, who laugh as you say the first few words of a memorable story and who cause you to smile when you see their number now on the caller ID on your phone. Ours is an abiding friendship. If divas are strong women, self-assured and confident, then the Valianettes have evolved into them. Renée chose the right name.

Almost twenty-five years ago we reconnected as friends. The rekindling of our friendship started out both with the bang of an immediate connection and with the tentativeness of a new relationship. The contact felt positive. We nurtured it, building new memories and sharing joys and heartaches. There are still the duos and trios who have stronger connective tissue than others. There always will be. It's human nature, but there is a thread that will always keep us together as a group. It is the thread of shared experiences, shared values, laughter shared and a few tears. Our connection is safe and comforting. It's simple. We are family. We are the Daughters of the Dream.

EPILOGUE

L TO R — RENEE MILLS, MARSHA WARE, MADELINE SWANN, VERONICA ABRAMS, DEBBIE RIDDICK, TAMARA COPELAND,
DEBBY SMITH — CHRISTMAS LUNCH 2016

On July 12, 2017, Madeline passed away. While two others in our group had died years ago, neither was a member of the inner circle, a part of the group that had been together now for sixty years. Madeline was the first to leave us. I was devastated. I was out of the country on sabbatical when I learned of her hospitalization. I had thought that something was wrong when I didn't get my typical birthday greeting from her. We shared July as our birth month, and always exchanged greetings. Even though in Italy, I still expected a text or an email from her. When nothing came, I noticed but didn't think anything about it ... not really. We all knew she was ill but weren't aware of how severe her condition had become. She was found weak, but alive in her home on July 9th. The next day, Debbie and Renée drove up from Richmond to see her. They were met at the hospital by Veronica and Debby. Text messages and emails kept me connected to the news, but not to Madeline and not to the group.

Our circle of love and friendship has now been broken. As the seventieth birthday gets closer than the sixtieth—yes, we must admit that— we know that one-by-one our group will get smaller and smaller. This past Christmas, we gathered for our first holiday luncheon without Madeline. We shared stories and felt a noticeable hole in our group. But love washed over our memories of her. We—and she—will always be as Renée describes us, DIVAs: Deeply, Interconnected. Valianettes, Always.

Tamara Copeland
May 2018

POSTSCRIPT

THE OTHER VALIANETTES

This story focuses on eight women in a club called the Valianettes. We have maintained our friendship for almost six decades, but there were others. It doesn't seem right to tell the story without saying a bit about them. Their names are Betty Jo Brown, Deborah Smith, Gloria Tyson Reid, Hope Herring, Ricki Ballard Williams and Wanda Randleman.

Ricki left the group in high school. She was the only Valianette to attend a private high school. Following her graduation from St. Gertrude's all-girls school in Richmond, she attended Fisk University for 2 years and then transferred to Virginia State University. Ricki was the oldest child of a prominent Richmond family. She married, but no one ever knew anything about her husband from whom she later divorced. There were no children. Sadly, Ricki died in 2011. Madeline, Renée, Debbie, Veronica and I visited her in the hospital before she died. We hadn't seen her in years. She didn't know we were there.

Betty Jo was always quick to smile. Barely reaching the 5 ft mark, the first thing you noticed about her wasn't her smile, but how short she was. This was particularly true since she was often with Madeline, one of the taller members of our group. Betty Jo attended Hampton University and like several others studied to be a teacher. After graduation, she taught for one year in the Tidewater area of Virginia. The following year, she accepted a teacher exchange appointment in St. Thomas, Virgin Islands. None of us has seen her or heard from her since high school.

Hope went with Betty Jo and Debby Anderson to Hampton University. Never having been a part of one of the close Valianette duos or trios, Hope's friendship bond to the Valianettes didn't continue in college. Even though everyone in the group eventually lost contact with her, Richmond is a small community, and ultimately folks learned that Hope had graduated from law school and returned to Richmond to work for a state agency. She never married and doesn't have children.

Wanda Randleman, like Ricki, left the group in high school. She attended the all-black Maggie Walker High School. No one can remember how Wanda became a part of the group and no one knows what happened to her.

Deborah Smith was Deborah #1 because we had three Deborah's— Deborah Smith (#1), Deborah Johnson (#2) and Deborah Anderson (#3), who would ironically marry Ken Smith to become our second Deborah Smith. Deborah was the only Valianette to stay in Richmond after high school. She was a psychology major at Virginia Commonwealth University right in Richmond. For a brief time, she and Deborah Johnson shared an apartment after college. Their time together was short because Debbie #1's behavior became erratic and troubling to Debbie #2. What we didn't know was this was the beginning of her multiple sclerosis. While it would ultimately affect her entire body, one of the early symptoms is a loss of judgment and difficulty reasoning. Deborah died from her illness in 1998 becoming the first Valianette to die. None of us attended her funeral. She was not a part of our new lives; the bond had been broken long ago.

Gloria was very much a part of the group, particularly close with Debby Anderson. But she, drifted away when she went off to Fisk University and established new friendship relationships. Much to our surprise, Gloria married after her second year at college. She had fulfilled Mrs. Dungee's wish for Veronica, Gloria had gone off to Fisk and married a doctor from nearby Meharry Medical School. We gathered for the wedding. Debby Anderson and Marsha were bridesmaids. While many of the Valianettes were there, the event wasn't much of a reunion. Gloria moved to Ohio with her new husband and soon became a mom to Kimberly and Bernard. Like many other Valianettes, Gloria divorced and returned home to Richmond. Gloria re-entered our consciousness when we learned of the tragic and early death of her daughter. She was the first Valianette to lose a child.

These women were very much a part of the story of the Valianettes, but their connection didn't rekindle when we reconnected as adults. Their lives had taken them in very different directions. For them, this particular group bond would likely always be in the past.

ABOUT THE AUTHOR

 Tamara Lucas Copeland is African-American, a child of the South, born, educated and still living there. This distinction provides a unique personal vantage point for issues of racial equity. She is also an only child, a circumstance that sometimes leads to friends being more like family. These factors contribute to her love for her forever friends, her perspective on the role race plays in America, and her authorship of *Daughters of the Dream*. For decades, Tamara watched her mother research the genealogical history of her family, talking to relatives, reviewing microfiche on hundreds of library visits long before the internet existed, as she labored to produce two published works. Motivated by her mother's determination to document her family and by her and her friends' realization of the importance of their five-plus decades-long friendship, Tamara took on the challenge of telling their story. Not a historian, but an avid observer of the overlay of history on the racial reality of America, *Daughters of the Dream* is the result.

Tamara is president of the Washington Regional Association of Grantmakers (WRAG). Founded in 1992, WRAG is a nonprofit association with over 100 of the most well-respected foundations and corporate giving programs in the Greater Washington, D.C. region as its members. Her leadership with WRAG's groundbreaking work, *Putting Racism on the Table*, has received widespread recognition for enabling the philanthropic community to understand so they might work for racial equity. She came to WRAG with extensive experience in nonprofit management and on children's policy having led Voices for America's Children, the National Health & Education Consortium, and the Infant Mortality Initiative of Southern Governors' Association and Southern Legislative Conference and having been Congressman Bobby Scott's (D-VA) Legislative Director.

Follow more of Tamara's writing at: www.DaughtersOfTheDream.org

DISCUSSION QUESTIONS

FOR A CONVERSATION ON RACIAL EQUITY

In today's America, structural racism and implicit bias seem to be revealed routinely in businesses, in government agencies, in the entertainment industry, in sports, almost everywhere, including in day-to-day interactions with friends and family. Even with chilling cell phone videos or revealing statistical data, some continue to believe that America offers a level playing field for all willing to pull themselves up by their proverbial bootstraps.

Daughters of the Dream uses the friendship of eight African-American women growing up and living in a racially-impacted society, to reveal what it is like to be black in America. This reality is likely to be unknown to many. Some may question the truth of this portrayal or its relevance. If you have picked up this book, you have already expressed your desire to explore America through the lens of ordinary, everyday black women.

The hope is that this book will open your eyes, enhance your understanding and prompt you to identify your role in working for racial equity. Exploring this side of America with friends and family will enrich your experience and deepen your understanding of others' views. The following questions may engender a rich conversation. Let me know.

1. Name five things that the book discussed that you didn't know. Should you have known these things. What about your education, formal or informal, failed to inform you? Does that failure continue today?
2. Think about the environment in which you grew up, how were you exposed to black/white people? How did that manner of exposure affect how you saw them?

3. When were you a minority in a situation? For how long did that situation last? Think about and try to actually define how it feels to always be the minority?

4. A story was shared in the book about the playing of "Dixie" as the high school fight song. If you are white, would it have occurred to you, as a teen, that the song might be offensive? If so, what would the teenage you have done? For any race, what is happening in your world now – not the larger society – that makes you uncomfortable and that you might change?

5. How has your sense of America's racial reality been shaped? What/who were the influencers?

6. As a child were you ever told how to act because of your race? If so, how were you affected by those messages? If not, what does that say about your status in this country?

7. Whenever the group featured in *Daughters of the Dream* gather, some aspect of race and race relations is discussed or experienced. What is the background music of your life? Is there a topic, an issue that always comes up? What is it? Why do you think it predominates in your life?

8. What factors have contributed to the racial reality in America today being so similar to the racial reality of the '60s and '70s?

9. If this book opened your eyes, what can you do differently? What will you do differently?

10. What is your most important/impactful take away having read *Daughters of the Dream?*

For a Conversation on Friendship

How often do you think about what it takes to make friends and to maintain and grow a true friendship? These questions are intended to help you begin a conversation and to help you nurture those relationships.

1. Who is your oldest friend?
2. How did that friendship begin? Is that the typical way that most friendships start? If not, what made this one different?
3. Does that person think of you as a friend? Are you sure? Why?
4. What are the critical elements necessary to maintain a friendship?
5. Does childhood or teenage friendship seem different than adult friendship? Why?
6. How do we ensure a balance between work, family, and friends?
7. The women in *Daughters of the Dream* were childhood friends, and then their friendship ebbed when they went off to college. Did you experience that with any of your friends?
8. The women in the book had a precipitating event that led them to rekindle their friendship after almost two decades. Do you think friendships can be re-kindled? Have you experienced that? Is there a friendship that you want to renew? What steps can you take to do that?
9. The women in the book have a bit of regularity to their gatherings – at a minimum, MLK weekend, a summer beach outing, and a Christmas lunch. Does having a routine help to maintain connections when life is often hectic? What regular gatherings can you plan with a close friend or friendship group?
10. Has this book prompted you to think about your friendships or to do something to nurture or renew them?